28 DAYS
IN
SRI LANKA

28 DAYS
IN
SRI LANKA

Andy Southall

Amapur Press Ltd

© Copyright 2020 Andy Southall

Andy Southall asserts his moral right to be identified as the author of this work.

All rights reserved. No part of this publication may be produced or transmitted in any form or by any means, electronic or mechanical, including photocopying, recording or information storage and retrieval systems, without permission in writing from the copyright holder.

ISBN 978-0-473-53545-2 (Soft cover)
ISBN 978-0-473-53547-6 (Kindle)
ISBN 978-0-473-53546-9 (EPub)

Cover Design by Sylvie Woods
Pexels image thanks to Digital Buggu
Edited by Lesley Marshall
Published by Amapur Press Limited
Printing by YourBooks
Author website www.andy-southall.com

While much of this account is based upon real places and events, several incidents are fictitious. Some names have been changed, and many of the characters are not real individuals but reinvented from several people we met. Other than the specific individuals named in acknowledgements, any resemblance to actual persons, living or dead, events, or locales is entirely coincidental.

A catalogue record for this book is available from the National Library of New Zealand.

Acknowledgments

A special thanks to all the people who have helped in the writing of this book: to all my Sri Lankan friends in Wellington – Chalaka, Kumara, Muditha, Dee, Chris and others – whose enthusiasm and warmth first inspired me to visit their homeland; to the intrepid and hardworking leaders of our tour, Sujan, Dharme and Saman; to all the friendly supportive people on our tour; to our guide/driver Sunil who patiently drove us for a week and showed us many beautiful things; to Priyantha and his wife for making our stay at Sega BNB so comfortable; to Shiroma for teaching us about tea; to the members of my writing groups – Angelique, Helen, Libby, Linda, Mary, Rodney, Tony, Vidya – who critiqued some chapters; to Helen for her guidance on the book cover; to Lesley Marshall for her kind yet thorough editing; and to Kate for putting up with blog writing while in Sri Lanka and for her comprehensive proofreading, suggestions and advice.

MAP OF SRI LANKA

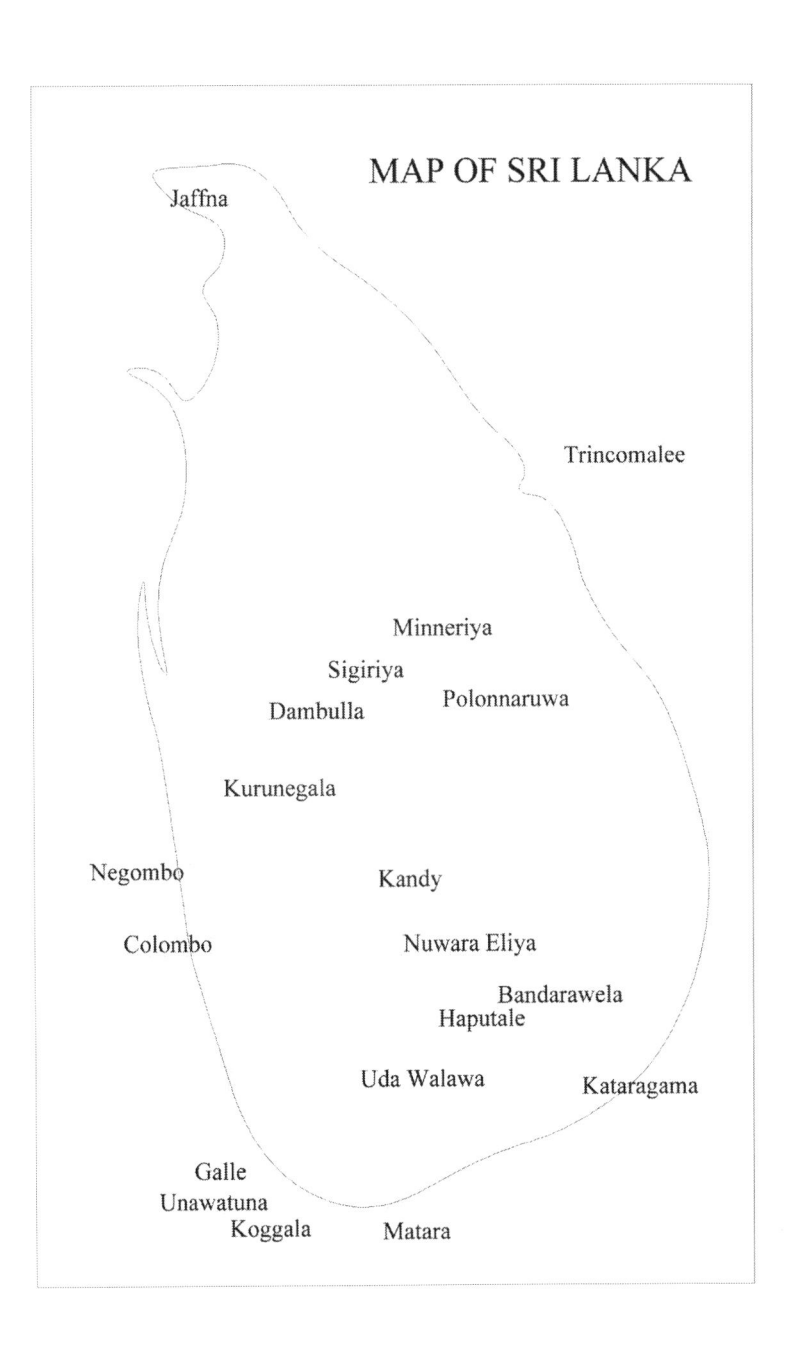

Jaffna

Trincomalee

Minneriya
Sigiriya
Polonnaruwa
Dambulla

Kurunegala

Negombo

Kandy

Colombo
Nuwara Eliya

Bandarawela
Haputale

Uda Walawa
Kataragama

Galle
Unawatuna
Koggala   Matara

Contents

Part One
With Others

1. Oshan's Eleven	3
2. The POMs on The Bus	10
3. On the Way to Dambulla	19
4. Sigiriya	27
5. Lion Rock	32
6. Wot, No Elephants?	40
7. In the Same Gear	46
8. The Elephants of Minneriya	54
9. Ancient City	59
10. Doctor Spice	70
11. Kool as Kandy	75
12. Gem Beetle	84
13. Rupees for Ranuga	91
14. Bamboo Torture	94
15. A Nice Cup of Tea	99
16. The Perfect Cuppa	108
17. Bridge over the River Kwai	113
18. The Never-Ending Loop of Nuwara Eliya	119
19. World's End	127
20. Breakfast at Bandarawela	137
21. Elephant Gap	142
22. Piñata	151
23. Five Go to Cinnamon Island	160
24. The Birthplace of Martin Wickramasinghe	166
25. Goodbye and Hello	171

Part Two
By Ourselves

26. The Stray Dogs of Sri Lanka	181
27. Over the Wall	189

28. Galle by Night	194
29. The Wrecks of Galle	201
30. Christmas Day at Unawatuna	207
31. Driving Mrs Kate	214
32. Baby Elephants and Other Things	222
33. Lipton's Seat	230
34. Seven-Forty-Seven from Haputale	235
35. Grandstanding the Grand	241
36. Tea Factory Visit – Take Two	250
37. Back to Kandy	256
38. John Key and the Cobra	268
39. The Man in the Wedding Photo	273
40. The Last Buffet	277
41. Rubber Band	281
About the Author	285

With Others

"Appreciation is a wonderful thing. It makes what is excellent in others belong to us as well."
Voltaire

ONE

Oshan's Eleven

We touched down at midnight, our limbs stiff and eyelids heavy. Bandaranaike International Airport flowed around us like a trance – dull yellow lights and long, featureless corridors, everything muted and slightly off-key. A female officer at immigration stamped our passports. At the baggage carousel our suitcases rolled up without delay.

Kate found a taxi while I watched the bags. Then we set off into the night, unresisting, vacant and warm. Our driver sped along empty streets, whistling tunelessly and saying nothing. It was twenty kilometres to our hotel. Yet it seemed hardly any time at all before he slowed, turned off the highway and drove through a grand concrete entrance.

A solid-looking façade bulked in front of us, pale lights glowing in some of its windows, and a thickset man guarding the steps. As our taxi stopped, the man stepped forward, his uniform grey in the dim light. Smiling behind his huge moustache, he lifted our cases from the boot and wheeled them up a ramp.

Inside, the Kokovano Hotel wasn't so severe. A lady

came out of an air-conditioned booth to greet us. She offered cold flannels from a silver tray, and then, despite our tiredness, tried to teach us elementary Sinhalese.

"*Bohoma istuti!*" she said as she handed over our key. "That means thank you very much."

"*Bohoma istuti*," I said clumsily. "We're on the Discover Sri Lanka tour. It's supposed to start from here later today."

"And it will!" Her eyes shone, radiant as the tray. "Oshan is your leader. He'll meet you in the bar at six tonight."

The man with the moustache – the night porter – led us around the side of the hotel, past a dark swimming pool and to our room. The bed was enormous, half an acre of softness. We didn't bother unpacking, brushing our teeth or undressing. After seventeen hours of flying we needed sleep.

When we woke up we found ourselves in a different place. Bright light cracked through gaps in the curtains, painting lines on our far wall. Outside, groups of Sri Lankan men stood in three-piece suits – *how hot they must be* – together with women in long dresses who looked after children and flowers. An event of some kind: a special anniversary or a wedding?

Jet-lagged, we spent the day in our room – sleeping, unpacking, and reading the joining notes for our tour. Rather than attempt to do everything for ourselves, we'd opted to join an organised trip for the first fourteen of our twenty-eight days. It was with a British company well known for small-group travel – and in the time available would be an efficient way of seeing things.

The pool outside screamed with children. The restaurant and foyer were busy too, another coachload of smartly dressed locals arriving. We had no chairs in our room, so we lay on the bed, heads propped on pillows, bare feet on the duvet. Then, a little before six, we put on our jandals and stepped out.

It was time to meet Oshan and the other members of our tour.

As we made our way into the bar, a handsome man in a black leather jacket stood up to greet us. His face was rosy, his eyes intelligent and his palm as hot as a furnace. "Jerry," he said as we shook, "short for Jeremiah. And this is Frank." He lanced a long finger at a second man who sat drinking at his table.

"Hi," said the man who was sitting down. He looked incredibly young, his face taut and his frame strong. He stood up and extended a muscly arm. We shook, his grip like a press.

"I put in for a single room," said Jerry, "but they've gone and stuck me in a shared." He laughed. "No lock on the lavvy, only one bar of soap and the beds are practically on top of each other!"

Frank laughed too. "I was supposed to be bringing my girlfriend. Then she found out there were snakes and bottled out."

"I'm Andy," I said.

"And I'm Kate." My wife leaned forward to shake their hands. She's good at meeting new people – her eyes brighten like Christmas lights and her smile stretches across the whole of her face.

A couple sat together at the next table – a bearded man wearing a khaki baseball hat and a lady dressed in a khaki suit. They looked as though they might be on the tour too, judging by how they studied a *Lonely Planet Sri Lanka*, one of them reading a page, then passing the book to the other.

Without hesitation, Kate walked over and held up our

copy of the *Lonely Planet*. "*Snap!*" she said in a gleeful voice.

Glancing up, the couple introduced themselves. The man was Tom, an ornithologist. His partner was Linda, a vet from Wharram-le-Street. "You won't have heard of it," she said in a strong accent. "It's only a small place. A smidge south of Scagglethorpe. One hundred residents. Though it's down to ninety-eight with Tom and me away."

"Is it in England?" Kate looked puzzled.

Linda shook her head. "Yorkshire."

Then, two by two, and one, the other members of our group appeared. Lucy and Bruce, a pleasant, good-looking couple from Leamington Spa who were escaping the British election. An older couple, Amy and Nelson, who announced they were here by mistake. They'd booked for India but had boarded the wrong plane.

"I thought Colombo was a detective on the telly." Nelson was a natural comedian, his cheerful face switching from aghast to mirthful. "You know – that chappie who wore a shabby raincoat and smoked a cigar? I never realised he was a capital city as well."

"The difference is you spell Lieutenant Columbo with a "u" not an "o"," said Jerry.

"You're clever," said Nelson. "How do you know this stuff?"

"I'm a quizzer." Jerry smiled. "Have you heard of the Runcorn Railway Workers Brains Trust? We came third in the British Quizzing Championship."

"No!" Nelson's jaw dropped to the lapel of his brightly patterned shirt. "We used to live just down the road in Frodsham!"

I backed away from them, sensing this might escalate into a catechism of mutually familiar places and then a conflict of mutually repulsive ideologies. England is a divided nation now. Even minor spelling disagreements are liable to develop into bitter tabloid wars.

Fortunately the final member of our eleven arrived, a lady with attractive red hair and glittery earrings, who said hello in a soft Welsh accent and introduced herself as Beca. She told us she worked for an aviation company and seemed easy-going, someone whose good sense would keep others out of trouble.

How wrong first appearances can be.

We were eleven in all, an apostle missing. Everyone was so busy introducing themselves we'd forgotten there was still a tour leader to come. Then Kate nudged my elbow and pointed at a Sri Lankan man who stood quietly to one side. He seemed amused by our group, the laughter lines around his eyes bending mischievously and his lips making a droll half-moon. As our chatter lulled he strode forward, not in any grand Hollywood way but as an ordinary man who required neither sequins nor sunglasses.

"Welcome to Sri Lanka," he announced in a fast, clipped voice, catching everyone's attention. "My name is Oshan, and I am your tour leader. For the next two weeks I will show you my country."

He came around shaking hands with everyone. He had no drink, and several people offered to buy him one, yet he refused them all. Gathering us in a circle, he described the highlights of our route. First, the fabulous cave temple at Dambulla. Then Lion Rock at Sigiriya, followed by the Temple of the Sacred Tooth at Kandy, the precipitous escarpment of World's End, and finally the historic walled fort of Galle. At Galle, Kate and I would exit the tour and commence our own independent travels.

Later at dinner, Oshan sat and laughed with us all,

offering advice on curries and telling jokes. Afterwards he took everyone to a conference room upstairs to conduct a more formal briefing.

"In cricket," he began, "Sri Lanka aren't doing so well against Pakistan. But that doesn't mean we can't win the T20s in 2020 because we always have to believe in ourselves."

"How about telling us something about our trip?" called out someone, probably Jerry. "All these fancy places we've paid to see?"

"I was getting to that." Oshan grinned and began handing out photocopies. "Here are forms for filling in your travel insurance details, and this map shows our route – all the places we visit and the hotels, yeah?" Then rather than describe days one and two, he jumped to day eleven and explained how our hill country railway ride might be brought forward to day ten. "Sometimes we can't get on board. The train is full. No seats, yeah? We have to stand."

"What about the whale watching?" asked someone else, probably Nelson.

"No whales on train, yeah?" Oshan pulled a face. "They are at Mirissa, where we charter our own boat. We don't go on the commercial boats. They are crowded and you can't move around."

I wasn't sure how much of this I'd remember the next morning – let alone in a week's time. The whale watching trip wasn't until day twelve, almost at the end of the tour.

Still going at breakneck speed, Oshan handed out more paper: notes on the island and a list of optional excursions. At that moment – the very beginning of our trip – time stretched endlessly. We had what seemed like a good group – jovial Nelson who'd make us laugh, young Frank who'd keep us honest, and intellectual Jerry who'd be our go-to man for anything complicated. We'd find out everything there was to know about Sri Lanka, we'd enjoy every moment and we'd return home wiser.

And with good delivery, a bit of spin on the ball, the Sri Lankan T20 cricket team might improve as well.

TWO

The POMs on The Bus

At breakfast the next morning I tried reattaching faces to names. Lucy and Bruce, the tall, dynamic couple from Leamington Spa. Beca, the well-spoken Welsh lady travelling on her own. And Amy and Nelson – Amy beaming through heart-shaped spectacles, and Nelson resplendent in a dazzling elephant shirt.

"Good morning." I set down the plate of orange segments, papaya and sweet yellow bananas I'd selected from the buffet and sat at the group table opposite Nelson.

"You sure?" He grinned, one eye larger than the other.

"I hope so. We're on holiday, aren't we?"

Out of the corner of my eye I could see Beca treading up and down the restaurant, glancing at the stacks of cups, apparently in search of a beverage to fill one of them with. Rising from my chair, I went over to fetch a coffee as well. Yet after scouring all the buffet tables neither of us could find a silver decanter, a filter machine – or even a tiny foil pack of instant. There appeared to be no beverages of any kind – coffee, tea, chocolate or hot water – and nor were there any staff members around to ask. Then Nelson came up too and from their omelettes Jerry and Frank, all of us waltzing around the dining room like suitors in a tea dance.

The kitchen door opened and a waitress in a smart blue uniform dashed out.

"Is there any coffee?" I said to her, and she smiled and promised to bring one to my table. And the same for Beca, Nelson, Jerry and Frank – whatever they wanted, all served to wherever they were sitting. Everyone happier, we returned to our seats.

Then, like an ambush, serving staff sprang from every direction. Waitresses in blue uniforms similar to that of the first one. Waiters in grey suits and black hats, even one man in a red pinafore that was almost pink. Converging on our table, they brought teas, coffees, little stainless-steel jugs of milk and ceramic bowls of sugar. We had more beverages than we could possibly drink – at least one tea and coffee each, and probably more.

A spirit of cooperation was forged as we worked out who'd ordered what and who would drink it. Altogether we were nine POMs, one Welsh lady and a Kiwi – Kate. Plus several exceptionally large pots of tea. A principle had been established. We had to be clear in everything we asked for.

KATE and I had rediscovered our love of travelling. Ever since spending the 2017 winter in Western Samoa we'd wanted to travel to somewhere equally exotic in another part of the world. It had to be during the New Zealand summer holidays, though, ruling out anywhere in the South Pacific that would be in the middle of its wet season.

Then we read about Sri Lanka. The country wasn't too big: it consisted of one island that was a fraction smaller than Ireland, and had a population of twenty-two million. There were two monsoon seasons, yet if we stuck to December and the southwest we'd enjoy dry, sunny weather. We didn't quite have the luxury of one hundred days as with Samoa; however, twenty-eight days should be ample time to visit all the country's highlights.

There were fun things to do: view elephants, eat authentic curries and sip the perfect cup of Ceylon tea. All the obvious things that sprang out of the brochures. We had a number of more serious objectives as well. To learn about the culture of Sri Lanka, with its markets, temples, museums, religions and peoples. To appreciate its antiquity, stretching back three thousand years – far longer than the chronicles of Britain. It would also be an ideal country in which to experience Eastern spirituality, for alongside many colourful Hindu shrines Sri Lanka is one of the best places on Earth for monks, meditation and Buddhism.

Kate's mum had been there recently and recommended several places. "You'll enjoy the tea," she'd told us, stirring a dark liquid inside her well-used teapot. "Fabulous stuff! They don't use teabags over there – only leaves."

Kate's brother had stopped over in Sri Lanka too and extolled its virtues with passion. "Make sure you go to Galle!" he'd said. "Amazing place. You can watch international cricket tests from the fort walls while drinking beer with the locals."

Similarly, the Sri Lankan members of my Wellington Toastmasters' club had been delighted when they'd heard I was planning to visit their country. Chalaka, the club's founder, told me a story of learning to swim off a pristine white Sri Lankan beach, flailing in deep waters and having to be rescued. Kumara and Muditha, cheerful compatriots from Galle, glowed with fondness as they remembered their native city.

"You can stay in my house," said Kumara, perhaps thinking we were taking our family and friends. "Four bedrooms, two bathrooms, a kitchen and lounge. And a roof terrace where the monkeys hang out."

So many reasons for going to this island nation with its surfeit of elephants, tea, monkeys, spicy foods and warm, kind climate. And as our journey progressed we knew we'd come across many other things we hadn't realised would be there – including stories from our new travel companions and self-discoveries about ourselves.

ALL THOSE BEVERAGES sat among our breakfast plates, some going cold, others still too hot. We blew across the steaming surfaces, stirred in milk and sipped cautiously from their rims. Then Nelson gulped down half his second coffee and, making his apologies, set off with Amy. Likewise Frank departed too, two of his cups still full. He was followed by Linda and Tom, then Kate, Lucy and Bruce, all busily chatting. Only Jerry, Beca and I remained.

"Have you been to Sri Lanka before?" I asked Beca.

"Oh no." She smiled and shook her head. "Well, I came here in my twenties, but it's so long ago I can't remember much."

"Is that why you've come back? To refresh your memories?"

"I don't know. I did think about going to Venezuela, but in the end I settled on here."

"I've been to Venezuela," announced Jerry from across the table, buttering an enormous slice of toast. "Went on this quizzing jolly to Miraflores Palace hosted by none other than Hugo Chavez."

"The President? Did you meet him?"

"I did, fella." He nodded at his toast, bit into it, then laughed. "I shook his hand."

I didn't know what to say. Then, glancing down, I was shocked to see the time on my phone. Almost nine. The bus would be leaving in a few minutes and it wouldn't do to be late. Oshan had been very explicit about punctuality. He'd devised an elaborate system of alarm calls, with precise times for waking up and leaving our suitcases outside our rooms.

All three of us raced out of the restaurant, looped around the swimming pool where a man with a net fished out leaves, then accelerated down the side of the Kokovano to the car park at the front. Sure enough, the bus fumed, ready to depart. Everyone else was on board, all the suitcases walled together like Lego on the back seat.

"Good morning." Oshan was perched on the front passenger seat, beaming. He seemed amused by our tardiness rather than annoyed. Some of the others viewed us less positively. Linda and Tom aimed enormous lenses, while Nelson pointed dramatically at his watch.

"Hey-ho, what time do you call this?" he said with a chuckle. "We should have left you behind!"

"You're mistaken, fella, cos we're dead on time." Calmly, Jerry took a double seat, while I sat next to Kate, and Beca waded down the aisle to the back. "According to my phone it's one minute to, so as a precaution –" he gestured at Nelson's wristwatch "– why don't you chuck that anachronism in the bin?"

Before Nelson could respond the bus shot forward, veering out of the car park and onto the main highway.

Straightaway our minds were wrenched from the trivialities of hotel etiquette and onto the more serious task of spotting traffic near-misses. For this was like no highway at home – New Zealand, England, or any other Western country where vehicles proceed on designated sides, left and right. Here, traffic obeyed no laws. It was a Buck's Fizz of swerving, weaving and bumper-to-bumper brinksmanship, and featured every different speed of road-user from lolloping dogs to thutting tuk-tuks to mighty white buses that stopped for no one.

Yet our driver seemed to know what he was doing. He was a small, cheerful man called Chanuka – or Mister C for those who couldn't remember his name. Skilfully he drew up behind slower red government buses, then – beeping and accelerating – passed them smoothly. Likewise, he avoided the stream of tuk-tuks that constantly tried to undertake, as well as the buses and trucks that thundered straight at us. He spotted all the sleeping dogs, the jostling pedestrians and – cleverest of all – the monkeys who climbed on overhead telephone wires to drop banana skins onto the windscreens of vehicles going too slow.

Oshan began speaking into a microphone, something he did a lot whenever we were in the bus. And once underway he seemed unable to stop talking, just as the pistons, crankshafts and wheels underneath the bus had to keep moving in order to convey us to our destination.

"How is everyone this morning?" he said, too fast for anyone to answer. "The word for today is *Ayubowan*. It is a particularly good word to use in many different situations. For instance if you are greeting people in a market you say *Ayubowan*. Or if you are trying to find a seat on a crowded train you can say *Ayubowan*. It is a Sinhalese word and means Long life. *Ayubowan, Ayubowan, Ayubowan!*" He had a hundred things to tell us, a thousand, a million, and not one of them could wait as words and facts spilled out faster than we'd ever be able to take them in.

"Hey!" Jerry raised an incisive hand. "Before we all freeze our assets, can you turn down the aircon?"

"Sure." Oshan fiddled with a knob and the temperature rose, closer to the sweltering heat outside. This would become another daily ritual: stepping from the fury of a hot day into the chill of an air-conditioned bus, then later back out into the oven, never entirely sure which was the most uncomfortable, the heat or the cool.

"Ta!" Jerry said loudly.

"You're welcome. And another word you can use in Sinhalese is *Stuthi*. It means thank you."

The bus made its way out of Negombo, the traffic growing denser. We might be on the first day of our tour, but it was Monday morning for everyone else. People were heading to work, taking their children to school and getting hairdos, manicures and the shopping. There seemed to be as many people on the edges of the road as there were vehicles whizzing past. Men standing in groups talking, other men carrying boxes, and a third group of men mending things. And women too, looking after young children, selling food at market stalls, and in one town leading goats along the pavement. The men were casually dressed in jeans, shorts, T-shirts or overalls. The women wore brighter dresses and saris, in purples and pinks, yellows and greens. Few people – men or women – glanced at our bus. One or two children pointed and smiled. We were not an oddity here but – *perhaps* – a commodity.

The weather was as oppressive as the traffic. Thick overcast clouds shut out the sun. The passing scenery was crammed together – dense green plantations one minute, then busy streets and shops the next. Palm trees with coconuts. Hair salons and nail parlours. A shop selling spare parts for cars. A greengrocer, a laundry and a spice emporium.

"This area is known as the coconut triangle, yeah?" Oshan gestured through the windscreen. "All the big plantations are around here. Green coconuts for drinking and brown for cooking."

"What are those ribbons?" Jerry pointed out at strings of orange ribbons hanging on both sides of the street.

"Those are for a funeral." Oshan's smile didn't falter. "Orange for a monk. White with a black line for Catholic. And plain white for everyone else. Land here is at a premium. Many people are cremated. We need plantations and paddy fields. The economy of Sri Lanka is dependent on these two commodities – coconuts and rice, yeah?"

Behind me, Nelson and Frank chatted to each other, not about coconuts but home brewing, and then the Silver Surfer's Club for the over fifties. I wondered how Frank could be remotely interested in this stuff – he looked like a twenty-five-year-old who'd drink in his local pub. Apparently this trip was his first time out of Blighty. The nearest he'd come to overseas travel before had been a day return to Brighton.

Meanwhile Oshan was reeling off more facts and figures, juggling the microphone from one hand to the other as he listed the vital statistics of tuk-tuks, Sri Lanka's ubiquitous motorised tricycles. They came with black plastic side-flaps and cost seven hundred and fifty thousand rupees – or seven years' worth of wages for the average worker. There were over a million tuk-tuks, one for every twenty people, and they served as taxis, couriers, produce shifters and family vehicles for families who couldn't afford cars. Most of them were cheap imports from India, although numbers had been restricted recently by the government in order to reduce road accidents and congestion.

Frank and Nelson seemed to be listening now, their side conversation ceased. Jerry, however, was talking to someone about the Liverpool Underground – "I tell you, fella, outside London it's the oldest underground in the world" – while Kate had started her own dialogue with Lucy in front about English houses and how small their entrance halls are. Clearly, there was going to be a *lot* of information on this trip: Oshan with his figures, Nelson with his quips, Jerry with his pearls of wisdom, and Frank on a tangent way beyond his norm.

These guys were all fully-fledged POMs – Prisoners of Mother England. And despite my emigrating from England to New Zealand twelve years earlier, it seemed that for the next two weeks I'd be an honorary POM once again, listening to British accents, meeting familiar regional isotopes, and hearing opinions on subjects such as NHS staffing, the BBC licence fee and Boris's forthcoming election as prime minister. My God, I prayed they didn't talk about Brexit. It had been painful enough to witness the UK's political quagmire from afar. It'd be disastrous to be plunged headfirst in the stuff while on holiday.

They say travel isn't about the places you visit but the people you travel with. Hopefully everyone was here for the right reason – to see Sri Lanka and forget about the country they came from.

THREE

On the Way to Dambulla

The first place we were scheduled to visit was the cave temple of Dambulla, with its five candle-lit chambers and one hundred and fifty-three statues of Buddha.

The bus stopped briefly at the town of Kurunegala on the way there – a chance for everyone to stretch their legs, and Oshan to rest his voice. It had been cracking a little during the last hour as he recited the names of previous kings and princes, a list far longer than the British Royal family.

Closer to Dambulla, we stopped again for lunch. This was our first experience of the ubiquitous lunch buffet, and initially it didn't seem too ominous, treading around a table stacked with stainless steel-trays, heaping little piles of rice and various vegetable curries onto a plate, then sitting down at a long trestle table to eat with everyone else. Some people chose from the à la carte – for instance Tom and Kate selected chicken curry which arrived as greasy drumsticks in a thin gravy, while Nelson risked prawns, perhaps a hazardous strategy this early on and so far from the coast. Although at the rear of the restaurant was a swimming pool, half-full of muddy brown liquid. Possibly the prawns had been reared there because the water didn't appear suitable for swimming. I didn't try sticking my toe in, though. Besides prawns there might be crocs. Even snakes.

Perhaps chicken really was the best option of all.

Hardly anyone finished their meals. The food was tasty, but all the buffet-goers helped themselves to far too much. This was a perennial problem with buffets. Lots of stodgy things in the first few trays: rice, noodles, then more rice. Stuff to fill you up before reaching the savoury dishes later. As my grandma always used to say, don't let your eyes rule your stomach.

Back on the bus, Oshan sat in his seat gargling with water. His voice had recovered, and he promptly alarmed everyone by announcing that the cave temple wasn't on the main road but up a steep, stony path only navigable on foot. The people who'd eaten too much at lunch would have to tighten their belts. Anyone with dodgy legs would need walking poles, boots, maybe ropes and crampons.

"Can the bus get closer?" I asked on behalf of several people who looked worried.

"It's close enough." Oshan grinned and spread his hands in a calming motion. "The bus goes to the ticket office at the bottom, yeah?"

"There isn't an escalator?" said Nelson.

"I doubt it," said Jerry. "Those caves were here before Jesus was born. They only had steps in those days."

At the ticket office the bus came to a halt and everyone tumbled off. Oshan sprinted over to the counter to buy tickets while Sakan – the third member of the crew – went around topping up everyone's water bottles. Sakan's grin was infectious. With his long, curly black hair he looked like a nineteen-seventies footballer – Kevin Keegan or maybe

Graeme Souness. Although the POMs had yet to mention the beautiful game. They were an untypical lot, making conversation without mentioning the weather, British railways or – *shriek, shriek, shriek* – the upcoming British election.

The path up to the temple wasn't as steep as everyone feared. The worst hazard wasn't the gradient or loose stones but the monkeys who assembled at the edges. They stretched out tiny pink hands and posed for photos. At first, only a few of them were visible, baby monkeys sent out as bait. But their numbers increased as more assertive brothers and sisters joined in. Then Mum and Dad – and even Grandpa, with wizened face and hair turning grey. The troupe formed a blockade in front of us, and behind too, every bit as determined as the miners who'd gone on strike in Britain during the nineteen-eighties. We had no Margaret Thatcher to lead us through. Nor the politician who'd inherited her throne, the inimitable Boris Johnson. Once again, the ordinary POMs were on their own – their leader, Oshan, nowhere in sight.

"Hmph!" Nelson made a show of waving his arms. "They're only monkeys!"

Behind him, Amy did a nervous breakdance, while Beca swiped at the air with her walking pole, all to no avail. The monkeys didn't budge. Grandpa monkey itched his privates, and the rest of his family took a step closer.

"We're surrounded," I said, taking stock of the situation.

"Looks a bit dicey." Frank nodded.

There were six of us – Nelson, Amy, Beca, Frank, Kate and me – surrounded by more than twenty monkeys. Still no sign of Oshan, nor the other five POMs, who'd gone on ahead.

"Look! There's a viewpoint up there. We might get some

nice photos." Amy indicated a gap in the trees ahead, seemingly oblivious to our peril. Either that or she was braver than me, prepared to shoo away the ten monkeys who barricaded the way.

"We can take some photos of the little fellows." Boldly, Nelson held his phone out at Grandpa monkey and began clicking.

The old monkey glared, the muscles around his eyes tightening and the pink of his lips receding across sharp-looking teeth. Concerned, I motioned at Nelson to step back. Yet Grandpa monkey didn't attack. He raised a clenched paw to his face and made a clicking sound with his tongue, pretending he had a phone too.

"Look! It's taking photos of you!" Amy giggled.

Then Grandpa monkey screamed and sprang forward. He snatched the phone out of Nelson's hand and disappeared into the trees, all the other monkeys shrieking and following.

For a whole minute no one said anything. Nelson stared into the trees as if he expected the monkey to return and hand his phone back, perhaps even say sorry. Amy stared at Nelson as if none of this had happened. And Kate, Beca, Frank and I stared at each other, our phones gripped in our palms and thrust deep into our pockets.

"Perhaps it thinks your phone is edible," said Frank. "It's an Apple, isn't it?"

Nelson's usual grin curdled. "It's a Samsung Galaxy."

"Chocolate, then," said Frank. "Didn't they have a Milky Way bar once?"

Above us, monkeys were making a lot of noise. Once or twice I thought I heard a sound like the Skype ring tone – *ding DONG ding, dong DING dong* – but of course it couldn't have been.

"We can go and look at the view now." Amy pointed at the empty path ahead.

"Hey-ho! What about my phone?" Nelson continued to stare upwards, though now the branches were empty; the monkeys had moved on. "I'm not going anywhere till I get it back."

"Come on, mate." Gently, Frank patted Nelson on his shoulder. "How about we catch up with Oshan?"

With a disappointed expression, Nelson followed us to a little hummock with a marvellous view of flat plains below. In the distance rose hills and the silhouette of a sheer barrow-shaped rock – the same rock we'd climb tomorrow.

"This would make an absolutely lovely photo," Nelson said in a small voice.

"Don't fret, dear." Amy touched his arm. "We'll get you another."

AS IF TO COMPENSATE FOR the shenanigans on the way up, the cave temple of Dambulla amazed us. We removed our shoes and handed them to an attendant for safekeeping in his hut. Then, passing through a whitewashed entrance building, we stepped barefoot into a smooth, cool courtyard. A lone monkey leered, probably a relative of the thieving troupe down the hill. A ginger cat strolled out too, remarkably like our ginger one at home. And there were plenty of other tourists – all nationalities, all creeds, most with serious-looking lenses hanging around their necks. The monkeys wouldn't pilfer those cameras so easily. The little critters would need a winch to hoist them up into the trees.

Around us, several people in our group prepared their equipment, removing lens caps and powering on zooms. Linda and Tom clutched especially big lenses, long enough to take someone's eye out. Everyone else had their phones, apart from Nelson who positioned his hands into the shape of two Ls in front of his eyes, framing the wooden door that led into the first of the caves.

"Sizing up your composition?" Jerry hadn't seen what had happened.

"Nah! The little bugger was too fast." Nelson misunderstood.

"There won't be any monkeys inside, will there?" Amy gestured at the entrance.

"No monkeys." Oshan laughed. "Only Buddhas."

And he was right.

Once we'd managed to squeeze past the stream of people coming out, we found ourselves in a long, narrow chamber almost entirely filled by a fifteen-metre reclining Buddha statue. People filed up and down the aisle at its side – some towards the distant head and others to the huge feet. Each toe was carved precisely in black-grey rock, the biggest the same size as a fridge. A few metres past the toes stood a statue of Buddha's faithful disciple, Ananda, who, after being appointed Buddha's principle attendant, accompanied him everywhere on his wanderings. Ananda had been endowed with the memory of an elephant and later was able to recollect many of Buddha's teachings.

We stepped out of the cave, blinking in the sunlight. Yet not for long. It was a moment's walk to the next doorway that led into the second cave. This one was huge, so big its walls appeared to be far, far away. From somewhere in the middle of all the Buddha statues and tourists, Oshan's voice unwound, explaining the cave's context and history.

"This is the Maharaja Vihara or Temple of the Kings, yeah?" His words cut through the hum and focused our eyes on a well-preserved wooden statue ahead. "The first was

King Valagumba of Anuradhapura who fled here from Tamil invaders. He came to this cave and converted it into temples." Then Oshan directed his voice towards a different corner, where a second statue stood, barely visible. "Another was King Nissankamalla of Polonnaruwa. A thousand years later he had the walls painted."

Despite all the people obscuring our view, the cave was a cathedral of artistic masterpieces. All the beautifully painted statues of Buddha laboriously carved from solid rock. And adorning the walls and ceiling – virtually everywhere we looked – a plethora of wonderful murals. Some showed scenes from Buddha's life: the little white elephant his mother dreamed of before he was born; later his temptations by the demon king Mara in various forms, firstly an army of soldiers brandishing arrows, then maidens attempting to seduce Buddha, and finally guilt for neglecting his duties as prince, father, husband and son. The murals were painted so their patterns followed natural contours of the rock, and in places they appeared more like hanging tapestries than anything solid. The most unusual artefact in the cave was a pot in one corner that rippled with water. Its source was a drip from the ceiling – rock water as holy as everything else here, and reputed never to run dry.

Eventually we left this soaring place to visit the three remaining caves. They were equally distinctive – smaller, yet still crammed with Buddha statues, wall paintings and people. In the third cave another long Buddha statue reclined, head resting on a stone pillow that floated like a delicate lotus flower. This cave had apparently once been a storeroom – as had cave five – before being converted into a temple. Caves four and five were rich in Buddha statues as well, some made of plaster and brick rather than hard rock. Too many statues, it seemed, could never be enough.

Perhaps a subtle reflection of the words Buddha is supposed to have used to repulse Mara's first temptation: "Mere numbers do not make the strength of an army. The sun can outshine a myriad of glow worms. If wisdom is the source of power, a single hero can defeat countless soldiers."

Behind me I spotted Nelson taking his imaginary photos, his hands framing, and his tongue clicking. His photos wouldn't be like the ones everyone else was taking – relegated to memory cards, computer drives, recycling bins and then forgotten. No, Nelson's images would be permanent, embossed within the synapses of his memory. Nelson had become our Ananda, storing forever impressions he'd never forget.

FOUR

Sigiriya

Once everyone was back on the bus Oshan walked up and down handing out *vadai* – ball-shaped, deep-fried snacks that tasted like spiced fish cakes yet were made entirely of vegetables. There'd been no sign of Nelson's phone on the path coming down, and though monkeys crowded along the edge, gibbering and gesticulating, none of them had been there to return stolen property.

Fortunately we didn't have much further to travel. Our hotel was at nearby Sigiriya, only fifteen kilometres northeast. Chanuka drove carefully along a highway bounded on both sides by thick trees. In front of me, Lucy and Bruce snuggled together as though on a date. Behind me, Nelson lamented the loss of his phone.

"I only bought it in September." It sounded as if he was talking to Frank – the two of them were rapidly becoming best buddies. "It cost me an arm and a leg, and all my photos are on it, plus a video of Amy doing hip-hop."

"Amy does hip-hop?" Frank sounded surprised.

"No, I don't!" said Amy. "I suggested ballroom, but in the end we never went."

"We saved up to come here instead." Nelson's voice rose in indignation. "And the little buggers nicked my phone."

Chanuka turned off the main highway and onto a dirt track that twisted this way and that like it was trying to shake us off. He slowed the bus right down and I stared through the passing foliage, less blurred now, hoping for another glimpse of the barrel rock we'd seen from Dambulla. We were closer now and ought to have a better view. Wherever the rock was, however, it stayed hidden. Oshan pointed out an electrified fence instead, then a rickety watchtower as tall as a tree.

"The farmer will sit up there at night, yeah?" he said in his sing-song way, his voice a little strained. "Watching out for wild elephants that wander in and destroy the crops. If the farmer sees one he will throw firecrackers and scare it away. The elephants can be very dangerous. Sometimes they trample on people."

"What about the monkeys?" An aggrieved sigh burst from behind me. "Do they throw crackers at *them*?"

"Yeah! They put on paper hats and laugh at the jokes." Frank chortled, somehow transliterating to Christmas crackers. "What do you call a monkey with a phone? An oh-rang-oh-tang."

Everyone groaned, especially Nelson. "You're a hard man," he said to Frank. "Mocking a fellow when he's down. You wouldn't be laughing if you'd seen the photo I took."

Five minutes later we arrived at Hotel Sigiriya. A team of receptionists, porters and waiters streamed out to greet us, offering us cold towels and glasses of refreshing fruit juice. Then after Oshan had handed out keys they showed us to our rooms and brought in our cases. Normally they'd be expecting a tip – tipping is standard in Sri Lanka for any kind of service – but while we were on the tour all tips would be provided by Oshan from a kitty we'd contributed to on the first night.

Our room was airy and spacious, with clean cream walls, and a fan slowly rotating from the ceiling. A pair of French doors led outside into a garden, while a more solid wooden one led into an en suite bathroom. The bed was comfortable too – just as well because we were staying for two nights. One night to psych ourselves up, ready for a near-vertical ascent of the rock we'd glimpsed from Dambulla, and the second to recuperate before we moved on somewhere else.

Suitably daunted at the prospect awaiting us, we crept to the hotel's bar for a drink. And there it was, in all its photogenic glory – Lion Rock, Sri Lanka's most popular tourist attraction. Now only a kilometre away, it towered out of the forest like a giant dinosaur's claw, dramatically aligned with the swimming pool. In the fading light, the rock's sides were an eerie red-grey and sheer too – so steep they'd make a skyscraper tremble.

For a while I sat with a beer, gazing in a kind of trancelike fascination. In turn, the rock glared back, unforgiving, unperturbed, impossibly high. By the pool stood a telescope yet I ignored it, preferring to keep the entire rock in my sights rather than be petrified by the detail of its sides. The thing was a relic, a fortress, a monastery, a battle site and a *huge, huge* shadow over tomorrow. It was only now that I was here, on the threshold of climbing it, that I could give it the attention it warranted and contemplate the mechanics of going up there one dread tread after another, a clanking iron staircase of twelve hundred steps.

When night fell, as swift and black as a power failure, the rock's menace faded a little. Climbing it couldn't be so bad, could it? Hundreds of tourists wended its procession of steps every day: young people, old people, people with sticks, people with phobias. And it wasn't so high. Taller in my mind than ever it was in altitude. At two hundred metres it barely reached halfway up the Sky Tower in Auckland. And Kate's mum and her four friends had already demonstrated the rock could be conquered, their combined ages in excess of three hundred years. We were younger and stronger than they were, and Lion Rock was an important reason we were here.

Bottling out wasn't an option. I had to climb.

That night as we dined in the restaurant, listening out for elephants and firecrackers but hearing only the clack of plates and babble of languages, I forced my mind off the rock and onto something else. Nelson's latest hi-def shirt, Kate's banter as she chatted with the rest of the table – and, of course, the food.

When it came to the dinner buffet Hotel Sigiriya had everything. Sweet corn soup in a big tureen along with seven different varieties of bread; a smorgasbord of salads, plus rice dishes, curries, and Western staples such as spaghetti bolognese, steamed vegetables and beef stroganoff. Best of all – judging by the twinkle in Kate's eyes – there were the desserts: trifles, crème brûlées, chocolate brownies and fresh tropical fruit. Perhaps we'd discovered our true reason for coming to Sigiriya. Not to climb the lion but to eat like one.

MORNING DAWNED, misty and fearful. Thick cloud spread over the forest, and the rock had vanished.

"It will clear later." Oshan grinned at us as we dawdled into breakfast. "Always around eleven. This is why we go up early – to avoid the heat and catch the best view."

"There'll be a view, will there?" Jerry appeared like a ghost, his hair wet and brushed, his face rosier than ever. He pointed at the telescope. "You can't see a thing through that. Looks like someone left the jug boiling."

"Yeah!" Oshan's grin grew bigger. "Don't worry. It's often like this. It will clear."

Everyone had to hope he was right. Although secretly I half-hoped he was wrong. In a near white-out like this we might not ascend at all. Even if we did, we wouldn't see much. And if I couldn't see anything, not even the boots of the person in front, I wouldn't have to worry about vertigo.

FIVE

Lion Rock

We set off in the bus, Chanuka chuckling as he drove and Oshan chatting by his side. It was a short journey to the official entrance, where lots of other buses were already parked. A large party of Asian tourists gambolled around one another in tightly fitting Lycra and fluorescent shoes. A crowd of Indian tourists formed into family groups, dads and mums leading children in brightly coloured clothes. One or two backpackers paid off their tuk-tuk drivers and then stood wondering what to do with their packs. None of them looked particularly fit. Yet no one appeared grossly infirm. They were average tourists like us, some fleet and brave, others slow and afraid, ready to give Lion Rock a go.

Oshan bought our tickets and marshalled us through the entrance. As he'd promised, the mist was starting to clear, and the rock rose like a huge ochre wall. Close up it appeared higher than it had from the hotel, and my heart skipped a couple of beats. I didn't want to stare up at the top yet momentarily I did, the summit thankfully still obscured.

"These are the water gardens." Oshan gestured at several rectangles of water. "If you go up there –" he pointed at an embankment on our left "– you'll see that together they form a square."

A few people climbed up to see. I stayed where I was, conserving my energy for the ascent proper. Now we were here – committed to doing this – I wanted to climb straight up and then down again.

Oshan, however, had more things to show us. An ancient fountain sprinkler from which water would have once spouted. A pink-and-red rock that looked like a hippo. A cave on the left-hand side in which, if we looked carefully, were traces of old paintings. Oshan pointed at something that could have been the image of an *apsara*, a celestial nymph. Equally, though, it could have been an ancient smudge. He told us about another cave on the right-hand side of the path, the sinister Cobra Hood Cave named for its resemblance to the snake's head. Fortunately he wasn't going to take us that way. The prospect of climbing up the rock was real enough without the fear of poisonous snakes as well.

"Are you saying there'll be cobras up there?" said Jerry, voicing everyone's thoughts.

Oshan smiled. "No snakes. But watch out for wasps. Nine wasp stings equal one cobra bite, yeah? And for monkeys. They bite too."

Nelson snorted. "I think Amy and I will stay down here. We'll take a little stroll around the gardens and wait for you to come down."

"Sure." Oshan didn't seem bothered. There were probably people on every trip who didn't go up.

I wondered if anyone else would opt out. Kate, maybe – but no, she held a walking pole in her hand, keen to reach the top. Likewise, everyone else stamped their feet and flexed their elbows. Besides me, only Jerry hung back. He was checking something on his phone – the weather in an hour's time maybe, or when the clouds would clear.

Oshan seemed oblivious to our impatience. Gathering everyone around him, he proceeded to tell us Sigiriya's history. The fortress and gardens had been built by King Kashyapa in the fifth century as a new capital to succeed Anuradhapura. Apparently King Kashyapa needed somewhere secure. He feared an invasion by his half-brother, Mogallana, whom he'd exiled to South India. Worse still, he feared revenge, for as well as cheating his brother, the rightful heir of the kingdom, he'd killed his father, King Dhatusena, by entombing him inside a wall.

Mogallana did return. He led an army of Tamil mercenaries that surrounded Sigiriya. Too rash to sit it out, Kashyapa came down to fight. His elephant, however, became stuck in mud, and thinking he was retreating, his own men abandoned him. Rather than be captured, Kashyapa fell on his sword.

There were a few oohs and aahs as Oshan finished. The bad king Kashyapa had reaped what he deserved, leaving the magnificent gardens and fortress as evidence of his ill-gotten reign. Oddly, this was an entirely different narrative to that of the pop video shot at Lion Rock in 1982, in which two band members of Duran Duran danced on the top of the fortress and sang "Save a Prayer". In their video, the sky had shone blue and cloudless, with crystal views of the forest – quite unlike the vaporous murk of today. Such is the provenance of beautiful, dramatic locations. One story fades, and a new one springs to replace it. More often than not, each is less about the place and more about the storyteller – a new generation looking at itself. In this way, Lion Rock can be the history of a king, the backdrop for a song, or simply a view.

At last Oshan ran out of stories, and we made our way into the boulder garden – several boulders lying against rock – and through an archway onto the first staircase, this one steep and walled in. Rain had fallen overnight so the stone steps were extra slippery. Even wearing walking boots I trod carefully, afraid of losing my grip and falling. The atmosphere was saturated with moisture, and reaching the top of this initial staircase I had to stop, lean against a wall and gulp water from my bottle. I felt as if I was boiling inside, everything too close.

"You all right?" Kate seemed in better shape.

"Yes." I nodded. "Just taking it slowly."

The vertigo hadn't kicked in yet, but perhaps apprehension of what was to come – all those sheer drops, those precarious staircases – was having an effect. And much as it was good to be in a group, I didn't want to hold everyone up. Maybe this was one activity I'd have been better taking at my own pace.

Another steep staircase followed. Then another and another. Each one more difficult, the humidity pressing in like a sauna without a door. These were the terrace gardens, a series of ledges hinged on sheer rock. Occasionally – nervously – I glanced back. We were above the tree level, the canopy of the forest stretching out like a dark green carpet. In the distance, other rocks protruded like pinnacles, while on the horizon wispy clouds drifted. It was a sublime, beautiful, transient view. And we weren't even at the summit yet.

The steps ended and we plateaued onto a ledge. I tried hard not to look down as we started traversing it, all too aware of the sheer drop on my left. There was a barrier of some description – yet I didn't want to look too closely at that either. Vertigo holds no logic; it cannot be easily dissuaded. I focused on the rock wall to my right and the solid path ahead, which abruptly and terrifyingly switched to metal struts with wide gaps of thin air.

Now I struggled to walk forward rationally. I wanted to huddle into a hyperventilating lump of hysteria on the floor. Giving in to my fears wouldn't help, though. I had to overcome them. Besides, there was no floor. Only cast-iron slabs, and God knew how many hundreds of empty feet beneath.

If I thought things couldn't get any worse, they did. We came to a cast-iron spiral staircase that corkscrewed perilously upward. It led to a cave in the rock face where – lo and behold! – flew a flock of colourful frescoes: buxom young women, painted from the waist upwards, all thought to be *apsaras* or celestial nymphs. These were the Sigiriya Damsels, incredibly old – and very famous. Originally there had been five hundred of them. Now only twenty-one survived. In their heyday the frescoes must have been magnificent. Even now, fifteen hundred years later, their colours and curves were still preserved, the nymphs offering us gifts of flowers and fruit.

A little way on, a three-metre-high façade wall had been constructed along the outside of the ledge. This was Sigiriya's mirror wall, coated at its creation with a highly polished plaster made from lime, egg whites, beeswax and honey. When King Kashyapa walked past – as surely he would have – he'd have gazed on his own wicked reflection walking with him. The wall's reflectivity had dimmed since then, yet to make up for this ancient poets had daubed the wall with nearly eighteen hundred pieces of graffiti. Some ditties expressed ardent feelings about the damsels, while others recorded the mere fact of their author being present.

I didn't read any of the graffiti. For one thing I was thinking about how I would climb down. And for another, all the writing was in Sinhalese, Sanskrit or Tamil – none of which I understood. Afterwards, on that modern equivalent of a mirror wall, the World Wide Web, I found these two examples in English. "Ah, the golden coloured one in the mountainside who entices one's eye and mind, and whose breasts, delightful to look at, diverted my mind to the intoxicated swans." And another, more straightforward: "Having climbed Sigiriya, I am delighted with the sight created by natural surroundings of Sri Lanka."

Another spiral staircase led down, back to the main path. A thick rock balustrade shielded any view of the drop. Reassuringly, there was a solid rock floor too. Then, abruptly, the balustrade ended. In its place stood a sparse metal barrier that – *don't look, don't look* – exposed how high we were. I gritted my teeth, clenched my fists, shut my eyes. Then opening them again – *horror, horror* – discovered the rock floor ended as well, tumbling into a railway line of metal slats.

I walked with my head up. No way would I glance down. Tricky, though. I had to look at something. The bare rock face? My white knuckles? The inside of my eyes spinning like a top?

With a flood of sweaty relief I spotted grass ahead. Far sooner than I'd expected, we had reached the top. Tentatively I lifted my eyes, looking out for those all-encompassing views – green treetops in every direction, rocks similar to Sigiriya in the distance, and beyond them the yellow-brown expanse of Sri Lanka's northern plains. The trees were dark, however, matted in cloud. Nor were there any plains, and we were not at the top. In my rush to finish I'd forgotten about the Lion Platform, two-thirds of the way up. On this flattish spur of rock a hundred or more people were collected in front of two giant stone paws. Each paw was the size of a car – and not a small car but a Mercedes Benz. Long ago they'd formed part of an enormous lion statue, a symbol of King Kashyapa's seized legitimacy to the throne. A staircase through the jaws had led all the way up to the summit. Rumour had it the steps had been entirely enclosed by a wall. King Kashyapa had suffered from vertigo too. Like me, he didn't want to look down.

The lion was long gone, fallen on its claws. The only way up now was a twisted, nightmarish fire escape – more cast-iron steps that criss-crossed the bare rock like they'd been specially designed to torment acrophobics. A line of people snaked upwards, laughing, shouting, taking photos. One or two trod more quietly, their faces frozen in stone, especially one Asian gentleman who'd stopped at a tight bend, petrified.

Once again I wondered about turning back. This was an option now since a different set of steps led directly down from the Lion platform, without having to climb the final metal skeleton to the top. I could claim I'd travelled ninety percent of the way up, only missing out the last fifty or so metres. Anyway, there'd only be swirling white clouds on the summit. None of the panoramic views of the "Save a Prayer" video, no soaring vocals, no singers in white pop suits.

But I'd come this far. All the way from New Zealand, all the steps up from the bottom. I couldn't quit – at least not without trying. Taking a step towards the iron hell, I again tried to kid myself – imagine I wasn't here but in 1982. In my head played a familiar riff, that rasping sequence of notes leading into their enchanting hit.

STEPPING up the last few treads, I emerged numb onto the flat top. There was no wind, no sunshine, only a blanket of cloud in every direction. I could see the grass in front of me, a few stone walls and, a little further away, a large rectangular tank of water. A hundred or so people milled aimlessly, occasionally posing for selfies. No one sang or danced. No helicopters with film crew and cameras flew by. The reign of mad kings and pop videos had long passed. Sigiriya wasn't a fortress anymore. Nor a stage.

Lion Rock had shrunk to an anthill, covered in tourists.

SIX

Wot, No Elephants?

"Was it good?" shouted Nelson from the bottom of the path. "Did you get to the top?"

"Just about." I was still perspiring, my clothes damp and boots wet.

Nelson, by contrast, appeared fresh and clean, his shirt uncreased and his trainers spotless. Amy too looked like she'd stepped out of a hair salon.

"Take a look at these!" With no device to take photos, Nelson had made several ink impressions of the Sigiriya water gardens in a notebook. With biro-blue fingers he flicked through the drawings, showing them to people as they boarded the bus.

"That's an elephant." He pointed at a splotch with two ears and a crude trunk. "And that big brown thing behind it is Lion Rock."

"There were elephants down here?" Kate loved elephants and would have stayed at the bottom if she'd thought she might see one.

"Only in his head." Amy shook *her* head. "He's just trying to make everyone jealous."

"But there *was* an elephant!" Nelson's eyes tightened. "All done up in tassels and fancy silk. One of those monks in orange was leading it. He said *Ayubowan* to me and smiled."

"I didn't see it." Amy shook her head again.

"You'd gone to the ladies."

"Why didn't you tell me about it?"

"I didn't think you'd believe me."

"I don't. You're making it up."

Whatever Nelson may have seen – a bona fide temple elephant, or maybe an elephant-shaped rock – we knew we'd be seeing more of the noble beasts later that afternoon in Minneriya National Park. Jeeps would pick us up from the hotel at two o'clock and take us on a fun-filled pachyderm safari. The park was part of an elephant corridor that connected two other national parks, Kaudulla and Wasgomuwa, and sometimes contained as many as three hundred of the animals. There was always a big elephant party in September when they drank, stamped and picked mates. A bit like us except a hundred times heavier.

Meanwhile we had the mystery of Nelson's elephant, conveniently unrecorded in any electronic format. Nelson himself was equally a mystery. Neither he nor Amy had told anyone what they did for a living. They might be teachers, academics or retired members of Her Majesty's Government. Whenever the topic of jobs came up they were experts at vagueness and diversion.

"Do you always go away at Christmas?" I asked Amy, trying to steer the conversation onto something other than the phantom elephant.

"Not really. Anyway, we'll be back just before. I'm

decorating the tree on the twenty-second and Nelson is picking up the turkey on the twenty-third."

"And I'm cooking it on Christmas Eve!" said Nelson, overhearing.

"You're a cook?"

"I know good food when I eat it."

"A food critic? A food photographer?"

"I can't take photos." He held out ink-stained hands. "I don't have a phone, remember? Or a camera."

"What's your job, though? What do you do when you're at home?"

"Oh, this and that." He smiled enigmatically.

"What do you mean?"

"Everything I have to and nothing I don't."

"Is it something sensitive? A secret?"

"I'd prefer to keep it to myself." He winked. "Maybe I'll tell you once we've seen our first elephant."

"But you have seen an elephant!"

He coloured at that and looked away. "Oh, yeah, so I have. But you haven't, have you?"

Back at Hotel Sigiriya our group sat in the bar area waiting for the jeeps. Some people ate snacks while others sipped drinks. Nelson had a big mug of beer on the table in front of him and so did Frank. Jerry ordered a glass of whiskey, perhaps inspired by the Christmas anthem "Good King Wenceslas" playing on the PA.

No one said much, staring into their drinks or gazing at the grey sky. The weather wasn't looking good. Clouds massed above the swimming pool, and Lion Rock was swallowed whole. Rain began to fall – just one or two drops to start with, spotting the surface of the pool. Then, with the suddenness of a car wash, the heavens opened, and rain came down in bucketfuls. The pool churned into a tempest while the roof above us became a drum. Even the ornamental metal chains at the edge of the bar cascaded with water.

It felt like we'd been transported out of our nice holiday, our nice hotel and nice travel group and into a disaster movie. Already a sheet of water was spreading across the terrace and rain ricocheted against our feet. This was a different place from the one this morning, especially considering this was December – the dry season.

"Just like being at home, isn't it?" Frank had a slogan for everything.

"I wish they'd stop playing those stupid Christmas carols," said Bruce, tugging at his hair. "We've had "O Little Town of Bethlehem" twice now, and last night it was "Rivers of Babylon" over and over again. It feels wrong, doesn't it? Carols out here?"

"Some of them aren't even carols." Lucy hummed the tune. "Just repetition."

Beca leaned forward. "Maybe if we asked, they could put on something more topical. "Raindrops Keep Fallin' on My Head"? Or "Singing in the Rain"?"

"I don't think I'll be singing," said Frank. "I'd rather read a book. And I will later, once you've all left."

"You aren't going on the safari?" I looked at him.

He shook his head. "Jerry's going. I'll stick here."

"I reckon we already see enough of each other." Jerry sipped at his whiskey. "Even best pals need a break."

As far as I knew Jerry and Frank were still sharing a room, despite Jerry's antipathy and Frank's stoicism. Now they were distancing, Jerry going out and Frank not – a bit like one of those fancy barometers on which the sun and the rain never came out at the same time.

Outside, water thudded down with no sign of abating.

The clouds had sunk so low we couldn't even see the trees let alone the rock. Only God knew what it would be like out on safari. We might not see any animals at all.

"The jeeps are covered, aren't they?" Bruce pulled at his hair again, a thick bunch of strands pressed between his fingers.

"They'd better be," said Lucy. "We'll get soaked otherwise."

The rain was making everyone pensive. Usually Lucy and Bruce were chilled out, relaxing in each other's arms rather than worrying about the weather. Yet now their concern was palpable. I too pictured the track churned into mud and big puddles forming in the dips.

"They won't go if it's too bad." Out of all of us, Frank seemed the least bothered, steadily drinking his beer, his feet stretched out on the table.

"What!" Jerry feigned surprise. "You mean I'm going to have to put up with you for the rest of the day?"

"Yeah, mate." Frank smiled.

Sure enough, a moment later, Oshan appeared, grinning like an artful genie. "*Ayubowan*," he said in a cheerful yet apologetic voice. "I'm afraid the safari will have to be postponed. It's too wet. You won't see anything. The elephants don't come out in bad weather. They take a rain check."

No one said anything. For a while we sat around, finishing our drinks and wondering what to do with an afternoon that had suddenly been cancelled. No point going for a stroll on one of the hotel's forest trails – it would be like walking at the bottom of the sea. Bizarrely, it was too wet to go swimming either – the pool was thrashing like a tiny typhoon. Perhaps Frank had the best idea after all, reading a book and relaxing, imagining we were somewhere else.

After making our way back to our room, Kate and I sprawled out on the wide bed with a book each. She read another chapter of *The Things We Cannot Say* by Kelly Rimmer while I stared at a blank page of my diary, unable to write. We'd been in Sri Lanka three days now, and there *were* things *we* could not say – such as the fact of my daily blog and its WordPress address. Until we knew the people in our tour a little better and how they might react to reading about our adventures it seemed prudent to keep the blog to ourselves. Later, once the group had bonded, I would announce what I was doing to anyone who was interested.

Three days then – and we'd yet to go on safari or drink a cup of good ole Ceylon tea. It was early days, though, even if it felt like we'd been here a while. The group was still getting started, with everyone on their best behaviour. They all seemed good-hearted, easy-going and funny – however things could change. The only certainties were the breakfast and dinner buffets that started and ended each day.

SEVEN

In the Same Gear

We hadn't known what clothes to pack for Sri Lanka. Lots of T-shirts and shorts for certain – the island was in the tropics. Yet the central hill country was rumoured to be chilly at night; we might need a warm jumper and a fleece when we reached that far. Then there were all the temple visits that required long-sleeved shirts to cover arms and shoulders, and trousers too that extended below the knees. I'd also brought my walking boots – hefty lace-up appendages that filled up my suitcase. They'd already ascended the slippery steps of Lion Rock and would later be used on the nine-kilometre tramp to World's End.

In the hot, humid climate we consumed clothes quickly. A fresh T-shirt in the morning would be malodorous by midday. Not that I changed that often, yet my supply of clean shirts was still diminishing. And as one hot day slid into the next I gave up trying to smell like a pomandered prince and became a rag-a-tag slob instead. A faint scent of stale sweat was part of being here, much like the aroma of dhal at breakfast, then the stronger smell of insect repellent in the evening. Anyway, our next scheduled activity was a bicycle tour of local villages. There was no way I was going to pedal for thirteen kilometres without perspiring.

The bicycle rental shop was a short bus ride from Giritale, where we were staying that night. As we drove up to the shop, the owner came out, waving at an array of bikes and helmets that stood ready in the glare of the morning sun. Straightaway the faster members of the group rushed over to claim their mounts – the bikes with the softest saddles and the best brakes. By the time I reached the fray only a black bike and a white bike were left. I selected the black one, with a black helmet – not because I like black, but because the helmet fitted.

Fortunately I'd chosen well. The saddle on my bike was the right height and the gears flicked easily up and down. The brakes were firm too – none of those soft spongy pads you only find out about on a steep downhill heading towards a come-smash-me brick wall. Hopefully, though, I wouldn't be needing brakes. The terrain was supposed to be gently undulating, without needing much effort.

Nine of us set off along a gravel track, Oshan at the front and a back-up man from the shop at the rear. Not everyone was cycling. Tom had pulled out his biggest lens yet and marched into the forest alone. He was set for some serious birdwatching and would meet us later at the lunch stop. Amy and Nelson weren't pedalling either. They were being chauffeured in a brightly coloured tuk-tuk. And Kate, not to be outdone, was driving her own tuk-tuk, with its usual driver sitting slightly bemused in the back.

"I've ridden heaps of quad bikes," she shouted as she zoomed past everybody, stones spitting and a jet of black smoke coming from the exhaust. "We herd cows with them in New Zealand. This is a piece of –." Her last word was lost in the wind.

I wanted to tell her to take it easy, but it was better I didn't. Cautioning her on speed would only make her go faster. Anyway, she was an excellent driver: observant, smart and decisive. The fact our insurance didn't extend to self-driving would remain irrelevant as long as she showed restraint. Though I couldn't help but remember a story she'd told me once. On one of her early quad-bike trips she'd taken out a fence at her parents' farm, allowing several cows to escape. Kate detests bicycles however – their pedals, their handlebars, their tyres and especially their saddles. For her, bicycles are instruments of torture designed for the athletically insane.

As she sped off into the distance, all of us cyclists tried to follow: Oshan, Frank and me pushing like crazy, and the others trailing behind. There was no way we'd catch her up. Apart from tyre tracks, she'd disappeared.

"She's done this before, yeah?" Oshan huffed and puffed.

I nodded weakly.

The track curved, then ran alongside a shallow cânal. Rickety wooden footbridges crossed to rickety wooden houses on the other side, and small children yelled bye-bye as they caught sight of us. The exact same greeting children had shouted in Samoa upon seeing a cyclist. Perhaps there was a connection, a reason they didn't use hi or hello.

Kate had to be way *way* ahead. We couldn't see her tuk-tuk, even after passing three junctions, several bridges and numerous confused-looking locals. Defeated, Oshan slowed, his brakes squealing. Coming to a stop, he pointed out a huge water monitor swimming below us in the reeds.

"We call them kabaragoyas," he said as the animal stared

balefully up at us. "We get thalagoyas too, but they're smaller and live on land. Sometimes the kabaragoyas eat the thalagoyas."

The kabaragoya wasn't the only creature in the water. A man kneeled at the edge, cleaning his teeth, while further away two women washed clothes. Oshan explained how the canal wasn't only for irrigating the rice fields but was a lifeblood to the villages, providing for many of their needs. The villagers used its water for washing, bathing and cooking. The canal was sourced from the nearby Giritale tank, a huge reservoir visible from the terrace of our latest hotel. Recent overuse of insecticides, however, had pushed up harmful metal levels in the water, forcing the villagers to now drink directly from water bottles.

We set off again at a gentle pace. The track was predominantly flat, and this wasn't a race. We were here to enjoy ourselves, to take in the sights and sounds, and to feel as though we belonged. Far better than being enclosed in a bus, seeing everything through glass.

Further on, another man was removing coconuts from their husks. He jabbed the fruits onto a long metal stake and twisted until the fibrous outer shells came off. A mound of discarded husks rose beside him. They'd be used for ropes, brushes and mulch, while the extracted coconuts would go to feed workers at the local rice factory. A little way beyond, we came to an area of brown mud being shaped into a paddy field. Low walls of moist earth separated the field into compartments, each to be watered and sown with rice plants.

Still no sign of Kate, though I wasn't worried. She knew how to look after herself – it would be the poor driver in the back who'd be clinging on for dear life as he watched the world rush by. Perhaps she hadn't come this way at all, especially since Oshan had murmured something about a shortcut to the house where we were due to have lunch. Kate might already be there, watching the cooks prepare our food.

Instead I relaxed and enjoyed the surroundings. Cycling can be so transcendental. My bike was easy to ride and worked perfectly. The tyres were fully inflated. The chain stayed on. The gears meshed seamlessly whenever I changed gradient, though that wasn't often. This was cycling at its best. No traffic, no punctures, no hills – and plenty to see. The irrigation canal stretched in a straight line with smaller canals branching off. Little shrines with brightly coloured statues of Buddha and Ganesh, the elephant god, sprang up along the track, while on the other side of the water sprawled households with huts, metal barrels, clothes drying on washing lines, children and dogs. Sometimes a dog might run out across a rickety footbridge, its tongue lolling. Only one ugly mutt bared its teeth and barked.

But we'd lost Jerry. One moment he was behind us. The next gone.

"Did anyone see him?" Oshan glanced reproachfully at the backmarker.

"I think he was taking a photo," said Beca. "Though he was taking a very long time."

"Perhaps he's watching us." I gestured at the bush behind. "Taking a photo as we speak."

As if on cue, Jerry came tearing down the track.

"Shit, now I've seen it all!" he shouted in a pitchy voice.

"A snake?" said Beca.

"A croc?" said Frank.

"Worse!" Jerry hopped off his bike and crouched, panting. "One of those water monitor things eating something, and – yuk – I zoomed in for a photo, and it was a bloody eye."

"An eye?" I felt my stomach turn inside out.

"It must have come from a pig or a goat or something." Jerry blanched. "This gunk shot out and went on my phone." He held up his Samsung Andromeda – slimed. He was going to have to clean the stuff off if he wanted to use the camera again.

"The kabaragoyas are scavengers," said Oshan. "They eat dead animals and sometimes, if the villagers are distracted, steal food."

After that everyone cycled a little faster, perhaps worried there might be other kabaragoyas about. We crossed a bridge to the final village and the track grew muddy and waterlogged. One by one we dismounted and pushed our bikes along its edge.

"I'm going to need a shower after this." Frank pointed at his legs, both splattered with wet earth.

"Heck, I'm gonna need a laundry!" Jerry turned around to show us his shorts and shirt saturated with mud.

"You should play for England." Frank laughed. "They need a tight prop."

"Ha, ha!" Jerry grimaced. "You lot should have waited for me. I had to grab the back of a tuk-tuk to try and catch up."

"And here you are!" said Oshan.

"Only just!" Jerry squeezed the bottom of his shirt, brown fluid dripping onto his legs. "The chain came off, the back wheel jammed, and I fell in this big greasy puddle."

We regrouped by the side of a nascent paddy field as Jerry sorted himself out. White ribbons dangled from wire fences, left there from a recent funeral. In the middle of the field, two flags fluttered sporadically from a crude flagpole. One appeared to be the Buddhist flag, with bright blue, yellow, red, orange and white stripes. The other was the official flag of Sri Lanka, a symbolic lion and more bold stripes.

"The colours are the different states in Buddha's life," said Oshan, noticing me staring. He pointed at the Buddhist flag. "Blue is compassion. Yellow, the path to liberation. Red, the Blessings of Practice. White, purity. And orange, wisdom."

"And the same for the other flag?"

"Those are for our peoples. The lion in the maroon rectangle for the Sinhalese. The orange stripe for the Tamils, and the green one for Islam. And the yellow border for everyone else."

No wonder everything in Sri Lanka was so colourful. The country was a tapestry of cultures, religions and peoples.

It was a short ride to the village house for lunch, where Kate, Amy and Nelson were waiting for us. A fire blazed in the courtyard at the front, heating a large metal pot suspended on sticks. Inside a lean-to, a lady chopped vegetables. And in a clearing out the back, beneath the branches of an enormous banyan tree, a table had been laid out with delicious fare: poppadums and a coconut chilli dip, dhal made from pulses, curried jackfruit – a yellowish brown fruit like breadfruit, white and red rice, and a local green vegetable diced and served with more coconut. The repast had been prepared by the family who lived at the house: a couple and their three young children.

Emerging from the lean-to, the wife showed us how to shred the white from inside a coconut using a metal scraper. Then she whisked it into coconut milk while her children smiled for photos. Oshan explained how the husband had once worked as a field labourer, but now that they received money from the tour company he was able to spend more time with his family. The husband would arrive home soon. He was out in the forest looking for Tom.

"Tom always gets carried away watching birds," explained Linda of her partner. "Loses track of time, gets lost and doesn't come home until dark. And it's no good phoning him. He's out of range or he's turned his phone off."

"It's the same with Lucy." Bruce put an arm around his wife. "I can never get hold of her when she's down the pub."

"I'm not watching birds, though." Lucy grinned, her smile wide. "Or blokes. Both eyes are strictly on the footie."

"Tom doesn't go to the pub," said Linda. "He brews his own stuff at home."

"I could murder a wine right now." Lucy's grin expanded. "It'd go down nicely with those curries."

She'd have to go without, however. There was no beer or wine with the meal, only cans of Coca-Cola and Sprite. Tom still hadn't returned, and waiting no longer we sat down to eat. Everyone was in a buoyant, après-pedal mood, heaping piles of food onto banana-leaf plates. The cycling had been therapeutic, providing some much-needed exercise and bringing our travels down to ground level. This was the way to see a country, wheeling through its rural heartland, one village at a time.

EIGHT

The Elephants of Minneriya

You'd think it would be difficult for elephants to hide, especially on flat grasslands where they were supposed to be grazing. Yet as our open-top jeep bounced along a rough dirt track, forcing us to cling to seats and handholds, we couldn't see a single animal.

We'd finally made it to Minneriya National Park – yesterday's trip rescheduled. Now, instead of rain, the sun blazed. Around us the damp landscape was drying out – puddles retreating, vegetation steaming, and mud hardening into cracked earth. The perfect conditions for a safari. Yet not one of the hundreds of elephants who lived here had made an appearance.

Tom, the ornithologist, didn't seem concerned. He rested a lens the size of a Saturn V rocket on one of the jeep's metal supports and aimed at a tiny black speck on a tree branch almost a mile away. The speck must be a bird of some kind, perhaps with colourful plumage, a greenish sheen on its breast. It was impossible to tell, it was so very very tiny.

You'd need the magnification of the Palomar telescope to see it properly.

"It's a green bee-eater," said Tom with quiet certainty. He peered into the viewfinder of his camera but didn't release the shutter. "They're two a penny around here."

The rest of us in the jeep – Linda, Kate and I – had to take his word for it. Neither Kate's phone nor my camera had particularly powerful zoom lenses. We'd struggle photographing elephants – presuming any appeared – let alone tiny birds. We stared at the impossible length of Tom's lens instead.

Linda noticed us looking. "When we went to Africa he had to get a special permit for his cameras. They thought he was a professional."

"That permit cost five thousand rand," said Tom gruffly. "Two hundred and fifty pounds in real money."

"It's not as if he's making a fortune selling photos to magazines," said Linda. "Most of his stuff goes to photo share sites. You don't get thruppence for that."

I didn't dare ask if he'd purchased a permit for Sri Lanka. Somewhere I'd read that one was required for all commercial photography at sites such as Sigiriya and Dambulla. Yet no one had been checking. Commendably, the guards at the entry points had been more interested in stopping plastic bags – an environmental hazard – than charging for cameras.

The bee-eater flew away and Tom put down his camera. With an almighty jerk our jeep shot forward, only to join a cluster of other jeeps blocking the track. Their passengers were standing on seats and aiming their cameras in one direction. No distant dot of a bird but a faraway grey rock.

"It's an elephant!" shouted Kate.

"Are you sure?" I said.

Whatever it was, it rose inert and wedge-shaped out of the foliage. It didn't look much like an elephant, but perhaps it was standing very still, concealing its ears, trunk and tail. Then, as our jeep edged closer, a mouth became visible and small black eyes. Nothing else though. The creature stayed behind its bush pretending it couldn't see us – and likewise we shouldn't see it.

"Don't they have such tiny eyes," said Linda. "You'd think for the size of them, they'd have something bigger."

"Their eyesight is piss poor." Tom pointed his lens at the elephant's head. "They can't see anything more than ten metres away."

More elephants came into view, these ones less obscured by bush and easier to see. Huge creased heads and parchment ears. Long, long trunks that arced forward gracefully to tug up wads of grass that they then curled into their mouths. Behind their heads, their big saggy bodies shuddered, grey folds of skin that reached to the ground. All of them were grazing, a slow, steady ballet of trunks, torsos and tails.

"They're premium, aren't they?" said Linda. "You know, if we had a zoo near to Wharram I'd get a job there like a shot."

"You hate working with big animals." Tom half-turned from his lens.

"Cows, yeah! They fart too much. But elephants – I'd give my right arm to work with one of those." She pointed at the animals.

"Can you get us the right lens?" Tom gestured back at his camera case. "I need the five hundred millimetre."

If he was having problems taking decent pictures with his moon-shot lenses, then I didn't stand a chance with the tiddler on my camera. How ironic that the world's second biggest land animal (Asian after African) still wasn't big enough to fill my frame. It made that expression "the elephant in the room" seem misinformed. As if anyone would ever have an elephant in a room other than a circus tent or zoo enclosure. Although there was a wild elephant called Natta Kotta in the south of Sri Lanka who liked nothing better than wandering into the lobby of the local Jetwing Yala Hotel.

The average male Asian elephant is nine feet tall, twenty feet long, and at a squeeze *would* probably fit inside your average living room. But it'd be there only a short while. Elephants are heavy, and the floor would probably collapse. Then there'd be an elephant – but no room.

The jeeps dispersed and we drove on, searching for other elephants that might be a little closer to the track. Five minutes later, we found what we were looking for. Four more elephants – two mothers and their babies – and much nearer. These elephants were eating as well, their trunks curving up and down as, one foot at a time, they shuffled forward towards untrampled grass. The babies sheltered underneath their mothers to start with, practically impossible to see. Then, becoming more confident, the small elephants made forays out into thicker grass, their little trunks looping, while their mums continued to graze and watch over them. It was a scene that was timeless and beautiful, and pulling out my camera I took a few shots. I'd have probably done better just watching. Yet, as always on safari, there was an urge to capture something.

Our jeep moved on, following others deeper into the park. The next herd of elephants was near enough for us to smell the vegetation they were eating – cogongrass seasoned with a strong scent of mint. Then on once more, to our closest encounter yet. Three elephants advanced to the side of the track, then – more agile than they looked – slipped single file between two jeeps and out the other side. A little frightening at first, but as cameras clicked and people sighed the elephants took no notice of us, and so it became the norm.

The best came last. Leaving the park and driving back to our hotel at Giritale, we came across several elephants right by the road, as close as close could be. Ignoring the traffic, these beasts lumbered over, so near we could have touched their hides. A sight worth waiting for – the ultimate pachyderm encounter. Proof you can shift any problem, but you can't stop an elephant.

NINE

Ancient City

At four forty-eight in the morning, according to the red LED clock on our bedside, a persistent rasping sound – *zah-Zah, zah-Zah* – woke me. Birdsong, I thought at first – the winged denizens of the beautiful Giritale tank greeting the new day. But as the sound went on, uninterrupted and spiking – *ZAH, ZAH, ZAH* – I realised it must be something else: a particularly annoying alarm call, a fire drill, maybe even a fire. Then, as suddenly as it had started, it stopped. Silence. But I was awake now and contemplating a new day. No elephants, no bicycles but a fabulous ancient city – the ruins of Polonnaruwa, once the capital of Sri Lanka's second kingdom, which dated from the eleventh century.

I found out at breakfast that the sound had been a fire alarm set off in error. Oshan wandered around the table, reminding everyone to wear plain shoes, easy to remove at the entrances to temples, and long-sleeved shirts – all shoulders covered – that would be respectful on sacred ground.

Then – time to go – Kate and I scooted out to the bus.

Our driver, Chanuka, was waiting for us, his firm hands around the steering wheel and a friendly grin on his face.

"*Ayubowan*," he said in a bright voice, clearly enjoying his job.

"*Ayubowan*," we said in return.

Nelson jumped on and teased Chanuka for being too cheerful. "You smile too much!" He waved a friendly finger. "You need to be more like our drivers in the UK and drive this bus like you're driving an elephant."

"An elephant?" Chanuka raised his eyebrows.

"Swear at everyone and blow your trumpet!" Leaning over, Nelson cheekily jabbed at the bus's horn.

BLARE!

Chanuka laughed, but behind us Jerry stumbled, spilling the coffee he'd been drinking all down his shirt.

"Heck! You gave me a fright." Jerry stared at us. "I've just had my stuff cleaned and all." With his free left hand he held up a yellow plastic laundry bag stuffed with clothes.

Nelson's face fell. "Sorry. I didn't realise."

Sakan, the luggage man, was laughing too. He'd finished loading the bags and now stood by the water container ready to replenish everyone's bottles. Oshan boarded as well, his expression as mischievous as ever. Whatever was amusing him – our accents, demeanour or how Nelson and Jerry fed off each other – he was always too polite to speak his mind. Instead he installed himself behind the microphone and, blinking rapidly, told us what we already knew: that we were heading to the ancient city of Polonnaruwa, then to a spice farm, and finally to our next hotel at Kandy. As usual there'd be an alarm call the next morning, though later than today, and hopefully not a fire alarm.

"Are there any shops in Kandy?" asked Nelson, still lacking a phone.

"Sure, yeah."

"How about earplugs? Soap? Sleeping pills?" said Jerry. "There's this persistent droning sound in my room – heck, a bit like somebody snoring – and I really need to get a decent night's kip."

"Yeah, yeah." Oshan nodded gleefully.

After three days together, the group was starting to gel. Amy and Nelson were hanging out with Beca, while Lucy and Bruce were hanging out with us. Linda and Tom were taking photos of everything, and Jerry wandered freely – at times a *de facto* leader, and at others his own man.

"Polonnaruwa is a UNESCO site and was once the centre of Sri Lanka's second kingdom, following on from the first kingdom of Anuradhapura," announced Oshan as we set off. "Its first Sinhalese king was Vijayabahu, but it was under King Parakramabahu – or Parakrama – that most of the city was built. That includes the Parakrama Samudra – the Sea of Parakrama – that we'll visit first."

Oshan could have referred to this sea as a "tank", a term the guidebooks used for manmade lakes in Sri Lanka. Thankfully he didn't, because then I'd have pictured a massive iron tank like the water cistern in the attic of an old house, yet none of these tanks – the English translation of the French word *reservoir* – were small or made of metal, but stretched out as huge expanses of water.

King Parakrama had been prolific at constructing tanks. He'd joined up five existing reservoirs to form the one vast Parakrama Samudra, and had overseen the construction and restoration of over two hundred other tanks as well. His motto had been, "Let not even a drop of rainwater reach the sea without benefitting man."

Fortunately for Oshan's aching tonsils and our fact-battered ears, it was only half-an-hour's drive to

Polonnaruwa. Chanuka took Nelson's advice and drove there using attitude, horn and irrepressible charm. As he parked on top of the dam bordering the Parakrama Samudra we marvelled at how big this glittering tank truly was. Fourteen kilometres end to end, and in places five kilometres wide. Midway across we could see a small island, Kok Doowa, once the site of a royal summer palace and now dotted with birds.

Despite all the history – this shining orb of ancient engineering – people in our group seemed more interested in an old bicycle standing upright by the side of the road. Frank knelt down to take a photo of it. So did Jerry with his newly sanitised phone. Amy and Beca too, everyone eager for an image of the bike's silhouette against the blue stillness of the water. Admittedly it was a sturdy, old-fashioned bike: a wire basket at the front, a crossbar, and a metal rack over a twenty-seven-inch rear wheel. The sort of bike your grandpa would ride on his way to collect the water or feed the goats. Functional nostalgia framed against picturesque antiquity. Yet for all the fuss people were making, the bike might have belonged to King Parakrama, or even his successor, King Nissankamalla, who'd bankrupted Polonnaruwa by having his name inscribed on practically every building. In all likelihood the bike was the property of one of the many vendors selling souvenirs. They strolled everywhere around the ancient city with trays of merchandise: straw sunhats, postcards, plastic replicas of carvings, and multi-coloured elephant jigsaw puzzles.

Back inside the bus, Oshan quickly ran through the itinerary for the rest of the morning. We'd drive to the archaeological museum first, two minutes away, to gain an appreciation of how the city was laid out: it extended several kilometres north to south. Then in short bus hops of a few minutes each we'd visit the Royal Palace complex, the Quadrangle of religious buildings, the Rankot Vihara – a huge brick stupa – and finally the rock carvings of Gal Vihara. There'd be a lot to see, more history and culture than most of us could absorb over several weeks rather than one short hot morning. Nevertheless, we'd do our best. We had plenty of brainpower between us – a quizzer, a vet, a teacher, a writer and an electrician. And Polonnaruwa was one of the most important archaeological sites in Sri Lanka. We had to do it justice.

The entrance to the museum was covered in scaffolding, with workmen in yellow vests hammering at things. Inside it was quieter, the subdued atmosphere of an institution. A series of musty rooms with stone relics guided us through the city's prolific history. In the first room stood a model of wood and polystyrene that showed the overall layout of the city: the Royal Palace a kilometre to our east, the Polonnaruwa Quadrangle a couple more to the north, and slightly further north again were Rankot Vihara and Gal Vihara. In later rooms various stone artefacts were perched on pedestals, and black and white photographs hung on the walls. There were few plaques to explain what anything was, other than cryptic numbers that referred to a yellowing list held at reception. Kate went back to borrow a copy, yet in the twenty minutes we had been allocated there were far too many exhibits to look up.

"It's all a bit lifeless, isn't it?" said Beca, one of the few people who hadn't rushed straight through. "I was hoping for something a bit more interactive."

"It's an ancient city, I guess. No one's lived here for hundreds of years."

I dawdled through the museum, trying to take things in, to become interested – and failed. I wished I'd read up more about Polonnaruwa before starting our holiday. Without question, there were going to be some incredible buildings later. It would have been good to have known more about them.

At the far end of the museum was a souvenir shop, where a large group of men in identical blue shirts and ties surged around one another like penguins, accumulating so tightly around the cash desk it was impossible to get near. They were all trainee guides, young and enthusiastic, yet perhaps too gung-ho for their future clients' good. Giving up on buying a guidebook, I went outside to find the others. If Chanuka drove off without me I'd have to follow on that old black bicycle.

Fortunately they were all there – Kate chatting to Oshan, Nelson to Amy, and Jerry going through his photos. Once everyone was on board, the bus took us to the ruins of the Royal Palace, first built in the twelfth century by King Parakrama. Even now, eight hundred years later, the facade still stood, a proud and imposing structure. Eight magnificent columns of red-and-black brickwork rose three storeys up into the blue sky, their surfaces changing to a beautiful mottled-green texture of lichen at the top. This building commanded like the tines of two enormous forks – a Pink Floyd album cover transposed to tropical jungle. Originally it would have towered even higher, with four additional wooden storeys that were long since gone. For ages I gazed at the strong, square base, the narrow-eroded waists, the thick joined-up necks and green-bearded tops, trying to imagine the palace restored. How tall and grand it must have been, the most exalted structure in all Sri Lanka at that time – the symbol of a king who ruled his kingdom of brick, water and people.

Other palace structures were sited nearby, such as King

Parakrama's council chamber – a three-terraced platform with stone pillars that had once supported a wooden roof. Ornate friezes of red-brown animals adorned the sides of each terrace – one of elephants, another of lions, and a third of dancing dwarves, all in different moods and postures, no two alike. The sheer craftsmanship to create these friezes must have been enormous; even now their carvings strode head to tail, intricate, detailed and perfect.

There was a royal bathing pool too – the same size as the pool at our last hotel – with two crocodile mouth spouts, three showers, and five stone seats for spectators. No one swam in the pool anymore, yet it still contained murky green water, piped in from a tank that in turn was supplied by underground pipes that ran below the palace.

The buildings were in amazing condition considering how old they were. The city had been overgrown by jungle for seven hundred years before being rediscovered in the twentieth century. No one had lived here for an exceptionally long time. The only permanent inhabitants left were dogs lazing in patches of sunshine, and toque macaques (reddish-brown monkeys) sitting cross-legged on low walls.

I stopped to photograph a young macaque that had long arms, long digits and a very long tail. It stared wistfully with dark, globular eyes, its face pinky-grey and its hair cropped black. I gripped my camera hard, remembering what had happened to Nelson, especially since he stood just ahead, framing a picture of a macaque with his hands.

"Don't give it your phone," he called. "Even if it offers to take a photo of you."

"These look a bit tamer than the ones at Dambulla," I said, pressing the camera button before my subject ran away.

"I saw one of them eating a sandwich. Bread from the hotel and a piece of bacon."

"They probably don't like dhal. Or cold rice."

God help the macaques if their diet did come from the buffets. They'd grow as fat as some of the tourists. Although local vendors wandered around selling food too: ice-creams, chips and nuts. Macaques would probably like nuts, even if they were less interested in puzzles and postcards. In all seriousness, though, they probably didn't eat enough. Their natural habitat was disappearing, and feeding them titbits made them dependent on transient visitors who wouldn't always be here. The species was already endangered. We had to respect their neighbourhood and give them space.

Back on the bus, it was a short four-minute ride to Polonnaruwa Quadrangle, where a whole multitude of ancient buildings clustered together. Once again I wished I'd read up more because these were undoubtedly a treasure trove of history. We came to the Vatadage first, an immaculately preserved, circular relic house, which had to be one of the most interesting and complex monuments in all Polonnaruwa. Before entering, we had to remove our shoes, leave them on the ground with dozens more, and walk barefoot across sun-baked earth. We had to remove our hats too, out of respect, yet unfortunately there was no roof, no shade, and without sun cream – *how unprepared we were* – I could feel my head burning.

It was worth it however to see the Vatadage, a circular stupa temple. Truly this was an amazing building, cleverly designed and expertly built. At each of the four entrances lay moonstones – ancient guard stones made in the shape of a half-moon. Each was intricately carved. An outermost ring of flames represented the cycle of life, and moving inwards came a ring of swans to choose between good and evil, a ring of elephants signifying birth, and a ring of horses signifying death. Unlike the moonstones at Anuradhapura

(Sri Lanka's first great city) there were no motifs for bulls or lions. Instead, these creatures had been transposed to the balustrade out of respect for Hindu and Sinhalese people, who wouldn't have wanted to tread on their sacred animals.

Inside the Vatadage there were four more of everything. Four seated Buddha statues, facing out to each of the entrances. And behind the Buddha statues, four small shrines, then in the centre a single low stupa or *dagaba*. Each Buddha statue sat in the *Dhyana Mudra* pose – both hands resting in his lap, the back of his right hand lying on the palm of his left. The heads however were different, again reflecting the intricacy and uniqueness of every carved image in Polonnaruwa.

Subsequently, I researched the different poses of Buddha, learning that distinct hand positions, or *Mudras*, represented specific moments in his life. In the *Abhaye Mudra*, the pose of protection and fearlessness, his right hand is raised, palm outwards and fingers up. In the *Dharmachakra Mudra* the tip of his middle finger on one hand touches the tips of the thumb and index finger of the other that have formed a circle to represent teaching. And in the reclining Buddha, as we'd already seen at Dambulla, and soon would at Polonnaruwa too, he reclines on his right side with his right arm supporting his head and his left arm draped along his body. This reclining pose represents the final moment of his life before he dies one last time and enters Nirvana.

For each of the four Buddhas inside the Vatadage there were twenty tourists taking photos. And every time I looked again they increased like bacteria multiplying on a Petri dish. Almost all of them scrutinised the images through their phones as if it were too passé to use only their eyes. Fortunately there weren't any selfies, for it was forbidden to pose for a photo with an image of Buddha in the background. If the police spotted this happening they would confiscate the camera and delete all its photos.

Leaving the Vatadage, I ignored my jandals and crossed into the Hatadage, another hot, pillared building that, along with the Atadage alongside, may have at one time housed the sacred Buddha tooth relic, now held at the Temple of the Tooth in Kandy. There were other ancient structures inside the Quadrangle too – the Thuparama Gedige or hollow Buddhist temple in one corner, and the Sathmahal Prasada or ziggurat monument in the opposite one. The Sathmahal was very striking and reminded me of a wedding cake because of how it rose six tiers high, each layer smaller than the one underneath. Unlike a cake, however, it was constructed of red and grey bricks, with an icing of green lichen. Given it had stood for over eight hundred years, it was amazingly well-preserved.

Time was melting in the heat, and after hurriedly finding my jandals among all the others I ran to the bus. A two-minute ride away we came to the largest wonder of the day – a brickwork dome the size of a stadium, with a single conical pinnacle at the top. This was the Rankot Vihara, a stupa that at fifty-five metres tall rose to a quarter of the height of Lion Rock. It wasn't climbable, however. Nor could you go inside. There is no inside. Apart from a number of tiny buried treasure houses, the stupa is filled with earth.

Again we removed our hats and footwear to ascend onto the stupa terrace and stroll around. Many colourful Buddhist flags flew from poles, but it was the stupa that magnetised us, difficult to believe this huge thing was entirely solid. Surely if I walked all the way around then I must find a door? By good fortune I went in a clockwise direction, eventually finishing – having spotted no doors – at the same place where I'd started. Later I read that this was another

Buddhist rule of etiquette. All stupas should be circumnavigated in a clockwise direction. This is an opportunity for meditation and brings good karma.

The bus took us for another quick ride, this time to the Gal Vihara, a popular and strangely enticing place. Here we had to show our tickets to uniformed guards before walking along a curved path to see four more images of Buddha, all carved into a single, huge granite outcrop. The first two images depicted Buddha seated, the third standing, and the last and easily largest showed him reclining on his right side. After the bright sun everywhere else the place had a serene, calming atmosphere. White butterflies flitted through the air, while from a cave somewhere came the sound of women and children chanting.

Yet we'd had enough. Ancient cities are like eating porridge – the first few mouthfuls sweet with honey, then every spoonful beginning to taste the same. Again, I wished I knew more. Yet would reading about these monuments and temples make sense before seeing them?

The sun was blazing hotter, the sky incandescent, and my brain was fizzing – too much history to absorb. Perhaps it was wise we weren't visiting Anuradhapura. There were even more buildings there. Its epic first kingdom had lasted thirteen hundred years.

After putting on our hats and jandals we made our way around a small lake back to the bus. This had been an epic morning, one both Kate and I would remember. In the distance Nelson crouched over something while Amy smiled, and Beca took a photo.

TEN

Doctor Spice

It was supposed to be a spice farm. A chance to see how the flavours of Sri Lanka were grown. Peppers, turmeric, cloves, curry leaves and cinnamon. Lemon grass, nutmeg, vanilla and ginger too. Yet as the herbologist led our group of eleven – no Oshan – deeper into the plantation, tugging at tree branches and sniffing from pots, it seemed he had other things on his mind.

"This is unripe pepper." With long, slender fingers, he pinched at a beady green fruit. "Cooked and dried to make black pepper. And not cooked but dried to produce green."

"And white?" said Jerry.

The herbologist frowned, clearly surprised at being interrupted. "White is from the seeds," he said in a lower voice.

He was a small, serious man. Thick glasses and a white coat made him look like a scientist, while ruffled hair and unruly eyebrows made him gangsterish. He ran his eyes up and down Jerry, perhaps working out if he was our ringleader. Then, flicking the flaps of his white coat, the man led us between coconut-husk-lined embankments to the next featured spice.

"This is cinnamon." He reached behind a tree and produced a canister with shavings inside. "From the inner bark of *Cinnamomum verum* – the true cinnamon tree. Aromatic and good for digestion. It is used in cooking, cakes, coffee and tea." After unscrewing the lid of the canister, he handed around a piece of the hard bark for people to touch and sniff.

Reaching behind again, he pulled out a glass vial filled with a yellowish liquid. "And this is cinnamon oil," he said, his voice intensifying. "Made by pounding the leaves, dissolving them in water, then distilling the liquid. It is good for toothaches, earaches and cleaning the lips."

He stared warily at Jerry as if dreading another question. But Jerry said nothing and shuffled backwards as though he might be allergic to cinnamon, or indeed to our precious herbologist.

"The oil is also good for the skin and for preventing chills." The man tipped a little of the liquid onto his finger, which he then dabbed onto Beca's bare forearm.

"Oh!" She blushed. "I wasn't expecting that."

"You feel the warmth?"

"Oh, yes." Her face turned redder. "It's quite nice."

One by one he dabbed a drop of the oil onto everyone's arm, even Jerry's, which he did last. The stuff felt viscous and soothing, yet since it was mid-afternoon – twenty-eight plus degrees – I wasn't sure there'd be any chills for it to counteract.

"We use the oil and coconut – and aloe vera too – in our special handmade *Ayurveda* face cream." Twitching, he led us through more lush vegetation and into an open-air classroom with neat rows of wooden benches. After standing and listening to him for half an hour, everyone was grateful for a chance to sit.

"Now our trained assistants will demonstrate the restorative properties of the special lotion," he said in a deadpan voice. "Please stay where you are and don't be afraid."

Several men appeared out of nowhere, all very muscular and profoundly serious. They spread themselves around the room, each of them shadowing one of us.

"Let me demonstrate on a volunteer." Without asking permission, the herbologist – let's call him Doctor Spice – sat down next to Lucy and began dabbing spots of white ointment on her face. She grinned in an embarrassed way, and as the number of spots increased, she appeared to have an infectious disease.

"Now we rub, deep into the pores." As if smearing a cake tin, Doctor Spice rubbed the lotion in broad circles across Lucy's cheeks and chin. She looked like a model putting on her make-up. "You will all try. It prevents wrinkles and makes your skin younger."

The assistants advanced. They each held little pots of lotion, their dabbing fingers ready. Everyone would receive the beauty treatment – no exceptions.

"Not me!" Linda jumped to her feet and ran to the back of the room. "I've got DEET on."

"I'm buggered if you're doing me either." Tom strode to the back as well.

One or two of the others appeared nervous, Nelson and Frank and probably me too. Facials were for women, surely? Anyway, weren't we on a spice farm?

Undeterred, Doctor Spice waved his little finger, and the assistants sprang into action. One began dabbing Jerry's face, while a second rounded on Bruce and a third cornered

Kate. An assistant came over to me, and unresisting I let him do his worst. Gentle, wet blobs were administered with a concentrated stare. Then a firmer touch as he fingered my forehead, cheeks and jaw. This is how personal rights are eroded – not by force but seduction. The lotion soothed and dried. Underneath my face felt tight.

"You are feeling the effects of the aloe vera." Like a James Bond villain proud of his stronghold, Doctor Spice beamed. "Your skin is fresher, the natural energy restored."

We all nodded, no one wanting to be the lone dissenter. And now that it was over, and hadn't been as unpleasant or embarrassing as we'd feared, we felt relieved, even amused. The charade had finished; we could return to the bus.

Except no. There was more.

"Next the massages!" Doctor Spice leered, the look of a man who knew he held us in his palm. "We will show you how the aloe vera – and the cinnamon oil too – will ease neck pain, back pain, leg pain and foot pain."

The assistants fanned out again, any initial hesitation gone, their faces set. By contrast, everyone in our group looked afraid, one or two crossing their arms, Jerry fingering his nose, and Linda and Tom fleeing outside.

"This is not part of the tour," went on Doctor Spice, "but there will be no charge. All we ask is a donation." He pointed at a large wooden bowl on the bench. "There is a choice of head, shoulders and neck massage, or feet and legs."

For one desperate moment I thought of running. Joining Linda and Tom outside in the land of sane people. Since when had spice gardens hosted group massages? But any chance of escape had gone. Already Kate had opted for a head and neck massage, which would be administered as she sat. And next to her, more enthusiastic than she was, Bruce and Frank wanted shoulders and back massages too, as they peeled off their shirts. From the front of the room came squeaks from Beca and louder sighs from Jerry as they sat with their legs stretched out, their feet in the grip of powerful forces. Meanwhile Doctor Spice strolled masterfully, his eyes circling, his forehead creased, his hair in turmoil as he directed and controlled.

I grimaced, realising I'd have to go through with this. But it was no longer a simple matter of getting it over with. All the assistants were occupied. First I'd have to wait and watch as they administered their treatment to others. See how thickly they spread on the potion. How with super-strong fingers they kneaded, pinched and pushed. Jerry groaned as his masseur pounded his ankles, and the ever-blunt Doctor Spice told him he was a tiny bit overweight. Similarly, Beca squealed with delight, and Doctor Spice pronounced a mild amount of water retention.

Then it was my turn. I chose the leg-and-foot massage as being the lesser of two evils. Tugging up the legs of my trousers and stretching out my feet, I readied myself for pain. Humiliation too. Yet as the assistant spread on the potion and tightened his grip, his fingers were unexpectedly relaxing. Perhaps I might enjoy this after all. Around me the others were talking again, no longer petrified but almost happy. Even Doctor Spice was smiling. Less the mad scientist and more a pioneer whose theories might be correct.

Cinnamon would never be the same after this. Nor aloe vera, turmeric or vanilla.

ELEVEN

Kool as Kandy

Half an hour until sundown, and the view from our balcony was atmospheric. Flocks of white birds flew along the axis of the valley, turning black as they rose into the bright sky, then dipping again towards the lake that shone between green hills. All around was the noise of crows cawing, leaves rustling and distant traffic – the white-and-red buses that flashed between trees. The wind strengthened, faded, renewed. Soon, there might be a storm.

A clatter of drums signalled a nearby dance show starting up. A roaring from a dragon instrument, moving closer. But no, it was a workman smoke-blasting the shrubberies below to rid them of insects. As more sounds drifted up – a clatter of plates, a chink of glasses, a muted conversation – the spell was broken. It was time to go downstairs to the hotel restaurant and eat another buffet dinner.

Somehow we'd escaped the spice garden and its extortionate shop. We'd come to Kandy, the capital of the last Sinhalese kingdom and Sri Lanka's second largest city. It was a bustling, chaotic, spiritual place. Over a hundred and twenty-five thousand people lived here together with their thousands of vehicles. Fortunately our hotel, the salubrious Twee Sri, was perched on a quiet, wooded hillside northeast of the lake. We could see the city and feel its hum without having to wear earplugs to sleep.

Ten minutes away – a gentle stroll down the hill – lay Sri Lanka's holiest Buddhist shrine, the Sri Dalada Maligawa or Temple of the Sacred Tooth. It stood white, black and gold alongside Kandy Lake, green water on one side, and green hills behind. A gleaming, white, crenelated wall surrounded the complex and inside rose a tiered octagonal tower, the Pittirippuva, plus several flared roofs, including one special gold roof that covered the tooth relic's chamber.

We'd visited the temple early that morning before the sun grew too hot. A crowd milled in front of the ticket office, while even more people – tourists with cameras and worshippers with lotus flowers – gathered on the forecourt inside. It was almost nine-thirty, time for the second *puja* or prayers for the day. All Sri Lankan Buddhists are expected to make one pilgrimage to this temple during their lives, and many of them visit more frequently, perhaps several times every year. Today being the second day after *Poya* (meaning full moon), they were here in their multitudes, enough pilgrims to pack the temple.

Oshan purchased our tickets. Then he showed us where we could leave our shoes. Etiquette was strict here – all trousers had to cover the knees and all shirts the shoulders. Security was tight as well. Before we could enter the temple compound we had to file through a turnstile where uniformed guards scanned us and checked our pockets. A Liberation of Tigers of Tamil Eelam (LTTE) bomb had exploded outside this entrance in 1998, killing twenty people and demolishing the façade. More recently, only eight months earlier on Easter Sunday 2019, bombs had exploded at three churches and three hotels in the Colombo area, killing two hundred and fifty-nine people and injuring five hundred. Many of these innocents had been young children, who hadn't even known what these crimes were about.

Trying not to think too much about past atrocities, we made our way through the crowds and into the temple. This part was the Drummer's Courtyard, where shortly musicians would play. Oshan didn't linger, however. Cutting a swift path through all the people – *Ayubowan, Ayubowan, Ayubowan* – he led us up a staircase to a busy chamber.

There he pointed at a richly ornamented brass door. "That is where the sacred tooth is held, yeah? When the prayers start we will file past, and if you're lucky you may glimpse the gold casket that contains it."

"We can take photos?" asked Nelson. He'd purchased a new smart phone from an electronics store only that morning.

Oshan nodded. "But be quick. You can't stop."

"No problem." Nelson grinned. "It's got a fast-motion thingy. Takes lots of pictures all at the same time."

"You know they've got monkeys in here?" said Frank.

Nelson laughed. "Pull the other one!"

"Elephants too."

"There will be elephants here for the *Esala Perahera* festival – hundreds of them," said Oshan. "It's held in July and commemorates the first arrival of the Tooth in Sri Lanka, yeah. The most important elephant carries the Tooth, and we call this elephant the *Maligawa Tusker*."

We trooped downstairs to wait for prayers to begin. When they did, all the tourists and worshippers would ascend the staircase again and file past the outer door of the Tooth Chamber. People were already pressing against us.

Kate and I decided to stay downstairs and watch the ceremony from there instead. *Pujas* or prayers happened here three times every day: at dawn, early morning and dusk.

Officials were already getting ready. Men in white tunics and two monks in orange robes walked to and fro in front of the shrine. Behind them was another closed door, its panels coated in gold and silver. Elephant tusks projected across its portico and above rose tiered friezes with ornate paintings of lotus flowers, lions and myriad other creatures in yellows, blues and pinks. Buddhist flags were draped everywhere, that same striped design we'd seen on cycling day. And lotus flowers too, covering the floor – nearly as many flowers as there were pilgrims.

With a sharp *pwack-pwack-pwack* proceedings began. The single, staccato drumbeat of a young man in ankle-length white sarong and tight red waistcoat, beating at his *davul*, a two-headed drum. A second identical drummer joined him, while a third man blew into a brass horn, producing an undulating sound that wandered, haunting and restless, around the chamber. This was only the start. The music went on – and on *and on* – drums and horn, horn and drums, each melody winding around the other like monkey and snake, baiting, thrusting, drawing, biting, never slowing, changing or ending. It seemed to last forever, strange and hypnotic at first, and then – as people flowed around us, shuffling to join the line for upstairs – becoming incessant and tedious, almost tortuous.

"How long do you think it lasts?" said Kate.

"I don't know. About an hour?"

We'd wait until the others returned. Yet there was no sign of them. Perhaps they were stuck upstairs, trapped inside a fast cycle of Nelson's new phone camera. Letting the drumbeat pulse inside me, the ever wavering horn too, I tried to imagine what the Tooth might look like wrapped inside its gold casket, which in turn, like a Russian doll, was wrapped in six caskets more.

The tooth is three inches long and made of ivory. It is supposed to be a canine tooth of Buddha's, removed after his cremation and presented to a King Kalinga of the east coast of India. For nine centuries it was kept in a temple at the capital Dantapura, but then as Hinduism threatened Buddhism it was smuggled to Sri Lanka. There the reigning king was pleased to receive the tooth and placed it in a special temple in his capital, first Anuradhapura, and then Polonnaruwa. Every year, a procession of elephants paraded the tooth through the streets as a sign of honour.

Over time the tooth became as important as the Crown Jewels, for whoever held it was the rightful sovereign over the island. Yet something so sacred could never be safe, and in the fourteenth century, an invading Indian army stole it, and the tooth had to be recaptured. In the sixteenth century the same happened again; the tooth was removed by Portuguese invaders who – under the orders of an Archbishop – smashed it with a mortar, burnt the pieces and threw them into a river. Somehow, the tooth was once more retrieved and restored. Since then it has been kept in Kandy at the Sacred Temple.

Suddenly I glimpsed Oshan, and the others trailing behind him.

"Got some fantastic photos!" Nelson beamed. "This phone is the real McCoy."

"Have you phoned anyone up yet?" I asked.

Nelson looked puzzled, as if phones weren't supposed to be used as phones anymore.

"You should call your old number," said Frank. "Tell that monkey what you think of him!"

Fortunately we saw no monkeys in the temple, though there'd been a lot of them climbing the telephone wires outside the hotel, as well as warnings in the rooms not to leave food or valuables on the balconies. Nelson would have to be careful, or he'd lose his new phone as well.

Oshan led us around the surrounding rooms: the Alut Maligawa with its many Buddha statues; the Audience Hall on a raised stone plinth; even a tiny library with centuries-old religious books. One place we missed that we shouldn't have was the devotional Raja Tusker Museum. Here in a glass cabinet were the stuffed remains of Sri Lanka's most celebrated elephant, the eponymous Raja. For fifty years Raja served as *Maligawa Tusker* – the elephant that carried the Tooth casket during the holy festival of *Esala Perahera*. Only special elephants can be selected for this role. They have to be male elephants, and all their seven appendages – legs, trunk, penis and tail – must touch the ground when they stand. They have to be twelve feet tall, with their tusks shaped like swords, and their backs straight. Raja filled his enormous footprints admirably, but ever since he died there have been several *Maligawa Tuskers*, none of them lasting nearly as long.

By now everyone was footsore and, after all that drumming, a little deaf. Like a godsend, Chanuka appeared with the bus and drove us on a quick tour of Kandy central. The Queen's Hotel with its faded colonial exterior. The various outlets along the main street – Dalada Vidiya – including Devon Restaurant where we'd later buy several delicious vegetable samosas. The white Clock Tower and adjacent market, plus the remains of the old Bogambara maximum security prison that was about to be converted into a cultural park.

After ascending a zigzag road to the viewpoint of

Arthur's Seat, we all disembarked from the bus to take photos of a breathtaking panorama. Below us lay an octopus of a city, swathes of buildings stretched like tentacles around the steep green hills, and in the middle a magical blue/green eye, the Kiri Muhuda or Kandy Lake. The lake is artificial and was constructed in 1807 by King Sri Wickrama in an area that used to be a paddy field. Labourers who complained it was a waste of time were impaled on stakes on the lakebed. More recently, in a fit of pique at being away from home, the British writer D. H. Lawrence threw his watch into the lake's depths.

Our quick tour over, Chanuka dropped us all at the Clock Tower for a free afternoon. We could do what we wanted and go where we liked.

Glad to be on our own for a while, Kate and I browsed through the central market. Downstairs were stalls selling fresh produce: colourful pyramids of bananas, papaya, vanilla and a hundred other fruits. Upstairs was a textile market where batiks, wood carvings and leather goods were on offer at stratospheric prices.

Crossing the road outside the market was impossible. Three lanes of tuk-tuks puttered down one side, and an everlasting line of buses dieseled up the other. We dithered on the kerb, unsure what to do. Locals dashed across, dodging and weaving, and we were thinking about following them when we noticed a subway that went underneath. It led into a subterranean area packed with local street artists. They sat with brushes and tins of paint, creating colourful, standout murals. One showed a traditional dancer pirouetting around a pillar. Another depicted a procession of vivid, flower-power elephants.

As we left, climbing up steps to the street, we saw the most amazing elephant of all. A real elephant standing calmly on the back of a flat-bed truck in the middle of all the traffic. It took us completely by surprise, and I wondered what was going on. Was it an orphan on its way to a sanctuary, or perhaps an older elephant simply hitching a ride? But of course it couldn't be. An elephant from the wild would try to escape and cause mayhem, injury and possibly deaths. This was a temple elephant, bred in captivity and trained for religious ceremonies. It might even be the current *Maligawa Tusker* on its way to a gig.

We made our way along Dalada Vidiya, the main street. The pavement was busy with people. Constantly, we had to stop and start. The traffic never let up either – noisy, smoky buses and trucks thundering past. The only way to cross at side-streets was to tag onto locals and run across with them. In this fashion, sidestepping and wiping our brows, we visited a shopping mall, two bookshops, three cake outlets, a mini rollercoaster, and even spotted a man in a red suit in a grotto. Santa was here! In Kandy, of all places, preparing for his big night.

But we'd had it with the heat, the humidity, the traffic, and the sheer overwhelming busyness of everything. Heading back to the hotel along a calmer path by the lake, we bumped into Frank who was watching birds. Dozens of them were gathered at the water's edge – egrets, herons, cormorants – while more circled the tiny islet in the middle.

The lake teemed with life. Unlike our next stop, the British Garrison Cemetery, which – the same as its inhabitants – was dead quiet. We found it at the top of a flight of steps, a secluded, sunny graveyard with trees at the end. A troupe of monkeys played in the shade, eyeing our phones.

"I don't think I'll be taking any photos in here." Frank

shoved his phone into his pocket. "One of them might be called Nelson."

We used our eyes instead, scrutinising individual headstones. They were well preserved, many repaired with local bricks rather than the original stone. The caretaker wandered up to us. He was a kindly older man with glowing white hair and a sun-treasured face. He turned out to be a natural storyteller and in a polite, well-educated voice explained how most of the people buried in the cemetery – all British – had died young. The oldest person buried here had been only forty, and many of the graves were for children. Some perished of malaria, others of cholera, and at least one man had been killed by an elephant.

"Are the monkeys any trouble?" I asked.

He smiled and shook his head. Not the monkeys, it seemed, but something else.

Then he pointed over a sturdy perimeter fence at a boar lurking on the other side. The animals liked using their tusks, he explained, to dig up graves. Before the fence had been finished he'd had to chase them off.

"But then His Royal Highness Prince Charles came to see us." His smile remained sincere. "He looked at four graves and asked about the fence. I had to tell him money had run out. A week later new funds arrived. The prince listened to my story and paid for the fence himself."

TWELVE

Gem Beetle

At the end of the corridor outside our room a spiral of uneven stone steps descended to the hotel swimming pool. The water rippled gently in the moonlight, and, had circumstances been different I would have jumped in for a dip. But it was half-past seven and we were on our way to dinner. The Twee Sri was a swanky hotel. Four stars, possibly five. The food would be good.

A tiled path led around the pool to the bar, then to the restaurant. The man with the smoke machine had gone, and the shrubs gleamed purple and bug free. No doubt some of the more persistent critters would return later – mosquitoes flying in from wherever – but for the moment we could stroll around with our arms and ankles exposed, assured we wouldn't be bitten. Although not all the bugs here were intent on jabbing spiky bits of themselves into our skin or flapping pointlessly around electric lights, because many of them were efficiently building colonies, and one or two were beautiful like the gem beetle.

Only that afternoon, on the steep road up to the hotel,

Frank had stopped, pointed down at his feet and whistled in amazement. "Blimey, what's that?"

Kate and I knelt to look at the insect. The creature lay on its back, its underside glowing iridescent green. It looked alien, as if it had emerged from a nuclear reactor or fallen from a spaceship. Too astonished to know what to think, we stared at it for ages. Then flicking with his finger, Frank turned it over. Its carapace shone brighter, a sleek, glassy viridian. Whatever it was – a beetle or a scarab or an emerald with legs – it didn't move. Its scuttling days were over. Flying too. Now it could only stun with the brilliance of its pigments.

"Let's take it to our room." Kate found a leaf and delicately wrapped the dead bug inside.

"Are you sure?" If it was a scarab beetle then it might come back to life. At least, that was what happened in all the mummy movies I'd ever seen and, pretty though the beetle might be, I didn't fancy chasing it around our room at one in the morning.

"It'll be fine." Kate put the leaf in her pocket and grasped my arm.

And now, four hours later on our way to dinner, she grasped my arm again, pulling me into an alcove by the pool attendant's hut.

"Look at these!" She pointed at a wall covered with large framed photos of elephants. One showed a tusked male striding magnificently out of the jungle. In another, four younger elephants squeezed together as if taking a photo booth selfie. There were twenty photos in all, arranged in a grid of five by four – perhaps the Sri Lankan equivalent of three ducks flying above a mantelpiece.

"Elephants rock!" Kate stared at the photos while I visualised vultures swooping on the hotel buffet and stripping it bare. I needn't have worried, though. There was plenty of food when we arrived, enough to satisfy everyone. Stalking like a predator among the stainless-steel trays, I lifted one lid, then another, checking what aromas wafted out. One tray was full of fluffy white rice and another of red. A hundred and one different curries, made from diverse ingredients such as chicken, pork, eggplant, beetroot and young jackfruit. Various sambals too, made from grated coconut, chilli, onions, and sometimes a green leafy vegetable called *gotukola* or Asian pennywort. The sambals were to be sprinkled on curries as a spicy garnish. And kottu dishes as well: these were made from shredded roti and stir-fried with egg, vegetables or cheese. Finally, there were even European foods: vegetable lasagne, chicken supreme, and fish steamed with onions and herbs.

The others in our group were all sitting at one long table, neatly laid out with a tablecloth, cutlery, wine glasses and tiny ornamental plants. At the furthest end, the trunk of a mature tree emerged through a hole in the floor, impaled the table, then branched towards the ceiling. The restaurant was surrounded by foliage: larger shrubs in planters, creepers dangling from the ceiling, and a well-groomed lawn outside on the roof terrace. It felt less like a place to eat and more like somewhere to meditate.

"The buffet costs a bit more than usual," said Jerry helpfully. "Three thousand rupees."

"That's still only eleven pounds," said Lucy. "Way cheaper than we get in Leamington, even at the Indian takeaway."

"And it looks nice." Nelson eyed us from across the table. "Especially those mousses and trifles."

For a moment, we ummed and ahhed. Did we go full Monty with the buffet or economise with à la carte?

Normally Kate's tooth was sweet. She'd want dessert. But after a samosa at lunchtime, followed by cake, she wasn't feeling hungry. Whereas I was ravenous; I could eat it all. So we compromised. Kate ordered a chicken burger with fries, while I made several trips to the buffet, first fetching rice and curries for myself, then returning, several times over, to carry back sweets for us both.

It was a lavish, indulgent meal, and afterwards I felt full. Eating was an important aspect of travelling, however – getting to know a country through its food. And there was certainly a wide choice of dishes in Sri Lanka. We were consuming three big meals every day – breakfast, lunch and dinner – our tummies becoming so solid we might have to consider diets when we returned home.

WE STILL HADN'T FOUND our promised cuppa – the perfect Ceylon tea. I wasn't doing so well on coffee either; nothing as mellow as a Wellington flat white. The coffee at the hotel – as I discovered the next morning – was thick and black and lurked at the bottom of carafes, left there by the drip-drip-drip of fluid through a wet, dark funnel. Nonetheless, I poured some into my cup, stirred in milk and sugar, then sipped. I needed caffeine to start the day – especially this one, our second in Kandy, with a trip planned to a gem workshop and then the botanical gardens.

Gems are an important industry in Sri Lanka, with nearly a quarter of its land mass capable of bearing stones such as sapphires, topazes and rubies. So it made sense to visit a gem workshop, even though Kate and I didn't want to go. The trip was a scheduled activity that, like the spice farm, we had to go through to reach other things.

On the bus out there none of the males were enthusiastic.

Frank sat subdued, Nelson silent, and Tom's chin hung so low his beard skimmed the floor. Whereas several of the ladies were smiling, thrilled at the prospect of jewellery. Linda had sketched a picture, all pretty greens and blues, of the bespoke necklace she wanted. Beca played with a credit card, and Lucy held up differently coloured lipsticks she'd use as a colour guide.

"I don't bother normally," she said, her lips shiny. "Bruce's the one with the make-up – all the sun block he uses – not me."

"Same here," said Linda. "But it's different when you're on holiday."

"Is this place mandatory?" Tom's expression was grim. "Can't we just skip it?"

"Don't worry. There will be no hard sell," said Oshan. "We go to the sales room afterwards, but you can leave when you want. You don't have to buy." He grinned slyly as if he didn't expect us to believe him.

Chanuka parked the bus outside a drab-looking building next to a bank. If the gems were as expensive as rumoured, then the shop was in a convenient spot. One by one we hopped out. Then, like members of a suicide pact – some reluctant, some eager – we followed Oshan up a narrow staircase, where there was absolutely no room to turn around and leave.

Inside, in a dull anteroom of hardback chairs, a lean, thin-cheeked man greeted us. He smiled like a stoat and shook hands like a bear. Politely he asked if anyone wanted to use the bathrooms. Then, once everyone was ready, he beckoned us through a mocked-up mining tunnel. The floor rose unevenly, and the ceiling dipped. Mannikins dressed as miners chipped at the walls. All of us taller than five and a half feet were forced to stoop and clutch at our wallets.

We came out into a conference room set out with more chairs. After seating us, our host took orders for tea and coffee. Then, darkening the room, he started the video. It was a little frayed at the edges, yet highly informative. We learned how mines were excavated and shored up with timber. Then how dozens of sacks of earth were hoisted out, washed and sieved for gemstones.

The video ended, and the beverages arrived. We sipped lukewarm tea – definitely not the magical cuppa we were looking for – as we walked into the next room. Display cases lined the walls, each filled with raw gemstones. Amethysts, sapphires, emeralds, onyx and rubies. And in the room after was a workshop where craftsmen peered through lenses and used drills to cut and polish stones.

"I hope you are enjoying yourselves," said our host in a voice like iron pyrites. "All our stones are authentic. When you buy from us you can be sure it is real. Now we go into the showroom, where there is no obligation to buy."

He led us downstairs to a large, carpeted room. Salesmen with gelled hair converged from every direction. They latched onto the women in the room, especially the ones with husbands.

"Would Madam like a bracelet?"

"A necklace?"

"What is Madam's favourite colour?"

I felt my heart sink as the nearest salesman opened a cabinet with compartments crammed with stones. Fortunately Kate shook her head and walked away.

The salesman followed us and opened another cabinet full of bracelets. "Please hold this one, Madam." Uncannily, he picked out a bracelet comprised of elephants. "It's all right to try."

Kate wavered, her eyes tracing the familiar shape of each

elephant. The bracelet was made of sterling silver. It was bound to be expensive.

"No, I'm fine." Resolutely, she walked away.

"How about some earrings?" Another salesman approached us as we strayed into his territory. He popped open a cabinet filled with earrings. This time Kate was tempted, drawn to a pair of light-blue earrings in the centre. Following her gaze, the salesman picked them out and attempted to drop them into her palm. He knew possession was nine tenths of the law. If she tried them on, a sale was virtually guaranteed.

Again Kate resisted. Yet her willpower was weakening, and as she studied the earrings – their smooth perfect ovals, the elegant silver casings, the adorable sky-blue colour – I could tell she was matching them to her favourite top and an empty space on her earrings rack.

"No." She shook her head determinedly. "I can't justify another pair. My mother was here a month ago, and she bought me some just like those."

"Are you sure, Madam?" The salesman pursued us. "I can give you a good –"

"NO!"

As we walked towards the exit I gave silent thanks for a lucky escape. Kate's mum had saved our wallets. We still had the gem beetle too, wrapped inside a leaf in our room. We'd found it ourselves, and its sublime green colour wouldn't degrade for hundreds of years. Nearly as good as an emerald, and a lot more unusual.

THIRTEEN

Rupees for Ranuga

It seemed it was our day for hustlers. As we walked through the central market looking for lunch, a man sidled up, inquisitive.

"You're staying at the hotel, aren't you?" he said in a silky voice. "I saw you at breakfast. You're from England?"

"New Zealand," said Kate straightaway.

"Yes! New Zealand." The man nodded vigorously as if the two countries were one and the same. "You like the food at the hotel? The eggs? I am Ranuga. I cook them."

"Oh, right." I nodded too, trying to work out if I'd seen him. The trouble was, there were lots of staff at the Twee Sri Hotel. I hadn't scrutinised all their faces at breakfast as I drank coffee and ate a Sri Lankan omelette. And though the omelette had been cooked to order – a delicious combination of eggs, tomatoes, onions, chilli and curry leaves – I couldn't remember the chef who'd whisked the ingredients together and fried them in his pan.

"I'm buying fish for tonight." Ranuga pointed at the market behind us with its stalls of colourful bananas, chillies, and vegetables I didn't know the names of. "I'm making red fish curry. And fried fish too."

"Sounds great."

He frowned, then held out a wad of crumpled, low-denomination banknotes, mostly red twenties and blue fifties. "But they didn't catch much, so the price has gone up."

I stared at him, unsure of what he wanted. Was he asking for a loan?

"Can't you buy less fish?" said Kate. "Add more vegetables?"

"It's fish curry!" His eyes bulged. "Vegetables are separate."

He was right. In Sri Lanka, if you ordered a fish or meat curry, usually they brought out various vegetable curries too in separate bowls.

"How much do you need?" I gestured at his money.

"Not too much. New Zealand is generous, I know – not like England. If you could lend me, I'll give it back tonight."

I didn't know whether to believe him. So many local people had approached us in Kandy, asking our nationality, where we were staying, then praising the All Blacks, or Kane Williamson, the captain of the New Zealand cricket team. They seemed to want nothing more than a friendly conversation. Ranuga was the first person to ask for money. Yet his story almost held water, a loan to purchase fish. I studied his features again – his startled brown eyes, his wide hooked nose – and became convinced I'd seen him somewhere, perhaps even at the hotel.

Kate shook her head as I pulled out my wallet. Ignoring her, I extracted a one-hundred-rupee note. "Will this be enough?"

"Another. We have many guests."

I tugged at my wallet again, his lips curling into a devilish grin.

Then Kate grabbed my arm, restraining me. "What's our hotel?" she asked in a do-not-bullshit-me voice.

He laughed. "You're staying at the Twee Sri."

Kate stared at him, undecided. As did I, still clutching my one-hundred rupee note. Easy enough to give it to him. It was worth less than a dollar – half a hoki fishcake in New Zealand. And our hotel employed dozens of staff, some of whom we'd seen and many more we hadn't. His claim might be entirely legitimate.

Once again my hand crept to my wallet. But this time to push it deeper in my pocket. His smile flickered, a little less friendly. I'd noticed the stalls behind him again. We hadn't spotted a single one selling fish.

"You know, the Twee Sri is a big hotel," I said slowly. "A lot of guests stay there, like you said. So I can't believe they wouldn't have food delivered, or that they'd have to send a chef out to the market."

"No, no, no." He grew flummoxed, his confidence slipping. "This is an emergency. The kitchen has run out."

We continued to stare, saying nothing. Then he turned and walked away. Not in the direction of the market, but towards the bus station.

We never saw Ranuga again. If he worked at our hotel he kept out of our way. I wondered if I should ask the hotel management about him but decided not to. They might arrange an identification parade of all the staff in the kitchens.

There was no fish curry for dinner that night, nor fresh fish. Unsurprising, really, since Kandy was in the central highlands, three and a half hours by road from the ocean.

FOURTEEN

Bamboo Torture

No fish or gems were on sale at the Royal Botanic Gardens of Peradeniya, six kilometres from downtown Kandy. This was the university district where gems were metaphysical – an insightful line of poetry, an idea to revolutionise science. Although there might be more scarab beetles and macaques posing for photos. Nelson would have to watch his phone.

The gardens delighted everyone in our group. Sixty hectares of beautiful lawns, trees and plants, enclosed on three sides by the river. After the confines of the gem workshop, then the bustle of the market, it felt good to be walking in the open, admiring flowers, and savouring pleasant, alluring scents. The sun shone and the grass gleamed. And once we'd made tracks from the packed entrance the crowds thinned out. The gardens were big. There were at least several hundred trees to each of us. For instance, the Double Coconut palm from the Seychelles that produces the world's largest nut. Or a line of cannonball trees, named for their ship-sinking fruits. Then there was an enormous Java fig tree, the girth of Goliath, dominating the Great Lawn. And so many different types of palm – three majestic avenues of them: Royal, Cabbage and Palmyra.

The gardens' talipot palms are a botanical wonder. After growing for forty years, they bloom only once in their lifetimes into the largest cluster of flowers in the world. "Their leaves are so big –" Oshan stretched out his hands "– in older times two leaves were sewn together to make a tent for a platoon of soldiers."

"Amy and I went on a camping holiday once," said Nelson as we walked across the famed Great Lawn. "It didn't go well."

"In Africa?" For some reason I imagined a trip similar to this one: a small party of fellow travellers visiting a remote tropical country.

He laughed. "Bognor Regis. At the Royal Camping and Caravan Park."

"Royal?" Now I pictured a vast lawn like the one before us, with a stately mansion at its edge.

"It was a right royal disaster. It rained all night and the tent leaked. We had puddles everywhere. Then someone tripped over the pegs and the tent fell down. Amy caught a cold and I got my phone wet."

"Sounds like a typical English camping holiday." I realised this was an opportunity to quiz him about what he and Amy did. "But still a break, hey? From the office where you work?"

"Not really." He shook his head. "Not for me."

"You work outdoors?"

"Sometimes." He laughed.

"What do you do again?"

"Oh, nothing really. Some call it a career. I call it biding time."

"What is it, though?"

"Let me see, now." He cupped his chin in his hand. "They've changed my job title recently and I never know which one to use. You're familiar with quality control, automated production lines and pointless paperwork?"

"Yes."

"Well, it's nothing like that."

As we reached the edge of the lawn I gave up. The gardens had to be my focus rather than being led up another of Nelson's winding garden paths. The Royal Botanic Gardens had been here since the twelfth century, first as a royal pleasure garden, then developed by the British into their present form. They'd served as a testing bed for imported plants – coffee, tea, nutmeg and rubber – and they'd been nurtured by tireless superintendents, notably the eponymous George Gardner, followed by Dr. Thwaits who looked after the gardens for an unbroken thirty years.

We came to the Great Circle, a large grassy area surrounded by a circle of trees. Each tree had been planted by a dignitary who, at one time or another, had been visiting the gardens. The first tree, a Bo Peepal, had been planted by Edward VII in 1875. Then in 1891, the Czar of Russia had planted a second tree. Since then a further seventy-six trees have been added by well-known figures such as Harold Macmillan, Yuri Gagarin, D.S. Senanayake the first PM of Ceylon, Princess Anne, Queen Elizabeth II and Lord Louis Mountbatten.

We wandered as a loose group around the circle, trying to identify the different trees and their famous planters. Some, established many years ago, rose wide and tall while more recent trees were hardly bigger than saplings. One of the most impressive trees was an *amherstia nobilis*, or Pride of Burma, planted in 1945 by Lord Mountbatten. Despite being seventy-four years old, it was still a modest tree with slender branches and a sprinkling of red flowers. Mountbatten had liked the gardens so much, he'd based the headquarters of South-East Asia Command in Peradeniya during WWII.

Further on were glasshouses. A wonderful collection of orchids, then succulents. This was followed by a spice garden and a lake in the shape of Sri Lanka. Normally the lake would be covered in water lilies, with marsh plants growing around the sides. Sadly, it was drained for maintenance, a big brown hole in the ground.

"Now we will see the giant bamboo," said Oshan. Beckoning with his little finger, he led us away from the empty lake to a grove of enormous bamboo. The stems rose twenty metres above us, some as thick as elephants' legs. "These are the biggest in the world, yeah? And bamboo is the fastest growing plant – it grows up to thirty centimetres every day."

"Here's your chance for some time-lapse photography." Frank pointed at Nelson's new phone.

"Better you take a pic of us all," said Jerry. "Use the timer. Set it for ten seconds and prop the phone on the ground somewhere."

Nelson chuckled. "I'm not daft. There're bound to be monkeys about. I'm not losing this phone as well."

"I can take the photo." Oshan stepped in and took Nelson's phone. After motioning us all to stand in front of the bamboo, he aimed and pressed. Then as he handed the phone back he said, "I have to tell you how the Japanese used bamboo as torture during the war. They'd tie the victim up and make them lie down. Then they'd force the bamboo to puncture their skin. It would grow through their body to the other side. Very painful. They always got a confession."

Nelson pocketed his phone, his face pale, and Jerry and Frank didn't say anything either as we walked back to the entrance. I wasn't sure I believed Oshan's story. Not on such a sunny day in this lovely place. Behind us the bamboo shoots towered, cutting into the blue sky.

FIFTEEN

A Nice Cup of Tea

We'd been in Sri Lanka a week, seven of our twenty-eight days, and still I hadn't found that perfect cuppa, the one my father, God bless him, had dreamed about all his life. Dad had made tea the old-fashioned way. Warmed the teapot, refilled it with boiling water, then stirred in two or three teaspoonfuls of loose tea leaves. Once it was brewed he grasped the pot by its warm handle and poured brown liquid into a cup already dribbled with milk, before stirring in one, two, three spoonfuls of sugar. Sweet and hot like morning glory. And milky chestnut, the shade of the tree that grew outside our house.

Tea was a concoction that, despite being my father's favourite tipple, had never convinced me. The perfect cuppa in my mind came without milk, without sugar, and was called coffee. I didn't know much about tea. All the different colours it came in: green, white, yellow and black. All the different types: pekoe, orange pekoe, broken orange pekoe, fannings and dust. All the various labels and brands too – which one was the best?

If coffee is best in the west, then tea is beast in the east. And after a week here in Sri Lanka I was beginning to see why. As well as Kandy, entire regions south of us – Nuwara Eliya, Uva, Uda Pussellawa, Dimbula, Ruhuna and Sambaragamuwa – were devoted to tea plantations, making Sri Lanka, after China, India and Kenya, the world's fourth largest tea producer. Time to put my coffee addiction aside, I decided, and start looking seriously for the perfect cuppa.

So after returning from the botanic gardens to downtown Kandy I wasted no more time and went straight to Devon Restaurant in the main street and ordered a plain ginger tea – plain meaning no milk, and ginger meaning ginger.

"This will be the one," I said to Kate. "My first authentic Ceylon tea."

She smiled, amused. "It's too hot for tea. I want something cold."

"Tea cools you down. It makes you sweat, and the sweat evaporates and takes away heat."

"I don't care. I want ginger beer."

When my tea arrived it wasn't in a teapot but a cup. A big cup. But still a cup.

I picked it up by the handle and held the rim to my lips. The liquid was hot, translucent and amber – and smelt strongly of ginger.

"This is it." I smiled at Kate, who was drinking her mediocre fizz. "The tea I've been waiting for."

I sipped delicately, unsure what to expect. Hot, yes. Gingery too, all the slices nestled like tiny newts at the bottom of the cup. I might have been drinking a potent ginger medication as fierce as Kate's ginger beer.

"What's it like?"

"Good."

"Can I try some?"

"Sure."

She sipped and smiled. "It's strong, isn't it?"

I nodded. It had cooled me down and went well with the vegetable samosa I'd ordered with it. Yet it wasn't my perfect cuppa, a tea so fragrant it brought olfactory enlightenment. For that I'd have to ascend to a higher plain – to the taller hills south of Kandy where the finest plantations grew.

The waiter came over. He was a heavy man with a moustache and looked like he should be a wrestler. He asked where we came from, and when we told him New Zealand he beamed, the ends of his moustache rising. In a calm voice he named half of the current All Blacks, followed by the highest scoring batsmen from the Black Caps.

"Kane Williamson!" He pounded the table. "Martin Guptill!"

"Sri Lanka are awesome too," said Kate. "Dimuth Karunaratne, Suranga Lakmal."

The waiter's moustache peaked higher. He was impressed by how Kate knew the names and could pronounce them. So often, as we travelled around, strangers would wander up to us, ask where we were from, then recite the names of Kiwi sportspersons they'd memorised. Mostly they had no ulterior motives. They wanted to be friendly and welcome us to their country.

As the waiter moved away Kate spotted our travel-savvy quizzer, Jerry. He sat alone at a table, thumbing his phone and forking rice from his plate. Kate waved to him, but he didn't notice and carried on eating.

"Maybe he's hungry?" I said. "He skipped lunch."

"I'll go and see." Kate slurped the last of her ginger beer, then weaved a path through the many tables to where Jerry sat. She tapped him on the shoulder and persuaded him to join us.

"The grub is good here," he said, setting down his plate opposite me. "Way tastier than at the hotel – and a quarter of the price."

I had to agree. The tea had cost barely anything, and the samosa hardly much more. For only a few dollars we could dine here like Mr. Creosote, the epicurean from *The Life of Brian* who ate so much he burst.

"What are you eating?" I pointed at Jerry's plate: several bowls of curry arranged around a heap of rice.

"Rice and seven curries." He looked proudly at the food. "Poppadums too." He indicated another bowl of crispy snacks to the side. "It's good. You should try some."

"I'm full." I gestured at the samosa crumbs on my plate. "But you should try the tea."

"Ta. I'm full too." He picked up my empty cup and sniffed. "Not bad. I'll wait till we get to Nuwara Eliya though."

I nodded, agreeing with him. Nuwara Eliya was at a higher altitude than Kandy – and the higher the tea bushes, the more delicate the flavour of their leaves.

"You must have enjoyed the gardens," said Kate to Jerry. "You seem very cheerful."

"I've got my own *room*." His mouth opened into a cavern of a smile. "Enough was enough. I've paid the single supplement."

"You are on holiday," I said.

"Yeah, I *am* on holiday!" He breathed in sharply, and his cheeks expanded. "And look, my pics have come out!" He held up his phone and showed us the pictures he'd taken in the gardens. They were all superb, the colours vivid and the subjects close. In one photo he'd zoomed in on a tiny squirrel at the top of a palm tree; the hairs on its head were individually distinct, and it looked as if it were only a metre away.

"Are you a professional?" said Kate.

He sighed. "I wish. It'd be a hell of a lot more satisfying than checking rail tickets."

"Is that what you do?"

His brow furrowed. "Not if I can help it. I'd rather be answering quiz questions and winning contests. You know, one day I'm going to get a job on that TV show, *The Chase*. They'll call me the Jerrymanderer, or the Ticket Puncher – something cool like that."

His bonhomie continued into the afternoon, because later he sent out a message on the tour's What's App group asking who wanted to go out for dinner. "Be in the foyer at seven-thirty," it read. "The world is a big place and has many good things to eat."

After showering, and brushing our teeth, we made our way to reception for seven twenty-five, wondering who else would come out – whether it would be all of us or just a few.

Not everyone was coming. Frank was eating at the hotel. Linda and Tom had other plans, possibly arranging a loan for the stupendous necklace Linda had bought at the gem workshop. Eight of us were intent on eating out, however. We all formed a conga line behind Jerry as he led us to the Empire Café in town.

"You'd better have a sweet tooth," he said. "The smoothies are flipping good. The milkshakes too."

"What about tea?" I was still on my quest.

"And Lion beer?" So was Nelson.

"There's no alcohol. But the food will make up for it. There're wraps and salads and pasta – all the healthy stuff you know you're missing."

The café was plush and quiet. A beautiful green batik of an elephant hung on the wall, far better quality than anything we'd seen in the market. A pendant light dangled above our table, its brightness playing onto everyone's faces as if we sat in a cinema. There were rattan chairs with huge peacock backs, and our own reflections in a mirror mounted on an antique sideboard. We might have been back in the days of empire, in a place where colonial chic met trendy cuisine.

Kate ordered a veggie wrap and coconut smoothie; I went for the macaroni cheese and another plain ginger tea. No single-leaf teas stood out on the menu – only slicker sounding concoctions such as classic Ceylon, green mint and chai cinnamon. I wasn't too concerned though. We'd be in the heart of the hill country tomorrow, on our way to Nuwara Eliya.

Beca had been silent, but suddenly she banged her spoon on the table and requested everyone's attention. "I met a friend this afternoon," she said in a confident voice. "Someone I knew in London before he moved back here to Colombo."

"Did you now?" Jerry's eyebrows rose.

"No, no! It's nothing like that. He's a colleague. I've known him for ages."

"Did you go anywhere nice?" asked Jerry.

"I'm not sure." Beca's voice dropped. "At one point I didn't think I was going to make it back."

"He didn't try to …?" Amy laid her hand on Beca's wrist.

"No, no! He's a gentleman. It's just we … how can I say this? We went to the wrong temple."

"The Temple of the Tooth?" Jerry gestured out of the window at Sri Lanka's most sacred Buddhist shrine.

Beca shook her head. "This one was miles away. The tuk-tuk driver recommended it, but had we known how far – it was right at the top of this awful hill – I don't think we'd have gone."

"Tuk-tuks can be scary, can't they?" said Lucy. "Squashed in the back, whizzing between all those trucks and buses."

"Oh, it wasn't the ride." Beca looked around the table, her gaze steady. "He went fast, but I wasn't scared. No, it was the temple! It was horrible."

She had our attention, everyone bending forward.

"How was it horrible?" Jerry asked. "Was it dangerous?"

"Oh, I should think so. We were the only tourists. Just Alex and me, and all those monks in purple gowns."

"I thought they wore orange?" said Nelson.

"I don't think they were Buddhists," said Beca. "And they didn't look Sri Lankan."

"So, what happened?" Jerry stared at her. "Did they threaten you?"

"Oh, no." Again she shook her head. "The opposite. They offered us lunch. But it didn't look very nice. It was one of those land monitors, like we saw on the cycling day, roasted and made into a curry, with its eyes still intact."

Jerry's face paled.

"And then while we were looking around we stumbled on this cave. It was too dark to see much, and we had to feel our way through. Then I remembered my phone, but I wish I hadn't because when I turned it on I screamed."

"There was a mummy?" hazarded Nelson.

"Worse." Beca blanched. "The walls were crawling with

insects – big cockroaches and spiders – and in the corner was a snake."

I felt my stomach turn inside out and, with all the horrified expressions around the table, it looked as though other people felt queasy too.

"What type?" said Jerry. "A cobra?"

"I don't know," said Beca. "It was curled up, and I wasn't going to touch it. I wanted to leave after that, but they insisted on taking us on this miniature railway."

"Miniature railway?" Jerry looked puzzled. "In a temple?"

"It was underneath the temple," said Beca with no hint of irony. "We sat in little carts."

Like Jerry, I wasn't sure I believed her story. This was rural Kandy not the London Underground. Yet there had been a mini rollercoaster in the shopping mall we'd visited yesterday. And Beca didn't seem the sort of person to tell lies.

"So, you hated it?" Jerry gazed at Beca.

"I didn't know where they were taking us. Or what was down there. I certainly didn't enjoy the suspension bridge at the end. It was falling apart, and we had to walk across. Below us was a river full of crocodiles."

There were more sighs and looks of disbelief. Yet something about her story sparked an old memory. A movie I'd seen that featured a banquet of elvers, eyes and monkey brains, a chase in mine carts, and a rickety rope bridge. The action-adventure film *Indiana Jones and the Temple of Doom.* I googled it later and learned that some scenes had been shot near Kandy.

Whether Beca knew all this as she told her story I had no idea. Afterwards she sat at the head of the table smiling to herself as she ate her empire salad. With lettuce, basil, coconut, tomato and onions it looked far more appetising than my plain old macaroni cheese. And as I thought about what she'd told us, I couldn't help but remember one of Nelson's favourite idioms. It's the quiet ones you have to watch out for.

SIXTEEN

The Perfect Cuppa

My search for the perfect cuppa continued. The next day, en route to Nuwara Eliya in the hill country, I came close to fulfilling my wish. We'd been driving uphill all day, the landscape changing from dense vegetation to uninterrupted slopes combed with tea bushes. Everything so green and lush, mist rising in the valleys, and in the distance the purple shapes of faraway hills.

"This is where the best tea comes from, yeah?" announced Oshan over the PA. "The higher the altitude, the more delicate the tea."

"Do we get a sniff of it?" asked Jerry, voicing exactly what I was thinking.

"Sure." Oshan nodded. "Very soon."

Some of the plantations displayed big road signs with their names. Familiar words such as Kenilworth Estate, Aberdeen Falls, Strathdon Tea Factory, Hatton Villa and Inverness, as though we might be motoring through a jumbled-up UK.

"The women do all the picking, yeah?" continued Oshan,

and sure enough, there between the neat lines of bushes were swaddled figures, their heads covered with scarves, and their hands plucking buds and top leaves into baskets.

"What about the men?" asked Jerry.

"They do the heavy work and look after the machines. They drink too."

"Tea?" asked Bruce.

Oshan laughed. "Sometimes."

"I could do with something wet," said Jerry. "What's happened to this tea stop? I'm parched."

"Soon."

Yet five minutes later, as Chanuka stopped the bus in a layby on the side of a steep hill, the only liquid in sight was a distant waterfall, surrounded by rows of tea bushes still to be plucked, processed and brewed in a pot before they might quench anyone's thirst.

"The St. Clair waterfall," announced Oshan. Then, once everyone had climbed out of the bus, he and Sakan guided us across the road, with its two blind bends, to a pleasant-looking green building on the other side. This, we discovered, was the St. Clair's tearoom where they served the finest St. Clair's tea.

The place resembled an English pub inside, all wood, spit and polish, with a couple of smiling barmaids in uniforms. Except they didn't sell ales but packets of tea. Yellow packets of black tea, green packets of green, and tins of pekoe, orange pekoe, broken orange pekoe and flowery orange pekoe, whatever these terms meant. The packets all carried a picture of a bearded man wearing spectacles and a banded grey hat: Bob W. Ryan, the Englishman who'd founded the estate and named it after his daughter.

Stepping back outside, we sat in twos at petit white tables on a pristine green lawn. So English – at any moment a mad hatter or a croquet party might appear. Yet it was a waiter in a white tunic who marched out. He served us slices of chocolate cake on little plates, then poured fragrant orange tea into china cups. This was the BOP variety, short for broken orange pekoe. Pekoe is an old Chinese word for tea, and orange generally describes the tea's colour. Broken means the leaves are broken a little – though not fragmented to small pieces like fannings or dust.

Both the tea and cake were delicious, each complementing the other. We sipped and nibbled, nibbled and sipped, feeling like an English prince and princess taking a break from royal duties. This had to be the closest I'd come so far to finding my perfect cup of tea. Yet until I tried another, a comparison somewhere else, I couldn't be sure. Finding an elixir was never going to be easy. It must entail sufficient difficulty to prove its worth.

Afterwards we journeyed on to Nuwara Eliya. The hills continued to swell like green stupas, etched in lines, curves and even helixes of tea bushes. In nature, tea isn't a bush – it's a tree, growing up to ten metres tall. Since this would be no good for picking top leaves, the bushes in plantations are pruned regularly, their height restricted to around a metre. And every few days the pickers pluck the top bud and two adjacent leaves from the end of each branch. It is these leaves – sometimes called flushes – that are used to make tea. As Oshan had told us, the quality depends upon the altitude, with high-grown bushes above twelve hundred metres producing the finest teas. There was still so much to learn. Fortunately we were visiting a tea factory in the morning, and there I'd find out more.

. . .

PEDRO TEA ESTATE was situated near a waterfall called Lover's Leap, a few kilometres from Sri Lanka's highest mountain, Pidurutalagala. After donning green aprons and swearing we wouldn't take photos, we followed a lady wearing a bright red sari into the factory. First, she took us to the dryers – long metal troughs into which the leaves are deposited and withered by hot air. Today, though, the troughs were empty. They contained not a single leaf.

"Are the pickers on strike?" asked Jerry.

The lady didn't laugh. "They don't work on Sundays. So no leaves today."

We moved into the next room where several large, circular machines stood motionless. These apparently crushed and fermented the leaves; however, with nothing to process there was nothing to see. Instead we had to use our imaginations. The same with the ovens in which the leaves were baked, and then with the filtering and sorting machines at the end.

All the equipment looked old. Some machines had been built in the nineteenth century. Originally the estate had been British, the first bushes planted by the epic Scottish planter, Bob Taylor. Since then it had been nationalised, the factory destroyed by fire and rebuilt, and subsequently sold to a private company.

Nothing was in use today, and hardly anyone was around. The lady explained about the different grades: orange pekoe (OP) made from whole young leaves and producing delicate, subtle tea; broken orange pekoe (BOP) made from broken young leaves and producing the same type of orange tea as we'd drunk at St. Clair's; then broken orange pekoe fannings (BOPF), the small particles of tea used in tea bags; and at the very lowest end of the scale came dust, the smallest particles that produce the strongest brews.

Our tour over, we removed our aprons and filed into the tea restaurant. Here we tried a cup of Pedro tea – orange like St. Clair but without any chocolate cake, and for some reason, perhaps a lack of twee white seats and a garden, less flavoursome than the broken orange pekoe we'd enjoyed yesterday. Overall, I was a little disappointed by our visit to Pedro, mainly as we'd seen none of the factory equipment functioning. We'd have to visit somewhere else – the Dambatenne Tea Factory at Haputale or the Uva Halpewatte Tea Factory near Ella – to have a second look.

My quest for tea had begun – yet was far from over.

SEVENTEEN

Bridge over the River Kwai

"When I shout FORWARD, paddle forward!" Oshan grinned from the back of the raft. "And when I shout RELAX, then relax!" He demonstrated by holding his paddle horizontal across the water. In his yellow plastic helmet and orange buoyancy jacket he looked quite unlike our tour guide and more like the other raft jockeys who steered their patrons down the river.

I held my paddle in the way he'd shown us. Right hand on the shaft close to the blade and left clasped over the end of the handle to prevent it from hitting anyone in the face. Although I didn't feel very relaxed. And little wonder, for only metres ahead, the smooth brown surface of the river transformed into a frothing, plunging rapid. My heart was beating on a knife edge as we drifted towards the point of no return.

There were six of us besides Oshan – all of us having wobbled into this fragile blue inflatable only moments earlier. Three of us had never been white-water-rafting before, while the remainder had done it so long ago they might as well be novices as well. Yet here we were, virgins and has-beens, breaking our journey to Nuwara Eliya to surge down the Kelani, Sri Lanka's fourth longest river.

Oshan sat at the stern while everyone else huddled along the gunwales: Bruce and I in front, Kate and Frank in the middle, and Linda and Lucy at the rear. It was anyone's guess who would fall in, but the odds had to be on Bruce and me, being so close to the prow.

"What happens if we fall in?" said Kate, as usual voicing what I was thinking.

"Don't try to swim!" Oshan crossed his arms tightly over his buoyancy jacket. "Hold yourself together and float feet first down the river."

We drifted centimetres closer to the rapids, like one of those nightmares in which space stretches forever and you never quite arrive. Ahead the water thrashed like a leopard's tail, a fury of white streaks and muscle. It was supposed to be a level two rapid, having a wide, clear channel with avoidable rocks and being suitable for novices. From this angle, however – staring over its razor-sharp lips – it looked far worse.

"Forward!" shouted Oshan.

Leaning over the gunwale, I paddled.

"Backward!" shouted Oshan, as if he'd just realised how dangerous it was and changed his mind.

Adjusting my grip, I tried to paddle the other way.

"RELAX!"

I pulled my paddle in and grabbed the safety cord that ran around the top of the gunwale. We swept into the maelstrom, water hitting the bow, and the shock wave soaking Bruce and me. Around us water boiled as everyone stared like helpless deadweights at the turbulence.

Fortunately Oshan knew what he was doing. He steered

the raft between two rocks and down a chute, the boat dropping like we'd hit an air pocket. Being at the front I could see every swirl and obstacle ahead. Behind me Kate and Frank cheered, while behind them Linda and Lucy screamed. Then before we knew it, the raft swept out of the rapid and into smooth, silky water. Relieved and exhilarated at surviving, everyone was shouting and whooping.

"Look! Fish." Oshan pointed into the water.

"Where?" Kate and Lucy peered down.

"There!" Oshan swished his paddle and dowsed them.

They shrieked and laughed. "You'll regret that," said Kate.

"Regret what?" said Oshan as, undeterred, he splashed them again.

"Regret this!" Kate tried to splash him back.

"Forward!" With a wicked smile Oshan steered the raft around.

We moved stern-first towards the next rapid, a longer and even more furious affair than the one we'd navigated, with a nasty trough at its end. Someone was going in here for sure – maybe the whole lot of us. And with Linda and Lucy now at the sharp end, their screams intensified.

At the last moment Oshan turned the raft around again. Once more Bruce and I gazed down the throat of the beast. Then we were tilting and twisting in a deluge of angry water. Close up the trough looked impossible, and as the raft fell into it I seized the safety rope.

A solid wall of water smashed us. The raft folded in the middle, bow touching stern, helmets colliding. Only the force of the water was keeping us upright, our own headlong momentum carrying us forward.

Then we were through, soaked yet still afloat. More

cheering as adrenaline flowed, the raft drifting into another stretch of calm brown water.

"That was awesome!" shouted Kate.

"Fan-bloody-tastic," agreed Frank, a big smile on his face.

But Oshan hadn't finished with us yet. "The next rapid is the worst, yeah?" he said in an ominous tone. "There is a chance of tipping sideways."

And this time, to increase the stakes, there were people watching, lined along the parapet of a bridge. No doubt they wished us well, yet perhaps they longed to see the occasional raft capsize. After all, more than enough came down the river each day. Besides us several other rafts had set off that morning, each filled with jaunty young Sri Lankans on a day trip from Colombo.

"Forward!" shouted Oshan, and we all paddled.

Then as he bawled "Hold on!" we hit the rapids, water spilling and slapping. We whirled around a rock, over a chasm, under the bridge. This time Oshan wasn't fooling. The water was rough and the rocks sudden. Expertly he navigated, taking us safely through. On the final drop, another V-chute, he sprang a surprise. He rotated the raft a full one hundred and eighty degrees so we went down backwards. The first were last and the last were first – as well as now being the suckers getting soaked.

After that the rest was easy. No more big rapids – only drifting and paddling across smoother sections of water as we journeyed on towards the river town of Kitulgala. At one point concrete stumps poked above the surface, and Oshan explained these were all that remained of the railway bridge that the movie director David Lean had blown up, train included, when filming *Bridge Over the River Kwai*. Although the film was set in Thailand, it had been filmed here in Kitulgala. For some scenes the then prime minister of Sri Lanka, S.W.R.D Bandaranaike, had attended with various government dignitaries to watch – notably the blowing up of the bridge. Yet to their chagrin things hadn't gone as planned. The explosives were all primed and the train running, but the cameraman hadn't been able to get out of the way of the blast in time. The scene had to be aborted, so Bandaranaike and his pals stayed overnight, waiting for the rescheduled shoot the next morning.

David Lean had only one chance to film the event, and to ensure this happened he used multiple cameras. But en route to London for processing the valuable film canisters went missing. After searching high and low for a week he found them baking underneath the sun at Cairo Airport. Fortunately the film was undamaged. The movie's most famous scene, as viewed by worldwide cinema audiences, survived.

The railway carriages still lie underneath the water. Although when we jumped out at Oshan's direction and swam this section no one spotted anything – not a lump of coal, nor a Ceylon Railways sandwich.

"This is the life!" shouted Lucy, her head and orange lifejacket bobbing above the water. "Beats going to work, especially in December."

"Lucy doesn't like Christmas much," said Bruce, wet hair plastered around his face as he oscillated up and down too. "That's why we go away this time of year."

"Yeah," said Frank. "Anything to escape the hype, all them same ole Christmas tunes, the TV, and those stupid flashing lights people put in their windows."

Lucy laughed knowingly. "Huh, if I had fifty quid for every call-out I get on those Christmas lights I'd be a millionaire. People wire them up wrong – they don't bother with an earth. Then when they switch them on – *kerfluff*! – the dicks, they fry all their circuits!"

"Lucy's a sparkie," Bruce said by way of explanation. "She did the lights at the Pump Rooms last year."

"Yeah, I was crapping myself when the mayor switched them on. They get hundreds of people at the opening ceremony. Imagine if something had blown!"

It was difficult to picture their hometown of Leamington Spa – or any other UK town – as we floated with the current, watching the forested hillsides, the little square houses with children playing. This was a beautiful place – the brown looping river, the rich green banks, the occasional platform house rising on stilts, and the sun shining down from an intensely blue sky. I felt as if I were a part of this world, no longer encapsulated inside my tourist shell but truly belonging.

Such a pity these white-water rafting trips wouldn't continue much longer. A new hydroelectric dam was in the final stages of construction upstream, and when it was completed – early in 2020 – would mean an end to rafting along this section of the river. Good for the environment if it meant cheaper, cleaner power. Yet a shame for future adventurers looking to escape Santa.

We drifted a little further, then Oshan grasped our lifejackets one by one and tugged us back on board. Soon we'd reach the Kitulgala Rest House, where the other five would be waiting for us. The same colonial hotel where David Lean had stayed in 1957 while filming his pretend River Kwai. Hopefully there wouldn't be a Christmas tree or lights in sight – so we could maintain our Santa-free illusion.

EIGHTEEN

The Never-Ending Loop of Nuwara Eliya

It was freezing cold in Nuwara Eliya, the temperature so low we had to rifle through our well-churned suitcases and dig out jumpers, trousers, socks and trainers. Our garb thus far – shorts, T-shirts and jandals – wasn't warm enough now that we'd fled the heat of the lowlands and ascended to the cooler heights of the central plateau.

"The British colonials used to come here for their holidays, yeah?" Oshan shivered at the front of the bus. "It was too hot for them in Colombo, especially in April, so they built all their summer houses at Nuwara Eliya instead."

He was wrapped in a light blue anorak with a fleecy hood. Mister C, too, was dressed for a winter skiing trip, with woollen gloves covering his hands, a blanket over his shoulders and a knitted beanie on his head.

"Things don't change." Jerry gestured at everyone in the bus. "We're still coming in our droves."

"They call it Little England –" Oshan hugged his chest "– because of all the Victorian buildings, the hotels, the park, the golf course, the boating lake and the racing course."

At first glance there didn't appear to be much to the town. The grey water of Lake Gregory was on one side with a few tall, worn houses on the other. Then the racecourse – though no horses – followed by a busy traffic roundabout with a gold statue of somebody in the middle, and on the other side of the road a large white stupa. A park too, full of deciduous trees. Truly, we might be in some anonymous town in southeast England rather than in Sri Lanka. The day was so dull, the sky cloudy, and everything had a washed-out, humdrum, no-one-ever-talks-to-you inevitability.

Which was unsurprising since the town was predominantly a British invention. In the first half of the nineteenth century the local POMs constructed a road from Kandy and developed local businesses, coffee plantations, and market gardens of English fruit and veg. Carrots, tomatoes and rhubarb prospered but coffee failed. Some bright spark, probably the tea pioneer Bob Taylor, then had the bright idea of growing tea.

Tea took off in a big way, requiring a glut of Victorian architecture to celebrate all this newfound wealth. The plantation owners built big houses, grand hotels, golf and racing courses, and anything else they could think of. Nuwara Eliya became a solid replica of England with a post office, pubs, sand bunkers and nags. It was a place to shelter during summer months while the rest of Sri Lanka sweltered.

"We'll give you a quick tour on the bus," said Oshan. "Then you can walk around on your own."

"What's there to see?" Frank seemed to share my doubts about the town's charisma.

"Flipping loads," said Jerry, who as usual must have done his research. "High tea on the veranda of the Grand Hotel for you posh chaps, and a game of snooker downstairs for the proletarians."

"Guess it depends what's your bag," said Frank.

"My bag is in my room," said Nelson. "I wish I'd brought my coat out now."

"Something else you need to know." Jerry held up his jacket, a smart worsted number that wouldn't have looked out of place at a gentleman's club. "Blokes have to wear a jacket and tie to eat dinner there, and ladies a dress."

"What about high tea?" I asked. "Do we have to dress up for that?"

"Nope." Jerry shook his head. "They serve it outside. You'll get away with shorts and sandals."

The sky remained dark, not a good omen for dining outside. Nonetheless I was keen to sample high tea at the Grand. In such a salubrious setting this might be the perfect cuppa I was looking for.

Chanuka swung the bus off the Grand roundabout and onto Grand Hotel Road. To the left rose a tall, modern white building that was a food court and hotel, while to the right stretched the trees and greens of the golf course. A moment later, to the sound of sighs and camera beeps, we caught sight of the Grand Hotel. The building stood out, handsome and vaguely Tudor-like: cream walls, brown timbers, paned windows and a terracotta roof. In front stretched a lawn, a fountain, unfurled flags and neat ornamental gardens.

"Looks like Great-Uncle Roger's place in Tunbridge Wells," said Jerry, laughing. "Twenty-six bedrooms, three dining rooms, a snooker hall, a greenhouse and one elephant-foot umbrella stand."

"The Grand has one hundred and fifty-four rooms," said Oshan, not to be outdone. "Plus four restaurants, including an Indian restaurant and a Thai."

"Looks too posh for me," said Nelson. "Especially if you have to wear a jacket."

"Better change your shirt too." Frank pointed at Nelson's elephant shirt. "No animals allowed in the dining room."

"Get away!" Smiling, Nelson prodded at the slogan on Frank's T-shirt – I'm With Stupid. "They won't let you in either."

Whatever the restaurant policy at the Grand, neither Frank nor Nelson would have stood a chance at the next hotel to appear on our left – a Scottish-looking stone building, again with an immaculate lawn and a tiled terracotta roof. This was the Hill Club, also with a dress code, billiards room and stylish, old-school dining room. The club had originally been established as a gentleman's club for British planters, with women being granted membership only in the 1960s. As well as being a hotel it was still a club, with a membership of several hundred.

The hotel area of Nuwara Eliya vanished as Chanuka drove into the newer, busier part of town. Modern buildings piled around us like the roads that snarled with traffic, and the pavements – where there *were* pavements – thronged with people. No neat lawns, no fountains, no graceful shrubberies lining the sidewalks. This was the commercial end of Little England, the half that had never been English but always Sri Lankan. In quick succession we passed the Windsor Hotel, a pub, a garage, a bakery, a bazaar, the police station and the post office, once more finishing up at the Grand traffic roundabout.

"We've gone round in a big circle," announced Oshan. "You can do the same now on foot, yeah? Just keep turning right and meet the bus back here at –" he glanced at his watch "– four o'clock."

As we climbed down the steps, he handed everyone copies of a hand drawn map. It showed the town as a figure of eight, the lake and racecourse in the lower circle, and the old hotels and main hub of town in the upper one. We had two and a half hours to explore. Surely that would be ample time?

"I'd like to try one of these high teas," I said to Kate, unsure if she'd agree. For as much as she enjoyed eating cakes, there were other places in Nuwara Eliya to visit such as a bazaar and Victoria Park.

"Are we going to have time for tea?" She looked doubtful.

"I think they start at three so if we get there promptly, we've got an hour."

"You know we're coming back here with Samid?" She named the guide we'd arranged for our very last week.

We wandered up to the town – left, left, left – in the opposite direction to the one Oshan had instructed, to take in the post office, the police station and then the bazaar. Things went wrong straightaway. The old redbrick post office, while immensely charming – especially a six-sided red pillar box from Derby – had lawns that might have been coated in stamp adhesive. No matter how many times I tried to wrench myself away, onto the next attraction on Queen Elizabeth Drive, Kate found something else to look at, be it the fancy red clock tower, the large poster of a reddish-brown Ceylon five pence stamp, the potted geraniums, even the trio of flagpoles.

"There's no rush," she kept saying. "We're on holiday. We have time to look around."

"But there are other things to see." The post office was indeed scenic – yet no more than any rural original in Blighty. "And I really would like to see if we can get high tea."

Eventually, as the grass beneath our feet withered, and the paint on the pillar box began to flake, we ambled fifty metres to the next interesting looking building, the senior police officers' circuit bungalow. It consisted of several buildings all close together – handsome white houses with turrets and green roofs. A sentry post was positioned at the top of the driveway, together with the sentry and two important looking police officers, so we knew better than to try to go in. I risked a few photos after a nod from the sentry, and then once again we tried to move on.

"If we're going to have time for those scones." I tried a little Devonshire persuasion. "Plus cream and jam…"

"All right."

In turn we visited a mall of shops, an underground market and a car-rental showroom. So far Oshan's circular map had been good. Everything where it should have been – even if it was taking us ages. Then we came to a junction where our navigation came unstuck.

"It's up there." Kate pointed at the road on our left. It appeared to lead into a park and golf course.

"That looks wrong." The road left didn't match the map. "We have to go past the pub, the petrol station and the Windsor hotel first."

"I'm sure it's up there."

"I think it's the other way."

Time was vanishing. We still had an hour and a half – but I wanted to reach the Grand with plenty of time for high tea. After more descriptions of cakes and petit sandwiches, we agreed to go my way. Straightaway, we hit a second big roundabout and the Windsor Hotel as predicted. We bumped into Lucy and Bruce too, who seemed to know exactly where they were going.

"We've been shopping." Bruce held up a bag bulging with gifts. "I love a bit of retail therapy."

"And now we're going to the pub." Lucy pointed across

the street. "Two lovely glasses of sauvignon blanc. Fancy joining us?"

"I think we have an appointment with another kind of drink." I nodded in the direction we were heading which, according to the map, would lead us to the two colonial hotels. "We want to try out afternoon tea."

On we walked, only to meet Amy and Nelson. Nelson had purchased another elephant shirt and Amy shielded her eyes from the pattern. They told us they'd visited the old hotels, so we had to be going the correct way.

"They've got everything inside!" Nelson danced with enthusiasm. "A ballroom, a big dining room, a billiards room, a conservatory and a lounge."

Yet as we plodded further into a maze of side-streets, the shops becoming smaller and scruffier, there was no sign of the green lawns that fronted the Hill Club and the Grand Hotel.

Kate pointed at a familiar blue tuk-tuk parked on the corner. "We've been past this before. We're just going around in circles."

"We're turning left, though." I waved the map.

"I'll ask somebody." She approached two bystanders who listened with puzzled faces, then waved us back the way we'd come. Following their directions, we walked for another five minutes, only to end up at the same blue tuk-tuk.

"Perhaps someone's moved it," I said optimistically.

"This is ridiculous."

It was after three. They'd have started tea service at the hotel, and anyone arriving on time – such as Jerry – would already be tucking into their second tier. In desperation, we headed along a mud path across a patch of parkland, then spotted our bus. Oshan wasn't on board, but Chanuka smiled from the driver's seat and pointed us in a new direction.

And lo and behold, we found ourselves on the same road into the golf course that Kate had pointed out hours ago.

"I said it was this way."

"But this doesn't match the map."

"It's still left."

All visions of miniature savouries, minute chocolate eclairs and tiny squares of Battenberg were fading fast. And of scones fat and creamy, of tea so delicate it could soothe the sorest throat.

We came first to the Hill Club, as fearsome and solid looking as it had appeared earlier. Then the Grand Hotel, resplendent, magnificent, the veranda sprawling with tables of happy people eating cake and drinking tea.

But it was ten to four. We didn't have time for even a single cuppa. Turning, we headed back the way we'd come, to the bus.

And the lesson of this story? Never trust a map drawn in haste by a man you don't know very well. Trust your wife instead, because she's probably right, and even if she isn't, then it doesn't matter because you won't be wrong either.

NINETEEN

World's End

A pair of large ears emerged from the mist, then the head and shoulders of a deer. It stared with round brown eyes, its fur dark in the rain. It was nearly the magnificent stag that graced a bottle of Glenfiddich whisky, yet we hadn't been magically transported to the highlands of Scotland. We were driving to a new dramatic sight in the hills of Sri Lanka.

"How much further?" said Jerry from the back of the minibus. "Are we nearly there?"

"Five kilometres," said the driver. Then, as if to contradict him, we passed a road sign that read, "Horton's Plain, ten kilometres."

Nothing made sense on this rugged, potholed road. We'd jolted over two railway crossings and seen no train. And twisted around dozens of hairpin bends, yet we were still going up. And now it seemed we were travelling in circles, the red taillights of the minibus in front really a memory of our own.

"Maybe we should turn around and head back down,"

said Linda. "This weather is unbelievable. It's too thick to see anything."

"Don't worry," shouted the driver. "The mist will clear when we reach the top."

This was hard to believe. The mist wasn't mist but low cloud. And "the top" – the highland plateau of Horton Plains – was at a height of two thousand metres, where conditions were likely to grow colder and wetter. If the cloud didn't clear we wouldn't see the incredible view we'd been promised at World's End, where the plateau came to a sudden and frightening end, plummeting a kilometre to the lowlands below.

We'd left the hotel at dawn for this jaunt. Our regular bus hadn't been able to take us – it was too big for the narrow roads – so we were travelling in two minibuses with local drivers. Too early for breakfast, we'd each been provided with a cardboard bag of food to munch on the way. One cheese and tomato sandwich, an orange, a banana, a carton of juice, and the pièce de résistance, a hard-boiled egg. The idea was to arrive refreshed and eager at Horton Plains visitors' centre sometime after eight, and then walk the nine-kilometre loop path (four and a half there, four and a half back) to the escarpment of World's End. Hopefully this would coincide with the usual brief mid-morning clearing of clouds and allow us to witness the trillion-dollar view.

We drove over another rail crossing and spotted two more deer. Tom pulled out his big lens for a close-up, yet even his equipment struggled in the poor light.

"Won't win any prizes," he said to Linda. "The colours will be washed out."

"Then don't bother." Linda was snuggled inside a bright-green cagoule, only her eyes and strands of hair visible beneath the hood. "Save it for another day."

But Tom took no notice. His shutter clicked like a metronome, and behind him Jerry aimed his phone too. Photos, photos, photos. No matter that you could take better ones of deer in the Scottish Highlands.

We stopped at some makeshift toilets, barely visible in the mist. Then a few minutes later the minibus stopped again. Dismounting and squinting, we could just about discern what looked like a Victorian hunting lodge in the murk. This was Farr Inn – the visitors' centre. Quite close – only twenty yards away – yet the cloud was so mulligatawny dense we might need guide ropes to find our way over.

"We'll be lucky to see sweet FA in this!" said Jerry. Nevertheless he was first off the minibus, his phone out again as he took more photos.

"It will clear later," said the driver in a small voice of optimism.

Disheartened, Kate and I followed Linda and Tom across the tussocks of grass, treading carefully between the puddles. I wore my boots, the solid, lace-up leather things that had taken so much room in my suitcase. At least up here in the cold we didn't have to worry about stepping on snakes.

Inside, the lodge resembled an old railway station. One musty room connected to another and then another like a Sunday afternoon puzzle, with odd chairs and old maps acting as clues. At the end of this labyrinth, the last room had been converted into a souvenir shop, displaying racks of sweatshirts, raincoats and woollen hats.

Reaching the lodge's exit we stepped outside, back into the mist. Down steps to a gravelled area where Oshan and the rest of our group waited for us.

"What kept you?" asked Nelson with his customary grin. "We've been over there already, and I can tell you, it's bloody marvellous."

"How come your shoes aren't dirty?" Jerry pointed at Nelson's unmuddied sneakers.

Nelson laughed in his good-natured way. "Guess I'm good at stepping over crap."

"You must be careful at the viewpoint, yeah?" said Oshan, half-grinning, half-frowning. "There is no barrier, only barbed wire. People have gone too close and fallen to their deaths." He didn't mention if any of these unfortunates had been on his tours – and seriously I hoped not.

We started out into the mist, each person following whoever was in front. Barely had we paced a hundred metres than the shape of another building solidified ahead. A security post of some kind, where guards in green uniforms lined up to check our bags.

"They are checking for polythene bags and the labels on plastic water bottles," shouted Oshan. "Anything that can be discarded and the wildlife will try to eat or get tangled in."

It seemed an admirable policy, the first of its kind in the world. And though we'd only seen sambar deer, there were other animals on this cold, damp plateau including stripe-necked mongooses, long-tailed giant squirrels, purple-faced langurs, wild boar, fishing cats and even the odd shy leopard. Plus all of Tom's birds: dull-blue flycatchers, Sri Lankan bush warblers, Sri Lankan whistling thrushes and yellow-eared bulbuls. Before the British colonials shot them all, elephants used to roam up here too. Horton Plains is now the only national park in Sri Lanka to lack elephants.

Past the security checkpoint we moved onto a paved path. Rain drizzled, dampening clothes, faces and spirits.

"Did you say there was a café up here?" Kate asked Oshan.

He smiled, knowing she was joking. "No. That's why you have hard-boiled eggs."

"Really?" She held out her hands in disbelief, the rain spotting the sleeves of her dark-green waterproof.

Kate decided to go back. Nine of us might be crazy POMs and one mad Welshwoman, intent on seeing the view at all costs – even at the risk of a broken leg or a chill, possibly sudden death – but at least one person, the sole Kiwi, had sense to forgo the excursion and conduct proceedings from the sanity of the bus.

Foolishly the rest of our group, me included, carried on. The path became red clay, possibly a watercourse, and slippery in the wet. Rocks blocked our progress in places and we had to clamber down, holding onto tree branches and embankments to steady ourselves. The danger of slipping and spraining an ankle was very real, especially for older people who weren't so sprightly.

I didn't spot any leopards, though that doesn't mean one didn't spot me. Nor did I see any of the rare purple-faced langurs, small primates with – as you might guess – dark purple faces, staring brown eyes, white beards and tufts of light brown hair.

Yet the landscape was ghostly and beautiful. Grasslands leading into cloud forest, with umbrella shaped trees called *keena* covered in lichens and moss. Many birds too, out of sight, warbling and whistling invisibly.

For a while I walked with Nelson, enjoying his wry sense of humour. We talked about our favourite music – bands from the seventies – and somehow arrived at the Dutch progressive band Focus whose single *Hocus Pocus* earned them international fame. The band members may or may not have toured Sri Lanka. But if they ever walked along this twisty, mostly flat path to World's End, their focus wouldn't have been guitar chords but watching their steps.

Our conversation drifted onto other topics: the price of

concert tickets, the resurgence of vinyl. Then, before we realised, we found ourselves at the first viewpoint of Little World's End. Luckily we were paying sufficient attention to stop in time. This was not a place to accidentally walk off the edge. Only a few strands of barbed wire bordered the observation deck; beyond that there was nothing for three hundred metres down.

Nervously I glanced over. Still mist, with glimpses of green hills. A shimmer of distant water too. The edge looked so innocent, yet beyond the tufts of grass it was deadly.

After walking a little further along the path we reached World's End proper. The same style of timbers made up the observation deck, the same type of grass grew at the edge, and the same token strands of barbed wire protected no one from themselves. Unseen, the escarpment dropped further here – eight hundred and eighty metres, almost a kilometre.

A year earlier an unfortunate nurse from Germany had fallen to her death after trying to take a selfie. In 2015 a Dutchman on his honeymoon had fallen as well. Miraculously he'd been saved by a tree fifty metres below that broke his fall. He'd been rescued by soldiers, who used ropes to lift him down. He'd then had to be stretchered through miles of bush before he could be driven to hospital. Clearing up accidents at World's End is further complicated by the top of the cliff being in one district and the bottom in another.

I wasn't going to risk any selfies. Instead I asked Frank to take a photo of me as I stood in front of a large green and white sign that read "World's End". First however I had to manage to stand there. Other people were taking photos of one another too, especially a large group of tourists who didn't seem to want to move on. No matter how long I waited for the space beside the sign to become free, constantly two or three of them hovered. They took every possible permutation of photo – hands at their sides, hands clasped together, hands raised above their heads. Then a photo of person A with person B, person B with person C, followed by persons C and A alone, and persons C and A together. One of them had even brought various costumes to wear – a bright yellow raincoat with beads, a loud red shirt and tie, even striped pyjamas with a knitted bobble hat. I'd be waiting ages for them to finish, or at least until they ran out of material or the batteries on their phones went dead. Seizing my chance, I pushed in front of them. Then, trying to smile – tricky under the circumstances – I motioned at Frank to take my photo.

Meanwhile more tourists were arriving – Europeans, Americans, Asians, – nationalities from all over the world. Despite the slipperiness of the path and the on/off drizzle they'd all braved the inclement weather and come to World's End for its amazing views.

The clouds pulled back like curtains. A vast plain stretched below. Faint lines that might be highways, and tiny cubes that must be houses. A sheet of shining water that might be ocean yet was probably the huge reservoir at Uda Walawe National Park. On clearer days you were supposed to be able to see the south coast – the entire southern part of the island. Truly a breath-taking sight.

The clouds closed, the show over. Although there were still the costumes to watch, plus some incredible footwear. One woman wore a pair of fawn knee-high suede boots. How she'd goose-stepped along the path God only knew. Others flapped flip-flops and sandals, clogs and high heels, even a pair of encrusted gumboots. All had their rightful places in this world – yet perhaps not on a strenuous nine-kilometre trek.

Thinking of Kate, hopefully warm on the bus, I hastened back. Now walking with Frank, who was as talkative as Nelson, I learned about singles' hotels near Tooting Bec and walking holidays in the Lake District. Funny, really, the things you talk about on a hike. Maybe everyone should try tramps like this more often. Without the distractions of eye contact or the temptation of electronic devices it's a good way to understand other people – and be understood.

After a couple more kilometres, including one particularly gnarly uphill section over tree roots and loose earth, we heard flowing water. A staircase of big, slippery steps led down to the noise. Arriving at the viewing platform, we gazed in wonder again, this time at the voluminous Baker's Falls, a rush of white water tumbling over black rock. Here we could stare, marvel and take photos without fear of falling. A solid metal balustrade ran along the edge, while a second platform lay below. Unlike at World's End, no one was dressing up either. The spray made everyone appear monochrome, apart from one Asian gentleman sporting a colourful golfing umbrella.

"Must get a snap of him," said Frank and, raising his phone, photographed the umbrella. "Stands out against the black and white, doesn't it?"

"Maybe he wants to be noticed," I said. "He's fed up looking like everyone else."

"Or his wife told him to hold it. She doesn't want to get wet."

There were plenty of other photo opportunities – if you liked taking pictures of tourists who all looked the same. Though we probably looked the same to them too, our pale European faces and choice of hiking clothes, and how we murmured in quiet voices. Apart from Nelson, that is, whose elephant shirt would eclipse the umbrella. Except Nelson hadn't arrived yet; he was still on his way.

For a while I stood and listened, letting the sound of the water overpower my thoughts. Several rivers started their journeys on this high plateau, radiating outwards to every coast. The Mahaweli, Sri Lanka's longest river, which flowed to Trincomalee in the west. The Kelani, the same river we'd rafted on two days earlier, which headed east to Colombo. And the Belihul Oya – the river of these falls – which joined the Walawe, and in turn reached down to Uda Walawe and Ambalantota in the south.

Waterfalls are fascinating things, I decided. How the sound spanned all audible frequencies and drowned out the chatter from every ethnicity of tourist. How the separate threads flowed together then broke apart, forming and dissolving over and over. How the crisscross of white glowed intensely against the pitch-black rock, and how luxuriant and green grew the surrounding vegetation. How the water kept coming and coming, gallons and gallons of the stuff, a permanent yet changing artscape, never stopping, seemingly inexhaustible.

The last few kilometres of path emerged from the cloud forest and undulated over grassland. The rain increased, falling faster, heavier, and soaking my fleece. In my hurry I left the others behind, and as the flora grew sparser had to hope I was going the right way. The landscape looked like Scotland – or New Zealand – rather than Sri Lanka, with its unique tropical dangers. Now there was no banter to sustain me – no debates about seventies rock bands, no *Hocus Pocus,* no discussions about vinyl. My focus was on getting back in the shortest possible time. And with relief I came to the place where the path had forked, then the security post, and finally the welcome sight of the visitors' centre.

I whizzed through, ignoring the sweatshirts for sale, the maps, the musty rooms. Linda and Tom were sitting outside staring at the mist, but I rushed past them too. Finally I reached the bus, glad of shelter out of the rain.

Kate sat quietly inside, warm and dry. She'd been chatting to the driver about Buddhists and Catholics, and how well they get on together. She'd eaten her sandwich too. And cracked open my hardboiled egg.

TWENTY

Breakfast at Bandarawela

Everything in our hotel at Bandarawela ran at an angle. The foyer was shaped like a triangle, and the staircase climbed ten degrees off true. In our bedroom all the pictures hung lopsided, and the window sloped far from the vertical.

"Bandarawela is an unusual town, yeah?" Oshan had told us as we arrived on the bus. "If you wander around you'll see there is not so much here for tourists, which is why we only stop one night. But it does have a very healthy climate. Some people say it has the best climate in the whole of Sri Lanka."

The view from our window hardly reinforced this. We couldn't see any of the lush, high green hills that surrounded Bandarawela, though we could see cloud and mist covering the sky. Even the best climate in the country has its off-days, I supposed, and in any case everyone's idea of a favourite climate had to differ. Kate and I had come to Sri Lanka for warmth and sunshine. Yet people who lived here endured heat all the time. Perhaps they longed for more temperate zones, even for rain.

We were high up on the third floor of the hotel and able to see several buildings of this plain-looking town. The green roof of the Municipal Council, the orange roof of the Tennis Club, and the grey-metal roof of the Uva Service Centre. The magnificent Grand Mosque too, with its elegant, onion-shaped gold dome. And a jumble of other places – a blue warehouse, and what looked like a canopy over a gas station. With its utilitarian feel, its lack of other tourists, its grimy, steel-town charm, Bandarawela might in fact be extremely interesting.

My legs still ached after walking nine kilometres to World's End and back, yet that was no excuse. I was only here once; I had to go out and explore. And after finding my way out of our Escher drawing of a hotel – descending its impossible stairs, treading one of its endless corridors, then locating the exit in its triangular foyer – I walked out through the car park and back along the road we'd just traversed on the bus.

As I neared the centre of town the traffic increased – trucks belching diesel, buses swinging dangerously around tight bends, and dozens upon dozens of tuk-tuks. It felt as busy as anywhere I'd been, perhaps busier, as if vehicles from all over Sri Lanka had to travel through here on their way to reach anywhere else. I stuck to the pavements, not wanting to get mown down or succumb to accepting a ride from any of the tuk-tuks that slowed alongside me. Lots of other people were out walking too, some empty handed and others carrying shopping bags, boxes and cartons of fruit and vegetables. They all seemed to be locals. There were no other tourists like me.

Many shops were open – shoes, textiles, spices, whatever you wanted – though much of the signage was in curved circular Sinhala lettering rather than the straight up/down lines of English. I'd read somewhere that Sinhala script had evolved this way in order to preserve the surface of the delicate leaves on which letters were once written. Straight lines were too incisive and would easily cut through. Curves were slower and gentler, unlikely to rip the leaf.

A little way out of town was the railway station. A large sign hung above the platform with Bandarawela written in Sinhalese, Tamil and English scripts. Many locals crowded wearily around benches, yet no train was due soon – they were all late due to the bad weather. We'd been due to arrive here by train ourselves, a short ride from Pattipola, Sri Lanka's highest railway station, close to Horton Plains. This indeed was the whole reason we were staying in Bandarawela. Our train trip had been cancelled, however. No one had wanted to spend several hours crammed into a railway carriage that might not arrive until late – so we'd travelled on our bus instead. A shame for all those railway buffs on the tour who wouldn't get another chance. Kate and I at least had another train ride planned for our last week when we came back to the hill country with our own guide.

My legs tired as I made my way back to the hotel. The streets were still noisy, though at one point I came across a triangle of flowers – white, pink and yellow roses – growing exuberantly in the middle of a busy road. Perhaps they thrived on fumes, their sweet scents counteracting all the particles in the air. The golden dome of the Grand Mosque was visible too – poking above a row of shops – a landmark to guide me back.

I hadn't discovered anything extraordinary in Bandarawela. Yet despite being a nuts-and-bolts town, it had been satisfying to explore, to glimpse what many other places in Sri Lanka must look like away from the dazzle of temples, elephants, beaches and tourists.

. . .

BREAKFAST the next morning turned out to be our best breakfast yet. Not because it had the widest choice of dishes or the most delectable foods. Nor for its view, which was another angle of buildings, roofs and concrete. The hotel was so ordinary, though, it was charming and possessed a unique retrospective. For the first time ever at breakfast there was no buffet. Here a band of cheerful Santa-hatted waiters served us everything.

We sat at a long, white-clothed table, no one yo-yoing up and down from their seat to fetch eggs, coffee or yoghurt but everyone altogether. Well, everyone except Beca who always seemed to arrive last.

"My alarm clock didn't go off," she said, dashing in. "I'm not late, am I?"

"Loads of time," said Jerry. "We don't leave until nine."

"The hotel's strange, isn't it? All those funny, sloping corridors leading everywhere. And the rooms are so odd. I counted seven walls in mine and twenty-three corners."

"Just don't look at the cobwebs," said Frank. "They get big spiders over here."

"Oh, I don't mind spiders." Beca smiled. "I used to keep tarantulas."

The waiters brought food on a never-ending supply of clean white plates. Slices of bread – brown and white, and one with specks of red and green. Fresh fruit too – papaya, pineapple and tiny bananas. Then slices of tomato, cucumber, pate and cheese. Olives, omelettes, pancakes, milk toast, curds and treacle. Finally glasses of juice and strong hot cups of coffee. Or tea for those who wanted it.

It was splendid. A feast. The finest breakfast in Bandarawela, the finest breakfast in Sri Lanka. An old-fashioned sort of breakfast where people sat and ate and talked, the way breakfasts in hotels used to be.

Bandarawela didn't pretend to be grand. Bandarawela didn't do airs and graces. Bandarawela stuck to its roots – to tradition – doing what it did best and doing it well.

TWENTY-ONE

Elephant Gap

It was hard to envisage we'd spend only three more days with the group. Time had passed quickly, yet slowly too, fooling us into thinking the tour would never end. It felt like we'd known this bunch of travellers for a very long time, despite it being little over a week and a half. Although I still didn't know what Amy and Nelson did. During the time left, I'd have to talk to them and find out more. My working hypothesis was that Nelson had been an entertainer of some kind, who may or may not have appeared on *Britain's Got Talent*.

We had another long road journey that morning. Once everyone was on the bus, Chanuka drove us out through Bandarawela's burly traffic. Thankfully it was lighter than the afternoon before, and, making good progress, we soon arrived at the neighbouring town of Ella.

Ella rocked. The main street swarmed with backpackers, while the cafes sold beer at knockdown prices and stayed open late into the night. The sort of place where young travellers would want to hang out, swapping stories and cigarettes, and hoping to overhear directions to The Temple – a legendary commune rumoured to lie deep in the jungle on the shores of a beautiful, nameless lake. We were older tourists though – mostly. Too unhip to attempt to blend in. With a chuckle and a wink Chanuka kept driving, taking us past a whole row of budget guesthouses and onto the tortuous road that led down to the plains.

He swung the bus around one tight hairpin bend after another. Above us, forested hillsides breathed with the mist of dragons. Dark, satanic peaks speared clouds, while closer, verdant hillsides tumbled down, with lonely teahouses perched on the edges. The view through Ella Gap was an inspiration. Faraway glinted the sunlit lands of the south. A different climate from here, a different country.

We slowed for roadworks, men and machines busy constructing a giant retaining wall. It rose like a contorted griddle several hundred metres up the slope, more ambitious than any similar scheme in New Zealand. How ironic that so-called third world countries construct first-world engineering. The Pyramids in Egypt, for instance, or the Taj Mahal in India – even the massive lion paws at Sigiriya. Perhaps this was another reason so many POMs had come on this trip. There was nothing new to see in England anymore – apart from plans for the Boris bridge joining Scotland and Northern Ireland, both of which aren't England and may soon vote for independence from the UK.

At Rawana Ella Falls we stopped to photograph a cascade of water zigzagging over black rocks. Forest bounded the sides, while tourists snapped at its heels. The road was narrow, and lined with buses, cars, minivans, tuk-tuks and motorcycles – all disgorging passengers who wanted to look. A plume of blue smoke rose from the cart of a vendor selling hot snacks: *achcharu*, a reddish-brown sweet-and-sour pickle; *vadei*, little cakes made from lentils; freshly fried triangular samosas; and bags of local nuts.

Back on board the bus, our journey twisted onward and downward. The highway seemed to descend forever and perhaps it did, one bend, waterfall and cloud after another, a continuation of that impossible staircase at Bandarawela.

Eventually the road levelled off. At the town of Wellawaya we turned left, onto the route signposted for Yala National Park. This is one of Sri Lanka's best-known wildlife sanctuaries, famous for elephants, crocodiles, leopards, sambar deer and monkeys. A place where the law of the jungle operates. The leopards eat the deer; the elephants eat the trees; the crocodiles eat each other; and the monkeys watch tourists taking their photos.

"You'll notice the fence, yeah?" Oshan pointed through the window at a meshed wire fence, three metres high, that bounded both sides of the road. "We're passing straight through the park. The fence is electrified to prevent the elephants getting onto the highway. But there are holes." He laughed. "Some big holes."

"And why would elephants want to get on the highway?" asked Jerry as if this was some kind of chicken-crossed-the-road gag. "No one's going to give them a flipping lift, are they?"

"The elephants try to stop the traffic for food," said Oshan, smiling. "Although it is discouraged, tourists feed them fruit. Now the male elephants demand their toll."

"Like meeting a Balrog," said Jerry.

"What's a Balrog?" said Nelson, and Jerry laughed.

Then out of nowhere a lone elephant appeared on the tarmac ahead. It was a big bugger, a fully grown male. It waved its trunk and stood defiantly on the left-hand side, blocking our way.

"Looks like we're in a spot of trouble here," said Nelson. "Any bananas, anyone?"

"I've got some cheese," said Beca, "but it's gone mouldy."

"No, no, no." Oshan waved his hands, thinking they were serious. "You mustn't feed it!"

No one had any fruit anyway. All the papaya and pineapple from breakfast had been eaten, the bananas too.

Anyway, Mr C had it sussed. He didn't even touch the brakes, but in one clean manoeuvre swerved right around the elephant. For one unforgettable split second the elephant's eyes fixed on us, its ears pinned back, and its trunk framed in the windscreen like a hold-up pistol. The next moment we were past it and speeding ahead on a clear road. Mr C didn't do angles. Nor did he stop to hand out fruit. He went as straight as his word, taking us from starting point to wherever we finished.

That day we ended our journey at Kataragama, a boulevard town at the southern end of Yala Park and, oddly enough, the third holiest site in the country. Every July and August thousands of pilgrims came here to worship as part of the Hindu Kataragama Festival. Some of them walked all the way from Jaffna, in the far north of the country, believing they were following the same route as the god Kataragama. During the festival itself the town grew incredibly busy, with devotees demonstrating their faith through mortifying acts such as piercing their skin with hooks, walking on hot coals, and bathing in the Menik Ganga River (full of crocodiles) then crawling to the holy shrine, Maya Devale.

We were here to spot elephants – and leopards – in the nearby Yala National Park. The entrance to the park wasn't far away, only fourteen kilometres from our hotel. So after quickly sizing up our room – all very spacious – we set off in mud-splattered jeeps for an afternoon safari.

I really hoped to see a leopard. There were dozens of the big cats living in the park, the highest density of leopards anywhere in the world. We made bets on how soon we might spot one – with Jerry bagging one o'clock, Nelson plumping for half-past five, and Beca settling on three. My estimate was mid-afternoon too, and I nominated a sighting time of precisely three-thirty. The leopard in question would be crouching on the branch of a tree, its tail waving as it stared at us with green eyes and licked its mouth.

The afternoon started off well. The dirt track to the park entrance was potholed, but various warm-up acts kept us entertained. Monkeys spying from trees, sambar deer grazing on grass, and bright-blue peacocks serenading less colourful peahens. Our group was split across two jeeps, with six of us in ours: Linda and Tom nursing their monster lenses at the front, Kate and me in the middle, and Jerry and Beca at the back happily chatting about that very English – and Welsh – preoccupation, the weather.

"Looks like it's gonna chuck down," said Jerry in a come-what-may tone.

"Definitely." Beca clutched at her backpack. "I made sure to pack an umbrella. You never know how wet it might get."

The jeep had a roof for cover, but the canvas sides were furled up. Of course if we did have to unroll them they'd prevent us from seeing any animals. For the moment the clouds held fire. The track had already received a dowsing earlier, leaving big puddles in the dips.

It must have been well after one by the time we reached the official park entrance. Jerry wasn't going to win the bet, no matter how many leopards we saw. Hopefully somebody else would get lucky. Yet with the threat of a storm and poor light there was no guarantee of seeing anything. Leopards are generally nocturnal and extremely elusive. Even under good conditions they are difficult to spot.

We trundled into the park, and it began to drizzle. The bush closed in around us, and as the rain grew heavier the grey sky seemed to sink lower.

"Where are the elephants?" said Kate. "I thought there'd be heaps."

"They go to high ground in the rain." From his cab at the front, the driver pointed out a hump-shaped hill. "To there – Elephant Rock."

He told us how the elephants had fled en masse to this rock on 26 December 2004. Elephants have sensors in their feet and had detected the earthquake long before the horrendous tsunami arrived. Over thirty thousand people on the south and east coasts of Sri Lanka were killed that day. Yet amazingly, no elephants drowned. We're supposed to be the smart ones. Sometimes elephants are smarter.

They were smart right now. They weren't skulking around in the bush, getting wet as they waited to be photographed. Not a single trunk or grey ear graced our viewfinders. The pachyderms had fled, off to Elephant Rock to contemplate zen, the melting of the polar ice caps, and weightless space travel. Just because elephants are heavy, it doesn't mean they don't want to go places.

Our jeep tilted and surged through a huge puddle. The rain fell faster and dripped onto our seats. Tom stood up and fiddled with the side canvas, perhaps wondering whether to pull it down. But as his brow furrowed in thought, he left it alone and sat again. He was always keen to get bird shots – and even now there might still be a chance.

"Look, there's a peacock." Jerry raised a finger at a peacock-shaped silhouette on a tree.

"I've got enough peacock photos," said Tom. "I really want a hornbill or a babbler."

"Can't help you there." Jerry pursed his lips.

"Wait! There's a bird down there," said Beca.

Sure enough, on the ground below us stamped a creature that looked like a Technicolor hen. Yellow-brown breast, blue tail, bright red wattle and comb. How everyone except Beca had missed it was a mystery because it stood out like a colour television in a Charlie Chaplin movie.

"Jungle fowl," said the driver. "The national bird of Sri Lanka."

He stopped the jeep for everyone to take photos. Then, once we were done, he jolted forward and stopped on a bridge. "Here," he babbled. "Something else to see." Not elephants, not leopards, but something in the water. Black snouts and the outlines of torpedoes. Every fish's worst nightmare – six or seven big crocodiles lying in wait for dinner. The longer I looked, the more reptiles I spotted. Another two on the grass, and one so close to a concrete buttress it was almost invisible. None of them moved, and it was no wonder people mistook them for logs. Very dangerous logs if you went too close: two metres of raw energy from tooth to tail.

"You see how they have their mouths underneath the little waterspout?" The driver pointed at a shallow lip in the stream over which water cascaded. "They will catch any fish that jump over. They have a fast shutter speed."

We watched for several minutes, rooting for the fish yet wanting to photograph jaws snapping on scales. The fish weren't jumping, however. If the crocs had fast shutters, then their prey had better lenses. The rain plummeted, the stream flowed, and water levels rose. If we stayed too long the jeep would be swamped. The crocs wouldn't be eyeing fish but us.

A terrific clap of thunder smashed overhead. One croc almost moved, its eyelid flicking down. Perhaps this was a signal to leave. The driver restarted the engine and revved forward, water splashing inside. The rain was now a deluge. Sighing loudly, Tom untied the right-hand side canvas and let it drape down, while Linda did the same on the left.

For a while we rode in semi-darkness. The only light came from the driver's cab at the front and a greyness from the jeep's open back. Underneath us mud churned, while above rain hammered. This was like no safari I'd ever been on before. This was more like camping in a storm, crouched in a small damp space and hoping the canvas wouldn't leak. It was the same weather Noah must have experienced before the Flood, yet at least he got to see two leopards and two elephants.

"Can't see that I'm going to need this." Tom began packing his big lens away.

"I'll try flash," said Jerry, holding up his phone. "It's got built-in halogen brighter than Land's End lighthouse."

"Except there aren't any ships," said Tom.

Jerry frowned. For a second it looked like there might be a discussion about the merits of SLR cameras versus phones. Then from the opening at the back of the jeep dawned light. A lake shimmered in the distance, punctuated by the silhouettes of several solid-looking, four-legged beasts.

"Water buffalo," said the driver, and suddenly everyone was taking photos, Tom included, despite the creatures being miles away.

Abruptly the rain ceased. The sky grew lighter. And we

heard a sound that was familiar yet entirely unexpected – the crash of surf.

Bizarrely, we'd reached the perimeter of Yala National Park on the southeast coast. And as Linda and Kate rolled one of the side canvases back up, furling it neatly with straps at the top, we caught sight of rolling white surf and a grey grey sea. When Jerry and I tried furling the canvas on our side, however, it spiralled out of control, the middle part sticking out like a sore thumb. Kate began to laugh, then Beca and Linda as well.

"What's the fuss?" Jerry stared. "It's rolled up."

"Ours is rolled up better," said Linda.

"I'm not getting out to roll it up," said Jerry. "Not if there're leopards out there."

If there were any leopards hiding in the trees they remained hidden, perhaps frightened by all the laughter, or else the sight of a badly furled canvas.

Out at sea, the horizon began to darken. Soon it would be dusk and unsafe to be driving in the park. We hadn't seen any leopards. We hadn't seen any elephants either, yet our safari had still been a great, wet adventure.

TWENTY-TWO

Piñata

I suspected something wasn't quite right the moment we walked into the rice farmer's courtyard. The broken ladder by the watchtower was suspicious. If an elephant decided to charge during our visit there'd be no one up there to shout a warning or throw firecrackers to scare it off. Then there was the rectangle marked out in the loose dirt, with six smaller rectangles inside. And what was the point of the three ceramic pots hanging from pegs on the washing line?

Jerry had noticed the pots too. "What are those for?" he said to Oshan. "Is that how they dry their plates?"

"The pots are for us." Oshan gave one of his enigmatic grins. "We will be playing piñata. The first person to break a pot wins the chance to go stilt-fishing."

Ominously, the chief farmer appeared with a thick stick. He smiled at us as if he knew something we didn't and then spoke in Sinhalese to Oshan.

"Who wants to go first?" Oshan looked at us all. "Linda?"

Linda stepped forward with a tense face. Her expression

grew even more worried as the farmer pulled a thick black cloth from his pocket – a blindfold to tie over her eyes.

"How am I going to see?" she said.

"You don't see, yeah?" said Oshan. "That's the game. You have to remember where the pots are."

The farmer bound the blindfold around the top of her head, rotated her three hundred and sixty degrees until she faced the pots, which were several metres away, then handed her the stick.

"No one to help her," shouted Oshan. "No feeling your way either or touching. And only one swipe."

Linda shuffled forward, one hand outstretched, the other gripping the stick. "I can't see a bloody thing!" she shouted as she veered left, away from the piñatas and into the undergrowth. "Please, somebody, help me."

No one said anything following the rule we'd been given. But as Linda almost collided with a tree Tom began shouting directions. "Left. Right. Forward. Stop!"

Finally Linda was headed in the right direction. Reaching the piñatas, she carried on past them and, drawing up at a wall, swiped hard at the farmer's house.

"Next," shouted Oshan as Linda tugged off the blindfold in disgust.

Lucy came forward, smiling optimistically. She did no better than Linda, advancing so far into the bush that had Bruce not rescued her we might never have seen her again.

Jerry, Frank and Nelson all tried – and failed. Everyone was laughing at each other's efforts.

Beca at least managed to connect with the middle piñata, but not with sufficient force to break it. By now, Oshan's rule about no help was being ignored as everyone howled advice. Tom was the most helpful, his cries of "Right", "Left", "Up a bit", "Down a bit" clear and precise. So far no one had managed to shatter a pot, yet the contestants were getting closer, the same as on that old seventies' TV programme *The Golden Shot* with Bob Monkhouse and Ann Aston.

My turn came and ended in ignominy too, the dark cloth tight against my eyes, bringing a sense of walking on the edge, about to trip over something or bash into a tree. It was much harder than it looked, shuffling forward in a direction I hoped was straight – yet probably wasn't – and experiencing a sense of disorientation like trying to cross an unfamiliar room in the dark of night. Encouraged by the others' shouts, I arrived at a position that felt like it might be close to the line. Drawing the stick back, I swiped madly. It connected with nothing, and I almost fell over.

The three piñatas hung intact. The stilt fishing prize remained unclaimed.

Then, looking like she meant business, Kate stepped forward. The chief took her through the same rigmarole. Blindfold, one complete rotation, then stick. Yet rather than dallying, Kate seemed to have an innate compass in her head. She marched in a dead straight line towards the piñatas as Tom shouted his stage instructions. Once she came within striking distance everyone else bawled, "Stop!" Raising the stick to her left, Kate paused, swung, and cut a perfect six for the Black Caps.

The first piñata flew off at speed, spilling its contents of milk and crashing against the farmer's fence. The second exploded, fluid and shards dropping to the ground. And the third followed a trajectory that took it smack bang into one of the legs of the watchtower where, with a crack, it snapped the thin wood in two.

Missing a leg, the watchtower became instantly unstable. The slightest gust of wind might tip it over. Proceedings ended swiftly. The proposed game of hopscotch was scrapped as too was the lunch of cassava, coconut, chilli and onions bubbling on the stove. Instead, the farmer ushered us onto his Formula One tractor with trailer and drove us out through the paddy fields at speed – five klicks an hour – back to the bus.

There was no stilt fishing prize. This had been a ruse by Oshan. As they say in Wellington, Madrid and Colombo, *que sera sera*.

EACH DAY we wove ritual into our journey. The art of pausing to laugh at ourselves, of using humour to understand better the people who lived here. Time on the tour was drawing rapidly to a close, the days speeding up like one of those pots tumbling to the ground. Half of the group – Amy and Nelson, Linda and Tom, Beca – were flying straight home afterwards, back to Blighty for Christmas lunch and the Queen's speech. Lucy and Bruce were apparently heading off on some mysterious extension in the Indian Ocean, while Jerry and Frank, like us, were departing the tour at the historic old fort of Galle.

Part of me was looking forward to moving on to the next phase of our trip. The tour had been excellent – everything organised for us and with visits to many fascinating places – but sometimes I felt too cosseted as we were bused around in our tight little bubble. We viewed things through the group's eyes rather than our own. We were shielded from the realities of independent travel: asking directions, negotiating bus stations and ticket offices, finding hotels and taxis – all the nitty-gritty details that can seem tedious and time-consuming as they happen yet afterwards provide valuable insight into a country. Sometimes, too, we focused more on other members of the group – most of whom now knew I was writing a blog – rather than giving our full attention to the sights we were visiting. As Robert Louis Stevenson wrote, "It is better to travel hopefully than arrive." Yet we must also choose where we travel to. Do we go in the same direction as everyone else? Or do we head alone into the unknown?

AT THE SEASIDE city of Matara we stopped for lunch: savoury pastries from a bakery, ice-creams from a supermarket, all happily consumed as we strolled along the beach. From a promontory at the far end a suspension footbridge arced out to an islet. This was Pigeon Island, the site of Paravi Duwa Temple. Had we had more time we might have walked over to take a closer look. It appeared to be unbelievably beautiful and would be stunning at sunset, but we were on a schedule. It was another twenty-seven kilometres to our hotel at Ahangama, further along the coast.

"The rooms are very spacious here," said Oshan half an hour later as the bus turned into the hotel's entrance. "The beach too, though only swim between the flags and avoid the coral. Watch out for the locals too – they will ask for money. If they mention the tsunami, just walk away."

Sure enough, as soon as I strolled towards the beach a sun-wrinkled lady popped up from the bushes.

"Where are you from?" she said in a familiar way.

"New Zealand." I frowned, half guessing what was coming.

"Ahh, New Zealand. The All Blacks? The haka?"

"Yes." I hoped she wasn't going to try to perform a haka. Or worse, expect me to.

"I have a stall." She pointed left along the beach. "T-shirts, sarongs, sandals."

"Great." I held up my towel, then nodded at the sea. "I'm going for a swim now."

"I have many relatives to support." She counted with her fingers. "Brothers, nieces, cousins, grandchildren. All unable to work since the tsunami."

As soon as I heard the magic word – tsunami – I made my excuses and dodged around her to a spot away from her stall. It's always good to support local businesses, but when they pester you sympathy evaporates. And as Oshan had pointed out, it was fifteen years since the tsunami. As a call for alms, it had passed its expiry date. The same lady accosted everyone else in our group who ventured to the beach. Linda and Tom became so wary of her they stopped going to the ocean and swam in the hotel pool instead.

Here at this spacious seaside hotel we could at last relax with free time to swim, sleep, read, and do nothing more strenuous than eating and drinking. There were no excursions planned. No temples to scorch our feet; no safaris to shake our bones. Though there was the option of whale-watching – of being woken at five in the morning to be driven to the nearby town of Mirissa, placed in a small boat, then bounced about in waves for several hours in the hope of spotting a tail.

The ocean off the south coast of Sri Lanka is one of the best places in the world to see blue and sperm whales. The enormous creatures migrate through these waters twice every year, from the Bay of Bengal to the Arabian Sea in April, and in the opposite direction in December. Yet despite several people – Amy and Nelson, Lucy and Bruce, possibly Beca – wanting to see these cetaceans, Oshan had been cagey about which tour operator was to take them.

"We have to charter our own boat," he finally said that evening, his voice a little more strained than usual. "One with two decks, an upstairs and a downstairs, so everyone has plenty of room. The whales may be on one side of the boat, then the other. You will need to move around. There are many unscrupulous boats who don't treat the whales well."

Then he told us the price. A scalp-tingling one hundred and fifty US dollars each. Unsurprisingly, there were no takers.

"Can't folk do their own thing?" said Jerry, probably having already researched all the other boat operators in Mirissa. "If Mr C takes them into town surely they can sort out their own trips?"

"I can't endorse it." Oshan seemed to be struggling with his conscience. "The big operators are not ethical, yeah? Their boats are overcrowded. You won't get a good view."

It was Beca who came to the rescue as she calmly announced she could arrange something ethical and for much much less. Her solution wouldn't even require a five o'clock start. If the other four people who were interested could rise at a leisurely seven and meet her on the beach, she'd make sure a suitable craft would be waiting.

"Fantastic." Jerry gazed at Beca, his eyebrows raised. "But how is it you can commandeer a boat from nowhere when Oshan can't?"

"Yeah!" Bruce guffawed. "With his bloody name – ocean – you'd think he'd have a fleet at his disposal."

Beca wasn't giving anything away. She smiled enigmatically and sipped at a Bailey's Irish Cream.

The next morning everyone gathered on the beach – the two couples who were going and the rest of us who weren't. We were all curious to see what sort of boat Beca had chartered, and how indeed she'd managed to persuade the captain to make a landing on the beach rather than depart from the regular port at Mirissa. Would it be one of the double-deckers Oshan had said would cost so much? Or a smaller vessel, one of the fishing boats he considered unethical?

"Where's Beca?" Jerry looked up and down the beach.

"Perhaps it's all a practical joke?" said Frank.

"I told you it's the quiet ones you have to look out for," said Nelson.

Amy shook her head. "I don't think Beca would do that. She's too nice."

Yet there was no sign of her. Or of a boat. Waves washed at our feet, the ocean empty and grey. On the horizon was the outline of a freighter. And, a little closer, an odd-looking cloud.

"I'm going back to bed," said Frank, rubbing his eyes.

"I'm going to breakfast," said Jerry, "before it gets busy."

"Hold on!" Lucy raised her hand and pointed upwards. "Can you hear that?"

A dull throbbing emanated from somewhere. At first it seemed to be coming from the hotel, but as the sound increased it shifted out to sea. And then the cloud, approaching faster than any cloud should, sprang rotors and hovered noisily above us.

"It's a helicopter," shouted Nelson.

Frank grinned. "And there was me thinking it was a seagull."

"Get back." Jerry began waving people up the beach and back towards the hotel. "It's going to land!"

Retreating twenty metres, we still felt the backdraft on

our faces. In a swirl of sand and water, the helicopter touched down lightly onto the beach.

As its door opened everyone gasped in surprise. In the cockpit a local pilot sat at the controls, and next to him, in the co-pilot's seat, was Beca, a blue-and-white Cardiff City scarf wound around her neck and a pair of headphones clamped over her ears. She turned and beamed at our incredulous faces. Beckoning, she gestured at Amy, Nelson, Lucy and Bruce to climb on board. They hesitated for a moment, but the pilot turned and beckoned as well. As the rest of us cheered, Amy and Nelson ran over, heads bowed, and jumped in. Then Lucy and Bruce, flopping into the seats behind and strapping themselves in. A final wave from them all, and the door closed.

The helicopter ascended and clattered out to sea.

TWENTY-THREE

Five Go to Cinnamon Island

It rained hard later, too wet to walk on the beach or even swim in the hotel pool, especially unpleasant when climbing out. We sat in our room watching raindrops race down the window and dark clouds mass on the horizon, wondering how the whale watchers were faring.

"Do you think they're back yet?" said Kate.

"I think we'd have heard them. That helicopter made a bloody din."

"They might have landed at the airport."

We'd checked Google Maps and discovered that Koggala Airport lay only a few kilometres up the road. Formerly it had been an RAF base with which Beca – or her old employer, the aviation company – might have had connections.

It was several hours since the party had left, far longer than we'd expected. Were they having such a buzz they'd lost all track of time? Or had they seen nothing at all and ditched in the ocean? The helicopter could only have so much fuel – and probably didn't float.

A sharp tap came on our door. I started, instantly worried it might be bad news. Oshan requesting we identify the bodies. The police wanting to interview us – why didn't we report them missing earlier?

"If it's the room boys –" Kate's expression was calm "– tell them we don't need any cleaning done."

"If it's the room boys I'm not sure I should open the door at all." I'd overheard a horror story after breakfast. Another hotel guest who, upon returning to his room, had found two room boys going through his wallet. He'd punched one of them and detained the other. Yet when the manager arrived, both room boys had denied all wrongdoing, and the manager had let them go.

It wasn't room boys at the door but Oshan. He grinned at me, clearly too cheerful to have heard anything bad about the helicopter.

"I've organised a boat trip to Cinnamon Island," he said. "Just wondered if you and Kate wanted to come?"

"Where's Cinnamon Island?" I didn't want to go out to sea; nor – after our last experience – did I want to go to another spice farm.

"It's in the Koggala Lagoon." His tone was reassuring. "There's a family who grow cinnamon there. They show you how it's processed."

"Okay." I nodded. It didn't sound amazing, but it was a chance to get out. Besides, both Kate and I liked cinnamon – she put it in her homemade muesli and I sprinkled it on cappuccinos. Cinnamon was also a commodity for which Sri Lanka had first become world-famous, long before tea or gems or tourism.

I locked all our valuables in the safe and we followed Oshan. The bus was already waiting, Chanuka revving the engine, and Linda and Tom sitting on the back seat.

"No one else coming?" I said, having assumed there'd be more.

"Frank is busy reading," said Linda, "and Jerry's gone off exploring."

I didn't ask her to elaborate. Obviously, the whale watchers still hadn't returned. I wondered if Oshan knew about the helicopter. He might be displeased after his finicky deliberations about the charter boat. Yet as he sat in his seat at the front he seemed his usual unfazed self.

The drive to Koggala Lagoon was short: three kilometres west, then right – ironically – towards the airfield. Peering through the window, I half-expected to see Beca's team riding tuk-tuks the other way.

The bus drew up at a little dock. A man gave us lifejackets to put on, then one at a time we stepped into a tiny boat. It swayed in the still water, especially when Tom heaved his lenses on board. The man jumped in last and tugged at the cord on the outboard. The engine wouldn't start though, and for several minutes we sat like seagulls bobbing up and down.

"This is quite an adventure, isn't it?" said Linda. "You know, I always wanted to be in one of those Enid Blyton stories where they row out to Kirrin Island for a picnic."

"You wanted their dog too," said Tom, "and look where that got us."

"Timmy?" Linda stared at Tom as if he'd said something he shouldn't have. Then she turned to us to explain. "We had this adorable mongrel I rescued from the practice. He was always going after rabbits, then one day he wolfed down our parrot."

"It was a beautiful yellow crested cockatoo!" said Tom.

"And I said we should keep it in a cage."

"What's this place – Kirrin Island?" said Oshan,

laughing. He probably knew nothing about the Famous Five stories, nor the dog Timmy that featured in them.

"Oh, it's not real." Linda laughed as well. "It's all made up. And I don't think they had much of a picnic there, either. They discovered a bunch of forgers or something like that, counterfeiting banknotes."

"In which case, there'd be no parallel with Cinnamon Island," said Tom. "The money here is already falling apart. You'd never tell the difference between counterfeit notes and real ones."

With a roar and a tang of black smoke the outboard burst into life. As the sound of the asthmatic engine echoed around us, the man steered us out into the dull waters of the lagoon. He stuck close to the shore, with mangroves at water level and trees above, perhaps fearing the engine would conk out again. We seemed to be the only living things on the water. Even the seabirds had flown away.

"Are there any crocs?" shouted Tom above the chug-chug-chug of the engine.

The man shook his head, then pointed out two eagles perched at the top of a tree. Immediately Linda and Tom scrambled for their lenses, the little boat rocking.

"They're probably parents guarding a nest." Tom aimed his camera and clicked. "One of them goes fishing while the other stays put."

As if to confirm his hypothesis, one bird lifted off and soared over us while the second bird remained.

The boat curved away from the shore into open water. Half a kilometre or so in front of us lolled the island, densely covered in trees. It was probably only a few hundred metres in width, yet there was plenty of cover for unseen activities: bark-stripping, spice-grinding, oil-making, maybe even the production of counterfeit rupees.

We landed at a small wooden jetty, each of us stepping gingerly onto not-so-dry land. A steep path led uphill between silent trees to a white stone house in a clearing. Oshan told us that three families lived on the island, all of them involved in making cinnamon.

On the porch, an older man with dense black hair sat cross-legged as he stripped a cinnamon tree branch of its bark. Once it was denuded he hammered the branch and then used a special knife to shave off the inner bark in long strips. These would then be dried into spiral quills. He passed the cuttings around for us to examine and smell. From somewhere else he retrieved a little bottle. It was full of potent cinnamon oil, drops of which he dabbed onto everyone's hand.

A grey-haired lady in a bright floral top stepped forward too, perhaps his wife. She dropped the remaining cuttings into a pot-sized mortar and pounded them with a wooden pestle as thick as an elephant's trunk. She might not have looked strong, yet she pressed and twisted with the strength of a machine. When she let each of us try we realised how hard this work was. Harder than pressing inked metal plates onto a roll of paper to make bank notes for sure – these people worked rigorously for their living. Because the process is so labour intensive, cinnamon is relatively expensive.

As well as selling the spice to tourists like us, the families supplied local markets. There are several different species of cinnamon trees across the world. The cinnamon in Sri Lanka is derived from the *Cinnamomum verum* tree, which is considered to be true cinnamon. Most of the cinnamon in our supermarkets, however, comes from the related, more strongly flavoured species *Cinnamomum cassia*, which isn't grown in Sri Lanka but in Indonesia and

China. Cinnamon contains a substance called coumarin that in sufficient quantities can prove toxic. There is a relatively high amount of coumarin in *Cinnamomum cassia*, meaning there's an upper daily limit on how much of this type of cinnamon can be safely consumed. By contrast, *Cinnamomum verum* contains virtually no coumarin, with no risk of toxicity at all.

The woman led us inside the house to show us her tiny kitchen. A fire of discarded branches blazed, heating a pan balanced on two slabs. Other pots and pans lay on the stone bench, spread out for production, or perhaps for show. Using an extracted kettle element wired crudely into a socket, she boiled water and made us cups of cinnamon tea. It tasted dry and spicy, quite different from normal black tea.

We thanked the people and boarded the boat to return. It was raining again, and fortunately the engine started first time. Everyone donned waterproofs – Kate in green, Oshan in red, Linda in black, Tom in yellow and me in blue. We were a motley bunch of cinnamon hunters, with more feathers in our caps than Tom's parrot. This wasn't Kirrin Island though, and no matter what we thought we weren't the Famous Five.

TWENTY-FOUR

The Birthplace of Martin Wickramasinghe

As a schoolboy, I hurried past William Shakespeare's birthplace every morning. The house is world famous, an object of pilgrimage for thousands of visitors every year. In my haste to reach school, however, I barely gave the place a second glance. It had always been there. It was just another timber building in a town already crammed with history. I'd rather have walked past a multiplex, a record store, or even a conventional bookshop.

My school wore its connections too. The oldest part of it – the half-timbered Big School – was where a young Shakespeare had once studied English and the works of Latin poets such as Ovid and Virgil. I didn't hold this room in great esteem either, especially when there were tests and end-of-term exams. Yet since then I've acquired a habit of visiting well-known writers' houses, such as Karen Blixen's home near Nairobi, Agatha Christie's summer house in Devon, and Robert Louis Stevenson's estate in Samoa.

Now at Koggala I had the chance to add another celebrated writer's house to my list: the birthplace of Martin

Wickramasinghe. A much-loved Sri Lankan novelist, he brought Sinhalese language and culture to the attention of a global audience. He wrote prolifically, with fourteen novels, eight collections of short stories, three plays, and numerous other works to his name. Many of his stories were set in Sri Lanka, and he even scribed a book about how D. H. Lawrence embraced the Buddhist practice of tantrism.

Our bus drew up outside the estate where his house was situated, and more slowly than usual, people climbed out. Today was our last day together. Shortly, at Galle, Jerry, Frank, Kate and I would leave the tour.

"Is an hour long enough for everyone?" shouted Oshan from the front.

There were nods all around, no one in a hurry. The whale watchers – Amy and Nelson, Lucy and Bruce, and Beca – stayed close together, murmuring among themselves. None of them had said much about their adventure yesterday, apart from Nelson last night in the bar.

"It wasn't much fun." He'd twisted his lips in a spiral.

I stared at him. "What did you see?"

"No whales. I can tell you that."

"Dolphins?"

"No."

"Large fish?"

He shook his head.

"Why were you out there so long? We were all getting worried. Jerry wanted to call the police."

Nelson smiled languorously. "I don't think the pilot knew where he was going. He hovered around a whale-watching boat, but they waved him off. Then he went around this oil tanker. I think they must have been heading the wrong way – towards India."

"So you didn't see anything?"

He shook again. "Nope. Not a sausage."

"When did you get back?"

"Late. The pilot had to follow this fishing boat to find his way in. There aren't any roads or signs out there, just water. He must have been low on fuel when he landed. These men in brown suits appeared, took us to a room, and questioned him and Beca. Something about logging the wrong flight path, endangering shipping, and none of us having insurance. I think the pilot was embarrassed. Beca too."

She looked a little tired now as she stepped off the bus. Her eyes were half-closed and her lips tight. Yesterday's surprise trip hadn't gone well and her holiday was about to end. She probably wouldn't be able to go whale watching again for a while – even though she lived in Wales.

Oshan bought our entry tickets for the Wickramasinghe estate, then everyone filed through the turnstile. Inside, the grounds were lush and shaded, with big trees in every direction. Most people headed for a set of exhibition halls that formed part of the estate, housing local Folk, Costume and Transport museums. But I was primarily interested in the birthplace. Splitting off from the others, I marched at speed towards the estate's north-eastern corner, where Martin Wickramasinghe's house was located.

Glimpsing it through trees, I felt excited and curious. It was a modest house, nothing grand. An open doorway in the middle, flanked by two sleepy, half-shuttered windows. A cerebral, receding, red-tile roof.

The house survives only by a quirk of fate. The British colonial authorities demolished all similar houses in the neighbourhood to make room for the nearby airfield, the same one where the whale watchers had been detained yesterday. Yet this house escaped, the wife of an officer taking a fancy to the place and persuading her husband that they should live there. A similar miracle may have happened to Shakespeare's birthplace – who knows?

I entered Martin Wickramasinghe's front room, where sofas crouched under the windows, and a desk – *his desk* – faced the inner wall. Bizarrely, my attention was caught by a steep ladder that led up through a hole in the ceiling.

"They kept food up there. Coconuts," said a kindly, white-haired old man, who seemed eager to offer information. He showed me a room at the back. "This is where Martin Wickramasinghe was born."

The birth room was tiny, with space only for a short bed and little else. No mirrors on the walls. No swaddling cot. A humble start to the writer's long, long life. The guide led me to another narrow room, where two beds stood end to end. "This is where he and his wife slept."

At the rear of the house in a large, airy extension were copies of every book Martin Wickramasinghe ever wrote – one hundred and twenty in all – displayed in glass cabinets. Many were written in Sinhalese, but a few were in English. Dozens of photographs of the writer were displayed on the walls, from a serious looking young man of twenty-four through to a more light-hearted octogenarian entertaining his audience. In his wedding photograph he embraced his bride. In another he received the Order of the British Empire from a young Queen Elizabeth II. In a third he stood next to Mao Zedong of China. Many of the photographs showed him wearing the same rectangular spectacles and wielding a probing stare. Yet he was enormously respected and well-liked – by other writers, by world leaders, and by his extensive family.

By the time I emerged from the house and into the sunlight outside the hour was almost up. Too late to visit the other exhibition halls and I could only manage a hasty glance at the *Samadhi*. This was a grass-covered mound underneath which Martin Wickramasinghe's ashes were buried. A black rock perched on top, taken from the Koggala reef. It symbolised his close roots to the area.

At the bookshop by the ticket office I bought three of his books: *Landmarks of Sinhalese Literature*, *Selected Short Stories*, and *Madol Doova*, a novel. A lot of his novels, such as the trilogy *Gamperaliya*, *Yuganthaya* and *Kaliyugaya*, deal with the effects of the modern world on traditional village life. This theme also influences his most admired work, *Viragaya*, about a young man from a Buddhist home who grows up in contemporary society.

Back on the bus, we'd have a short drive to the main gate of Galle Fort where, along with Jerry and Frank, we'd be pulling off our bags and setting off on our own. We'd have to say goodbye to everyone else – Amy, Nelson, Lucy, Bruce, Linda, Tom, Beca, Oshan, Chanuka and Sakan – who'd be continuing to Colombo. It would be a sad moment, leaving all these new friends, our group. Hopefully we'd stay in touch through social media and perhaps one day visit some of them in the UK.

No more Nelson, no more Beca, no more Oshan. How on earth would we cope?

TWENTY-FIVE

Goodbye and Hello

But the tour wasn't quite over. With typical sleight of hand, Oshan revealed we all had to stay on the bus for another of his infamous whistle-stop recce tours, taking in the highlights of Galle Fort: the shady tree by Sun Bastion wall; the steps to the Maritime Archaeological Museum; the inscription above the old gate; and Court Square with its big wide trees and Saturday art market. The lighthouse too, plus Flag Rock and the western ramparts.

There are two parts to Galle. The new town, where most of its one hundred thousand inhabitants live. And the historic Galle Fort, where most of the tourists hang out. We'd booked to stay at a guesthouse in the new town for our first night. Then we'd move to accommodation directly inside the fort for three more.

But first we had our bus tour.

Chanuka drove carefully around the perimeter of the fort. Although the fort area is small – a promontory of roughly fifty-two hectares – it was full of tuk-tuks, motorcycles, pedestrians and seemingly dozens of dogs. It was an enclosed, well-defended place with few spaces for traffic to disperse. A solid, high stone wall protected the northern land border, with only two narrow tunnels in and out. More stone ramparts ran along the eastern, western and southern boundaries, each one looking out to sea.

As we cruised down the eastern rampart we passed street after street of elegant colonial buildings. The *uber*-salubrious Amangalla Hotel, the solid-looking Dutch Reformist Church, and the ochre-coloured Maritime Museum. At the lighthouse on the southern tip the bus turned west, then headed north along the other rampart back to our starting point. The recce tour over in a record eight minutes, Chanuka parked underneath the shady tree. Now he, Sakan and Oshan would be taking a break while the group disembarked and traversed the old fort on foot, including the four of us who were leaving at Galle – Jerry, Frank, Kate and me. This would be our final *final* tour of duty before we returned to the bus for the very last time, collected our bags, made our farewells, and set off on our own.

"Two hours, yeah?" Oshan beamed at all of us, leavers and stayers alike. "Back here by two for the big goodbye."

By now the clouds of the last few days had cleared, and the weather was baking hot. We wouldn't be rushing anywhere as the sun hammered down like a forge. After dawdling past the National Museum, then the Amangalla Hotel, I reached up to staunch the torrent of sweat dripping off my chin.

"You haven't got another shirt, have you?" Kate's forehead creased. "You're drenched."

"I've got one on the bus, yeah." I was starting to sound like Oshan. "I don't have one on me."

"Maybe we should get an ice-cream or a cold drink?"

Before we melted completely, we ducked inside the Dutch Reformist Church. Here, thank God, there was shade, and the temperature dropped a few degrees. The church was one of Galle Fort's most prominent buildings and full of other tourists like us seeking respite from the heat. Yet a fascinating place to look around. The floor was made of what appeared to be gravestones yet were in fact inscribed memorials to Dutch settlers. High in one wall was a stained-glass window of yellow, red and green squares, and I thought it wouldn't have looked out of place in a modern art gallery.

We sat on a pew, Kate glancing around while I fanned my face. A man in front of us shouted orders in Sinhalese to several helpers. He was supervising an event of some kind, and suddenly I remembered this was the last Saturday before Christmas. Despite all the trees, tinsel and carols of our previous hotels, we'd become so consumed with events of the tour we'd forgotten it would soon be the twenty-fifth. Here in the Dutch Reformist Church it all came tumbling back. Christmas Day was on Wednesday, in only four days' time. At our next port of call – the Anglican All Saints Church – a choir of children sang carols in beautiful harmonies, reminding us that no one escapes Christmas, no matter where they might go.

"They were singing in Sinhalese earlier," said Beca, suddenly standing up from one of the pews. She seemed a little brighter than before, her eyes dancing in tune with the music. "You know, I'd quite forgotten about Christmas."

"Us too." I said. "You don't think about it when you're watching elephants and crocodiles and –"

"Whales?" she tittered, positioning her hand in front of her mouth. "You know we didn't see any, don't you? I should probably give them their money back, but there was a penalty for landing on the beach, and of course I still had to pay Pedro."

"Pedro?"

"The pilot." She took her hand away from her face and smiled. "That's his call sign. He used to work at my old company before he moved back here. I don't think he's done whale watching before, though. Normally he flies people up to Lion Rock."

"Onto the top?" I recalled the video for "Save a Prayer" – with its panoramic shots that could only have been filmed from a helicopter.

"Sometimes." She looked at me curiously as if she might be thinking the same. "If it's allowed. I don't think they like people landing there."

The choir took a break. I needed a bathroom after all the bottled water I'd been drinking, so Kate and I left as well. There didn't seem to be any public toilets, however. Certainly not at the Galle Fort Post Office that, apart from a single red pillar box on the grass, appeared to have been abandoned. Nor were there facilities in Court Square – named after Galle's functioning courts. Here, the only stalls were ones selling paintings of sunsets and elephants. By now I was growing desperate, my walking becoming prancing, and a new river of sweat further embarrassing my shirt. There were Indian rain trees along the edge of the square. A massive banyan too. Yet nowhere a corner I could secrete myself.

"We have to find a café soon!" My voice was bursting, as tight as my bladder.

"All right. Just hold on." Kate stayed calm. "I'm sure we'll find somewhere."

Up ahead stretched a long white building. The renovated Dutch Hospital: two storeys of gem shops, boutique cafés and restaurants. There had to be a bathroom too – surely? And stopping at the first place that looked like it might have facilities, Kate ordered Coca-Colas and Key lime pie while I dashed inside. Into a room chocked with tables, chairs, a bar yet no side-doors. No signs. And running into the next café, it was the same dilemma there.

Any longer, and I'd have to go in the street.

Why had I drunk so much coffee at breakfast? So much water on the way here? Why hadn't I searched for a toilet earlier?

A waiter pounced. Pointed. At the centre stairwell of the hospital where white porcelain gleamed through glass doors.

I ran there faster than greased lightning. And sighed as I stumbled inside. Thank God, the toilet was free. Fumbling and swearing, I made it just in time.

Back at the table with our cold drinks, I sipped in a state of relief. Then, glancing at my phone, I had another shock. The time was ten to two. The bus left in ten minutes. If we didn't rush up there and take our bags off, Mr C would drive them all the way to Colombo.

We ran back – along what we hoped was the quickest route. Lighthouse, swimming beach, and Flag Rock where, for a fee, daredevils hurled themselves into the faraway waters. Then up a lane that led north. From a corner of my eye I spotted a man playing a flute, directing the tune at a sinister-looking wicker basket. We couldn't stop though. If there was a cobra inside it would have to wait. We shot past a poster shop, a place selling toilet paper made out of elephant dung, an art gallery, a café, a restaurant, a post box. We didn't have time. *We didn't have time. We didn't have time.*

We needed time to say thank you – to Oshan for his wit and guidance, to Chanuka for his humour and safe driving, and to Sakan for bringing our bags this far. We needed to say goodbye – to the five of our group who were returning straight to England: Nelson with his jokes, Amy with her good nature, Linda and Tom with all their amazing photos, and Beca whose calmness kept everything balanced. And we had to say goodbye to Lucy and Bruce as well, expert conversationalists and rafters, who'd be heading on to their mystery destination.

With a minute to spare, we reached the bus where our group were gathered for the final time.

Then Lucy and Bruce surprised everyone by announcing they were flying on to Male in the Maldives – not for a holiday or diving but to join a maharishi's retreat. A bit like when the Beatles went to meditate in Rishikesh, only this time there'd be a beach.

"You get maharishis in the Maldives?" Jerry looked surprised.

"It's Bruce's gig. He's always wanted to go transcendental." Lucy's eyebrows sloped towards one another. "Ever since Sergeant Pepper."

"No, the White Album!" said Bruce. "Coming here has inspired us. The temples, all the statues of Buddha. We want to declutter ourselves and become who we are."

"Yeah, get our lives on track." Lucy nodded but didn't look convinced.

We'd miss them both, their friendly banter. We'd miss the others too. And Jerry and Frank, though they'd be staying in Galle for a few days like us, so we'd continue to enjoy their company a while longer. Our tour had been enriched by every single one of these people. The last two weeks had been a reaffirmation of Englishness, and Welshness, of different accents and personalities working together and proving how rewarding small group travel can be.

Tomorrow we'd be four. Then in a couple of days down to two, just Kate and me. It would be like old times, yet it wouldn't be the same

By Ourselves

"When I follow my own head, I am, in general, much more correct in my judgment than following the opinion of others."
Horatio Nelson

TWENTY-SIX

The Stray Dogs of Sri Lanka

Venice had its Doge, and London its Isle of Dogs. Fort Galle, however, had the real thing – or things: legions of four-legged creatures that wandered from street to street, barking at people they didn't like, then in the heat of the afternoon sleeping underneath cars. There were all colours and patterns: black dogs, brown dogs, black dogs with streaks of brown, and brown dogs with white spots. They were as ubiquitous as the ornately carved doors, the art shops, the cafés and restaurants. And uniformly distributed, roughly three dogs for every street.

"As long as they don't start following us around," said Kate as I stopped to take a photo of a particularly lazy-looking specimen. I knew she was thinking of a dog in Rarotonga that, no matter how many roads we crossed or corners we bluffed, had attached its snout to our heels more tenaciously than superglue. We had to join a local bowling club to escape it, swinging in through one wire gate, then ten minutes later fleeing through another gate on the opposite side.

"The ones here don't seem that interested," I replied. And honestly, they didn't. They patrolled in ones and twos like policemen, flicking casual brown eyes in our direction yet largely ignoring us. One bark meant "I'm coming through", two warned "Don't you dare take my photo", and a growl was "Get the hell off my tail". Together with the tuk-tuk drivers who asked if we wanted a ride and the crows who perched like gargoyles on telephone lines, the dogs were one third of the triumvirate that ruled this town.

The crows were generally scarier. They massed in big groups – *murders* – preening and squabbling, pecking and flapping, their black beaks and shiny noir feathers guaranteed to silhouette any sunset.

The tuk-tuk drivers, on the other hand, were persistent, asking over and over if we wanted a ride when it was obvious we didn't – we were doing something like sitting down outside a restaurant for dinner, stopping to tie up a loose shoelace, or even climbing out of another tuk-tuk that only moments earlier we'd arrived in.

The dogs weren't afraid of the crows, and the tuk-tuk drivers didn't offer rides to the dogs. The crows perched and shat on the tuk-tuks while the dogs sometimes barked at the drivers. There was a healthy equilibrium between the three groups – *air, road, gutter* – with none of them dominant and no one oppressed.

The welfare of the dogs was every citizen's concern. A billboard advertised a school that trained dogs for duties such as guarding, entertainment and *ajilaty* – presumably agility. A shop specialised in selling doggie T-shirts, shoes and bones, with a percentage of the profits going to assist the stray dogs of Sri Lanka.

The rats were less fortunate, as rats usually are. No one seemed to be raising funds for them, and though they kept themselves out of sight they were definitely about. During our first afternoon in Galle I spotted the whiskers of one rat sheltering in a drain. That's where they lived – in the sewers, where the Dutch, rather foolishly, had once introduced them. The plan was to harvest rats for musk. The rats, however, harvested the Dutch of food. And now, like the dogs and the crows, they're part of the Fort Galle scene.

GALLE IS the fourth most populous city in Sri Lanka. It is far more extensive than its historic fort area, with Galle new town stretching north and east, a mishmash of modern buildings, traffic and busy people. For our first night after the tour, we'd booked to stay in a boutique villa hotel near Mahamodara Lake, up in the northwest of the city. The place was too far to walk with our luggage. Anyway, we'd never have found the route on our own. Galle was much bigger than Nuwara Eliya – and we hadn't even been able to find our way around there.

As a final gesture of goodwill Oshan procured a tuk-tuk for us and negotiated the fare.

"He will do it for seven hundred rupees, yeah?" he said with his customary smile.

"Okay." The fare would be higher because of all our luggage. Somehow, however, the driver squeezed our main bags on, plus all the satellite ones we seemed to have accumulated. My monster suitcase had to be jammed onto the back shelf, while Kate's slimmer red number rested on the right-hand end of the seat. This left half a seat where we could sit, wedged in as tightly as buns in a baking tin.

Tuk-tuks are incredible machines. Basically motorbikes with a passenger seat and canopy strapped onto the back, they can weave nimbly in and out of traffic, threading gaps that four-wheeled vehicles are unable to contemplate. Not only do tuk-tuks convey tourists, but they also carry laundry, parcels, gas canisters and building materials. They're versatile, multi-purpose and agile.

Our driver started the engine, and with a stuttering, lawnmower purr we sped away. Around the big roundabout outside the main gate of the Fort, past the green space of Galle International Cricket Stadium, then into the turbulence of a major highway. The vehicle's little engine whined up to an ear-shattering crescendo, while on either side of us much bigger diesel engines thundered in a stink of black smoke – the red cliff of a government bus; the dirty-yellow maw of a truck. If either of them veered slightly in a momentary lapse of concentration we'd be crushed. Yet our driver seemed to know what he was doing, his head bobbing left and right like one of those nodding Churchill Insurance dogs people once placed on the back shelves of cars. Even more miraculously, our luggage stayed put too – Kate's suitcase rocking beside me and my big monolith solidly behind.

With no indication, the driver accelerated, then swung across oncoming traffic into a secondary road on the right. A minute later, merging with a stream of throttle-happy scooters, he veered left and we found ourselves on a quiet avenue lined with palms and frangipanis, behind which reposed spick, handsome villas. Stopping outside one of them, he shut off his engine and helped us carry our bags to the entrance.

Inside sparkled paradise. A pristine blue pool, its surface so perfect even the touch of a butterfly would leave ripples. And beyond that, a carpet of green grass that led to a beautiful stone house, that was faced by fluted columns. Two angels ran forward to take our cases. They guided us across an Indian-green marble floor and up an elegant staircase.

And so, we came to our room – an immaculate, comfortable, first-floor suite with a spacious balcony and a powerful monsoon shower.

There didn't seem to be any other guests anywhere. We had the pool to ourselves, a relaxing way of cooling down in the heat. That evening, as we ate curry and fruit salad at a table in the foyer, it felt like we might have rented the entire villa to ourselves. Quite a change from busy buffet meals in hotel restaurants and constant interaction with others.

"I wonder how Nelson's getting on?" Kate had a slightly quizzical look on her face as she spooned up papaya and pineapple.

"Mounting another attack on the French and taunting everyone with his jokes."

A moment later, as if he'd heard us, both our phones *ting*ed. A What's App message from Nelson, announcing the bus had arrived in Colombo to find a firecracker wedding underway at their hotel. The noise was horrendous. Nelson's early-evening snooze had been impossible, even after fastening all the windows and sticking plugs in his ears. A poor way to end a holiday and prepare for a long flight home. Ever optimistic, he'd included a photo of himself wearing a yellow apron with the motif "Stay Calm and Curry On". It probably wouldn't help with the noise, but at least he'd look cool at breakfast.

THE NEXT MORNING, we whizzed back to the fort in another tuk-tuk, a short ten-minute journey. Same procedure – my big case in the back, Kate's on the seat, and the driver's head bobbing from side to side. Now that we were used to the motion, of being so dangerously close to buses and lorries, it was a lot of fun. Again we went past the cricket ground, around the big roundabout, then clattered through the stone tunnel that was the fort's main gate. Once inside the fort, the streets were calmer. There were other tuk-tuks and scooters but no grumbling juggernauts. Our driver sped along the eastern rampart, past the lighthouse and mosque, then turned right into Church Street.

Here was our base for the next two days, the welcoming and comfortable Sega BnB. Downstairs it was a shop selling artwork, postcards, carvings and glitzy embroidered wallets, while upstairs, somewhere, must be our room.

We'd hardly stepped over the flagstones than the shop's owner, Priyantha, came out to greet us. He was a modest, charming man, his smile broad yet not overdone. Immediately he manhandled my suitcase and, despite its weight, carried it up a flight of narrow stairs on one side of the shop. We followed him, I now carrying Kate's suitcase, and Kate carrying my backpack. At the top, a landing led past several closed doors, then a second flight of stairs ascended on the other side of the shop. By now Priyantha was struggling, his smile flat and his face red. Somehow sensing his discomfort, a young man – presumably Priyantha's son – bounded out from behind one of the doors, took the case and bore it up to the top.

Our accommodation was a pleasant, light room with windows looking south and west. If we gazed in one direction we saw Flag Rock and the Indian Ocean. And if we gazed in the other we were met by a jumble of rooftops and turrets that stretched to the eastern ramparts. We'd never tire of this room, of its marvellous views. It was like being in a secret observation chamber, spying on everyone else, south, west and east.

Priyantha wasn't finished yet. Leaving our luggage in the room, he beckoned us up another flight of stairs that led along the outside wall of our room to the roof. And here, his face beaming, he showed us the jewel in the crown: the rooftop terrace.

I could hardly believe my eyes. The floor wasn't concrete but springy moist grass. Shrubs and flowers grew along the side, and in the corner – *holy goldfish* – a water feature rippled. The views were expansive. East, the mosque and lighthouse. South, Flag Rock. And beyond, in every direction except north, the wide blue ocean.

Priyantha indicated a table and chairs. "If you want, you can bring a beer up here and watch the sunset." Then he gestured at an area of shade under the stair turret. "Or during the day, sit up here and read."

Our host was delightful, wanting to do all he could to make our stay enjoyable. So far we weren't doing too badly away from the tour group. Things were different, perhaps slightly more challenging, yet in other ways more fulfilling.

Back in our room we installed our stash of chocolate in the fridge, then sat on the edge of the four-poster bed. A gentle knock came at the door. I opened it to find Priyantha's wife holding two tall glasses of chilled mango lassi. She smiled, her warmth authentic like her husband's, and placed the drinks down on the table. After explaining something we didn't quite understand, she bowed and left.

This was our first homestay on this trip. Such a refreshing change from the armies of hotel receptionists, porters, waiters and room boys we'd encountered everywhere else. Here there were only Priyantha, his wife and son, plus a grandfather who waved us into the family living room next morning for breakfast.

During our stay, Priyantha told us about the neighbourhood. The good people who helped tourists and a few less straightforward individuals we might need to look out for. Meanwhile Kate joked with Priyantha's wife, gently rebuking her for getting her rain forecast wrong. Instead of a deluge at four as she'd predicted, the bad weather had veered north, and the sun stayed out instead. Yet the following evening, a storm came our way, loud thunder and a blaze of lightning. Sadly, we had to skip our sundowner beers on the roof. A shame, really, because the livid sky would have been an incredible sight.

TWENTY-SEVEN

Over the Wall

The fort grew sleepy in the afternoons, and we drifted into a lazy routine. Late lunch at a tiny café followed by thirty-nine winks on our bed. A big aircon unit hung on the wall, yet it was quieter to leave the windows open. Outside there wasn't much noise – the occasional passer-by with a loud voice, a motorcycle rumbling in the street. Closer to sunset there would be the amplified voice from the mosque as the faithful assembled for prayer.

We became familiar with the fort, wandering its patchwork of streets. A few doors down from us were several jewellers and tea purveyors selling loose leaf tea. And a little further on blazed the lavish cornucopia of Barefoot, Galle's equivalent of a Trade Aid shop. Opposite Barefoot, a hole in the wall led to a family store selling everyday necessities such as sweets, chocolate, chips, biscuits, and plastic bottles of Sprite and Coca-Cola.

Along Leyn Baan Street, parallel to Church Street, there were more jewellers, a spice shop and an outlet selling paper manufactured from elephant dung. An art gallery too, displaying ephemeral, otherworldly paintings so expensive they must be destined to hang for all eternity on the high pastel walls.

Pedlar Street always pulsed with a beat – shops with tacky tourist-ware such as "We Are Doomed" T-shirts and chainmail made out of ring-pulls, as well as every possible flavour of café, restaurant, bistro, teashop and ice-cream parlour. People thronged night and day along the street – it was the one place guaranteed to be busy, with a continual flow of tuk-tuks and pedestrians accumulating at its junctions like silt.

Every instance we strolled we took a different route. Sometimes we saw the same things, places we'd seen yesterday and the day before. Other times we stumbled into new things – a line of world flags, a miniature whitewashed stupa, two bowls of lotus flowers on either side of an image of Buddha, a tuk-tuk moulded and painted to look like an elephant, and, most bizarre of all, two handcuffed youths walking through the archway of the magistrate's court. Each walk was like a voyage around the fish tank – seeing mostly the same fish, yet occasionally being surprised by something rare, undiscovered or dangerous.

One sticky afternoon I broke the glass wall. Walking towards the main gate out of the fort, I didn't slow or stop or turn around but kept going. Apprehension filled my heart, my feet becoming heavier, for in the couple of days since arriving here I hadn't been out of the fort area.

As I reached the fort's massive northern wall, even as I walked through the short, dark tunnel that led outside, it became clear this was not only a historical boundary but a psychological barrier too. It separated old from new, make-believe from make-do, tourists from inhabitants, the sleepy fort from a busy modern city. And emerging on the other side, suddenly I felt as if I'd stepped into a different place. Traffic increased by several orders of magnitude – trucks, buses, cars, all the big vehicles that couldn't fit inside. More people too, standing in large groups, leaning against things, rushing with an urgency that didn't exist back within the fort walls. Previously calm and green, even the cricket ground was darkened by the shadow of a huge rain cloud. Worst were the crows – whole black armies of them. This side of the wall they didn't just caw and pose; they fought furiously over scraps of food, their cries loud and raucous.

I froze in horror. Did I really want to venture into this havoc, all alone and without any backup? I might be robbed, knocked over, or lose my way. And deliberating – alarmed by the traffic, the people, the crows – I almost went back.

But this was more than a fright-seeing trip. There was an ulterior motive. In two days it would be Christmas Day, and all the restaurants and hotel bars wouldn't be allowed to sell alcohol, even to tourists.

I wanted to purchase a bottle of wine. A can or two of Lion beer as well. There were no wine shops inside the fort, however. The nearest one was in a street around the corner from the bus station, which in turn was on the other side of the cricket ground.

First, though, I had to cross the busy highway leading to the roundabout. Buses, trucks and tuk-tuks shot past in both directions with scarcely a break. This was far harder than crossing a road in Kandy; and unlike me, none of the locals were attempting it.

I skirted the road on a grass verge all the way to the next roundabout. Here at least visibility was better. I was able to preview what was coming – an extra couple of seconds that might make all the difference.

Several lorries thundered by. A couple of buses, their

drivers like zombies. Then as the traffic petered to a flock of scooters I dashed between them. Arriving at the middle line, I flattened my body as a big truck went the other way. Then before I could think, I ran again, toes thrusting and heart thumping, nearly skinned by a car and causing a tuk-tuk to swerve, yet I made it, breathless, to the other side.

Now striding more calmly around the cricket ground, I came to the bus station. Here the pace went breakneck. Buses and trucks snarled at each other while tuk-tuks hooted like angry birds. It was a fight to the death, a war over road space. Even pedestrians ran berserk, rushing, dodging, sidestepping. These were the poor people, the worried people, the people with children, problems and deadlines.

There were shops too. Far more than existed inside the fort – and selling not souvenirs but real goods such as furniture, TVs, clothes and food. For a while I was excited. The energy here was in such contrast to the languidness of the fort. And joining these people, rushing with them, on and off the pavement, alongside the railway station, in and out of the road, I set off in search of the wine shop. This felt like the bona fide Galle – the living, working city rather than the colonial dream world I'd just left. I was suddenly the hero of a dystopian movie – Ewan McGregor fleeing *The Island* or Patrick McGoohan escaping the village – stimulated and bewildered by everything I saw.

A huge thalagoya – or land monitor – sheltered in a doorway, its tail sticking out like a snake. I gave it a wide berth, remembering those things could bite, especially when cornered.

Further on, the wine shop was a heavily fortified slot in the wall. All the merchandise was secured in wire cages, accessible only to the two salesmen who glowered more like guards behind the thick, solid counter. At first I couldn't get served as local men pushed in front and bought cans of Lion beer. Then I caught the eye of one salesman. He extracted three bottles of red from a cabinet, and I chose the one that looked the least unpalatable, an Australian shiraz. Two cans of Lion as well, just for safe measure. After putting my booty into my backpack, I crept back the way I'd come. Slower now, the buzz gone. This might be the real Galle, the place where locals lived, fought and drank, yet my place was back inside the fort – no more the sanctuary of Dutch soldiers but of soft-bodied tourists like me.

TWENTY-EIGHT

Galle by Night

As the waiter brought over the three-tiered silver platter stacked with goodies, Kate's eyes bulged. A trio of pastries lay on the top tray: savoury leek, strawberry cream and chocolate mousse. On the tray beneath, a selection of various cakes: coconut-and-pineapple, ginger, chocolate éclair and Millionaire's shortbread. And on the bottom tray, sandwiches, sandwiches, sandwiches: cucumber and cheese, egg paste, tomato and basil pesto, and salmon with cream cheese.

If all this wasn't enough, the waiter reappeared with two samosas, one chicken and one vegetable. Then two generous scones, accompanied by saucers of clotted cream and homemade raspberry jam. Kate sighed, unable to believe her luck. This was like three Christmas lunches rolled into one, and it was still only Christmas Eve. Forget ham and pavlova, bottles of Steinlager or wineglasses of sav blanc – those customary Kiwi tipples; this was the real business.

We were enjoying high tea at the Amangalla, Galle's swankiest hotel. Hardly an inexpensive treat, even by New

Zealand standards. Yet we were on holiday, and the cakes and pastries looked splendid. As too, when we were able to tear our eyes from the sugar feast, did the decor and ambience of the hotel. At the front, a classic white-columned façade with graceful arches and a wide, airy veranda. And inside, on a floor patterned with maroon, black, yellow and blue tiles, were plants in enormous green pots dotted between wickerwork sofas and chairs, teak and brass Dutch chests, and sideboards with enormous, polished mirrors.

The building had originally been the Dutch governor's house, constructed in 1684. In 1863 it was converted into the New Oriental Hotel. And now it was a fabulous, five-star hotel with twenty-eight rooms, a spa, a pool, and top notch service – plus prices to match. Though as we sat on the veranda overlooking the street, preparing to sample the delicacies in front of us, we weren't thinking much about history or rooms or what this high tea might cost. Instead we imagined we were a lord and lady of somewhere, latter-day colonials in a Somerset Maugham short story escaping the daytime stupor with a pot of hot tea and a plateful of sweet comestibles. After we'd missed out in Nuwara Eliya, this was a treat well overdue.

Below in the street, as if to emphasise the setting, a film shoot was underway. A handsome Sri Lankan couple strolled arm in arm as two wiry photographers pursued them, holding a light umbrella and brandishing a camera lens longer than an elephant's proboscis. Who they were and what they were doing we had no idea. Maybe they were fashionados, addicted to posing in front of UNESCO heritage buildings? Or models for a TV campaign promoting the picturesque virtues of Galle?

We could only focus on them for so long. High tea demanded our attention, especially as the cake stand rose twelve and a half inches tall. Starting with the bottom layer, Kate carefully selected each item of food and cut it into two. Samosas and sandwiches into neat little triangles, infinitely delicious yet swallowed in a flash. Cakes and pastries as well, and finally the scones. The scones won tongues down, piled with so much cream and jam Kate had to ask for more.

The tea too was a buoyant, aromatic, soaring nectar. Each sip, each cup, went perfectly with the edibles, one pot containing Lover's Leap broken orange pekoe, and another an oolong local speciality. As both pots drained dry, the waiter removed them and refilled them, ensuring we never ran out.

An hour later we'd finished, not a dollop of cream, a speck of jam or a crumb of cake remaining. We were too full to stand, so we sat and watched the street again, the beautiful couple – the real stars of this place – still prancing and dancing as directed by their film crew.

That high tea had to be one of our best experiences so far. Perhaps I'd found my perfect cuppa – one of the reasons I'd come to Sri Lanka. Time would tell. Every tea has its moment, and every day starts and ends with a brew. Meanwhile we stared and mused, tempted to order another high tea, yet knowing we shouldn't.

JERRY AND FRANK were staying in Galle, and Kate messaged them to meet up that evening. It'd be good to swap stories, to find out about the places they were staying in and how they'd experienced life post-tour. Unbound from the group, we'd see them in a new light – as the unique individuals they surely were. Jerry would charm and entertain us with his knowledge. And Frank was a friendly, down-to-earth young fellow, full of jokes and energetic good humour.

But first, I wanted a swim. The sun pressed down, still hot and close. We had no pool at our accommodation other than the water feature on the roof. Yet a short glance from our room was a little beach sprawled beneath the lighthouse – a miniature lagoon of black rocks and shallow water, where dozens of local families bathed.

After making my way over there with a rolled-up towel, I descended a set of stone steps and waded into the tepid water. For a short while I felt conspicuous: the only Westerner on the beach, let alone in the sea. As the water soothed, though, I relaxed and enjoyed the view. The sun sinking towards the horizon and into a tiny islet of silhouetted palm trees. The coastline curving east, dotted with ships, gantries and buildings. All the people in the water: boys splashing footballs, fathers holding children, and old ladies paddling up to their knees. And the lighthouse too – white, slim and tall, rising up behind the ramparts like a protective uncle. This might not be the best beach I'd visited, nor this the best swim. Yet it felt good to be part of something – of all these people – rather than a wandering tourist.

DUSK TUMBLED. Streets that an hour before had been packed, fell dark and deserted. No longer fearful of being hit by a tuk-tuk, we strolled leisurely, taking in the streetlights and illuminated shop fronts. Galle at night is haunting. A place of long shadows and eerie walls, of buildings invisible by day, and alleyways silent with intrigue.

Reaching the Bungalow Galle Fort, an upmarket boutique hotel and restaurant, we found Jerry and Frank drinking together in the bar, strangely best buddies now they didn't have to share a room – or even a hotel.

"This is a great place to eat." Jerry looked spick and span – his skin slightly pink, his hair freshly washed and combed back. "Try the red fish curry."

"How about we take a gander round town first?" Frank too appeared smarter, his shirt crisp, his jowls smooth. "A guy at my hotel said Hoppa is pretty good. You can sit outside and people-watch."

But when we reached Hoppa, a tiny restaurant in Pedlar Street, the place was full – too popular for its own good. Which was a pity because the hoppers it served – bowl-shaped rice pancakes filled with chicken or seafood curry – smelt delicious.

"What about Galle Gourmet?" I pointed at a white building in an adjacent street. "Look, they're doing a Christmas special."

After studying the menu Kate was unimpressed. "It's forty-nine US for three courses. That's way too expensive."

"There's lobster curry, though." Frank's finger stuck on the pedestal menu. "And pork belly, lamb shank, mushroom risotto, roasted cauliflower and tuna sashimi!" He smacked his lips.

Jerry peered over his shoulder with sharp eyes. "You don't get them all. You only choose one. And look." He pointed at the small print. "It looks like there's a government tax of twenty-two percent."

"Wow!" Frank's eyes widened.

"Let's go back to the Bungalow." Jerry nodded at the street ahead. "I had the red fish curry last night, and it was probably the best meal I've had all the time I've been here."

We left the enticing smells of Hoppa and turned right, back the way we'd come. But as the lights grew fainter and it started to rain we slowed. Underneath the dimness of a blue lantern, Jerry looked about with a puzzled expression. "This isn't right. That's a police post. We're nearly at the main gate."

There wouldn't be any restaurants immediately outside the fort, at least not the sort we were used to. Turning around, we blundered up another poorly lit street before realising we were lost. Around us the darkness grew darker and the silence more subdued. The shadows had ceased being photogenic. They'd become ominous.

"There's a place down there." I pointed at a distant light, winking like a tiny lighthouse. "Maybe that's somewhere we can eat?"

We advanced towards the light. Still no sound, not even a dog barking, and I wondered if we were in danger. What if the light were the ghost of a suicide who'd jumped to their death from Flag Rock? Or a knife-wielding psychopath wrapped in a red mackintosh, come to slash our throats? Galle by night wasn't only haunting; it could feel spooky too.

The light grew brighter, making me shield my eyes. Then beside me Kate laughed. We weren't heading towards a restaurant but to one of the lighting crew we'd seen earlier, still filming the elegant couple.

"I have to get a pic," said Jerry.

"Perhaps they'll know somewhere or give us directions." Frank too pulled out his phone.

Then – *ting, ting, ting, ting* – at precisely the same instant all our phones sang.

"It's a message from Nelson!" Kate exclaimed. "He's sent a photo."

Jerry, Frank and I all glanced at our screens too, thinking it might be a picture of Amy and Nelson arriving home. But no, this was Nelson, and nothing could be that simple. It was a photo he'd taken in Galle, about as subtle at that moment as a four-hundred-gram steak with fries. In a shop front in Pedlar Street hung that same novelty yellow apron he'd been wearing in Colombo. Now its caption taunted us. "Stay Calm and Curry On."

TWENTY-NINE

The Wrecks of Galle

We found the Bungalow eventually, in the opposite direction and tucked away in a side street. As Jerry had forecast, the fish curry was excellent, the sauce piquant and deeply red, yet not overpowering the fish – which had probably only been caught that morning. We drank delicious sauvignon blanc from clear glasses shimmering against a pristine white tablecloth. Every knife, fork and spoon were impeccably aligned as well, every bamboo placemat in perfect position. This was Sri Lankan dining at its finest. Diligent service and sublime food. So good to have shaken off the lukewarm buffets and mishmash of cuisines we'd experienced at all the earlier hotels.

And this was an opportunity to tap Jerry's brain – the quizzer who seemed to know a little about everything – and ask him what he thought about Amy and Nelson.

He looked at me strangely, the lines in his face emphasised in the restaurant's low light. He sat silent for a moment. Then, blinking, he took a long sip of wine. "Well, for starters, I don't think Nelson's his real name. He's made it up, or been reading loads of history books about the Napoleonic Wars. You know that Lady Hamilton, Lord Nelson's mistress, started life as Amy Lyon?"

I hadn't known this – yet I wasn't surprised. "You mean Amy's name is made up too?"

His pupils darkened. "It's probably all her idea."

"Amy's?"

"Yes. As Nelson likes saying, it's the quiet ones you have to watch out for."

He had a point. Sometimes Nelson's banter had diverted from Amy's thoughtfulness. While he joked and chattered, she carefully listened and observed.

"So why wouldn't they tell us their real names?"

"Obvious." Jerry twirled the wine in his glass, a swirl of yellow light reflected across his face. "Who's been in the papers recently? Who wouldn't want folk knowing his – or her – real identity?"

"A contestant off *Britain's Got Talent?* A senior manager for Southern Rail?" I was clutching at straws. "A disgraced member of the royal family?"

"No!" He chortled. "To be fair, you won't know cos you live in New Zealand."

"Well, I don't live in New Zealand –" Frank came to my aid "– and I don't know either."

"Guess I'll have to spell it out." Jerry smiled, clearly enjoying himself. "You've heard of *My Underwater Romance* – the book that's topped the UK bestsellers for weeks on end?"

Frank stared at Jerry in disbelief while Kate and I looked blank.

Jerry's smile intensified. "It was shortlisted for this year's Booker Prize too, yet no one really knows anything about the author, one A. Neston. No interviews or book signings or anything; whoever wrote it is like the Banksy of the literary world."

My jaw dropped. I'd been in the company of a famous author and not even realised. "And you think Nelson is this A. Neston?"

"Nope." Jerry shook his head. "Not Nelson – Amy."

"Amy? Why?"

"Simple." He beamed knowingly. "Neston is a place near Liverpool where the real Amy Lyon – Lord Nelson's mistress – was born. And *our* Amy has used it as the pseudonym for her book."

I wasn't sure I believed him. His logic didn't prove anything – least of all that Amy was a reclusive bestselling novelist. Yet Jerry was a smart cookie. He could be uncannily accurate with his predictions. If his hypothesis held water maybe there were more clues in the identities of the two British legends Nelson and Amy had chosen to impersonate: Vice Admiral Nelson of the White Squadron of the Fleet, and Lady Hamilton, née Emma Hart, born Amy Lyon at Neston in Cheshire. One a maritime hero of his generation, dispatcher of the French and Spanish navies; the other a beautiful, talented socialite who wowed a decade.

So the next morning, when I read about the Maritime Archaeology Museum in Galle, I resolved we must visit. The museum wouldn't necessarily shed any light on Nelson, Vice Admiral or otherwise. But it still had a maritime theme and, however unlikely, might trigger something I hadn't thought of yet.

We found the museum easily. It was a long, ochre building that formed part of the fort's northeast wall. Sitting in an anteroom, we watched a video about maritime archaeology. Then we wandered through a dimly lit yet spacious hall to view the exhibits.

One that stood out was a large-scale model of the *Avondster* – a Dutch East India Company ship that had slipped anchor in Galle Harbour one calm June night in 1659, hit the coast, broke in two and sank. Its skipper and first mate were later arrested and ordered to pay damages. Meanwhile the cargo of areca nuts the ship had been bound to load on board and convey to the Coromandel Coast in India remained in the warehouse. No other ships were available to take them. The nuts were instead sold to the burghers – free citizens of Galle – at a fixed price.

Further on in the museum, a war-room-style map displayed the locations of all the shipwrecks around Galle: the *Arcturus*, for instance, a British steamship that sank near Rala Gela – or Brown Rock – to the east; the *Dolfin*, an East Indiaman that was leaking so badly all the ship's men and all the ship's pumps couldn't keep her afloat; the *Crispigi Cross* that sank right in front of Galle Hospital; and the *Hercules* that foundered while leaving harbour when a sudden cross-wind dashed her onto cliffs on Gibbet Island. There was even a cargo ship called the *Lord Nelson* – sadly, the museum's only new revelation about *our* Nelson – which had gone down in 2000.

The waters around Galle were choc-a-bloc with wrecks, a reflection of the old port's prime position in the world, at the confluence of so many trading routes – European, Arabian, Indian and Asian. In the 1990s the Galle Harbour Project had been established to map and explore all these local wrecks. Sadly, eighty percent of the retrieved artefacts were swept away by the 2004 tsunami, lost forever. The current museum building was also badly flooded in the tsunami, though the rest of the fort was largely protected by its high, thick walls.

Like a rabid, murderous sea monster, the tsunami tore

north into new Galle instead. It demolished the bus station and cricket ground, and in one foul blow killed four thousand people in town. That's the same number of passengers in thirty double-decker buses, standing room only. Or ten Boeing 777-300 long-haul planes, every seat occupied. Too many to lose in one day, and it wasn't even a day because when the waves surged in – unannounced, unexpected, literally out of the blue – they lasted for a mere ten minutes, drowning, crushing and destroying anyone who happened to be in the wrong place at the right time.

Later I discovered that the biggest wreck wasn't recorded in the museum at all.

There is little trace of it now – no red pin on the map marking its location, no underwater site where divers can swim between its rotting ribs, no bottles, crosses, bells, whistles or other artefacts waiting to be discovered on the seafloor. Yet of all the wrecks it was by far the worst – an enormous loss of life, all in one place, almost in one moment.

The *Queen of the Sea* wasn't a ship. It was a train, and early on 26 December 2004, it departed Colombo Fort station, as it did every day, bound for Galle. The locomotive *Manitoba* pulled eight carriages, all packed to capacity – nearly two thousand people altogether – for it was both a Buddhist *Poya* day and a Christian holiday.

As the train reached the village of Peraliya, twenty-four kilometres north of Galle, the first wave of the tsunami struck. It flooded the tracks and stopped the train. Locals climbed onto the carriage roofs, while others sheltered behind the train, believing it would shield them from further waves.

Ten minutes later the second wave crashed in. This wave was bigger, as high as a three-storey building. It picked the locomotive up and carried it one hundred metres, smashing the carriages like rattles against houses and trees. Inside, the carriage doors could not be opened. Too many people, too much water. Unable to escape, passengers drowned as successive waves of water washed over them. Others, sheltering by the tracks or on the roof, were crushed, some dying of their injuries hours afterwards as they waited vainly to be rescued.

Because of the state of emergency, the train wreck wasn't discovered until four in the afternoon. Rescue teams had to come from far away and didn't arrive until much later. Upon first hearing news of the tsunami, the railway authorities had tried to halt the train at Ambalangoda, an earlier station. All the staff there had been busy though, ensuring a timely departure, and hadn't answered the phone.

More than seventeen hundred people were killed altogether, the worst train disaster in the history of the world. The precise number isn't known because some passengers boarded the train on season passes or government permits. Nevertheless, this was a wreck to out-wreck all other wrecks – a huge, awful, unimaginable tragedy.

A monument now stands at Peraliya to remember the people who died. Yet as we left the museum and wandered around the fort ramparts in bright sunshine – the cricket ground in the distance, the bus and railway stations bustling – it was difficult to picture the terrible events of that Holy Day.

Around us the ocean lay calm and flat, yet its power remained undiminished. Ripples of ripples, even fifteen years later. All the spaces inside people's minds – the daughters, sons, mothers, fathers, sisters and brothers who should still be here, and aren't.

THIRTY

Christmas Day at Unawatuna

It was Christmas Day and time to move on – ten kilometres from Galle to the seaside resort of Unawatuna. In most places in the world this would have been challenging – and expensive, with taxi-drivers charging generous Christmas rates, double or treble what was normal. Not in Sri Lanka, however. A tuk-tuk was already idling in the street, the driver smoking a cigarette and fiddling with his sound system.

"Please can you take us to Unawatuna?" I pointed at the map on my phone. "This hotel – the Aurora."

"Aurora." He stared as if he knew it, somewhere he took guests every day. Then his brow creased, and he scratched his head. Perhaps he didn't know – perhaps he'd take us in the opposite direction, to Colombo if he thought that was where it was.

"It's just off the main road." I pointed again.

"Yeah!" His jaw dropped, he sneezed, and long black hair cascaded over his eyes.

Suddenly I didn't trust him. He was still lolling against

his vehicle, making no effort to load our suitcases. And peeking inside I saw there was no room for my case anyway. The back shelf was occupied by a huge loudspeaker. He wouldn't be transporting us on three wheels – we'd be blasted into another dimension on a wave of sound.

We scouted a second tuk-tuk, driven by a less rhythmic man who did have room for our suitcases, and for us too. And once everything was on board, Kate and me wedged like commuters in the back, our driver nodding in the front, he accelerated down Lighthouse Lane and out through the main gate. Immediately we were engulfed in traffic, a red bus ahead of us, motorcycles and tuk-tuks on our right, and a giant truck behind. Not that I could see the truck because my case was in the way, but I could hear its monster engine rumbling, and its horn trumpeting close to my ear.

It was practically a stampede to Unawatuna, charging along the main highway, cutting up motorcycles, and undertaking buses. Everyone in a hurry, yet never impatient and always practical. This is how they drive in Asia. Plenty of swerving and tooting, but only to say "Watch out, I'm coming through" rather than "Bugger off, you cretinous road-user".

We didn't arrive at Unawatuna so much as become absorbed. The outskirts of Galle were the outskirts of Unawatuna, and nothing lay in between. A couple of times our driver pulled off the road to ask directions of other tuk-tuk drivers. Even he didn't know where Aurora was despite his firm chin and an even tighter baseball cap. Then, just as I thought he might be completely lost, he cut left up a narrow lane and we found ourselves outside an impenetrable black metal gate.

If this was Aurora, it didn't look much like a hotel. More like an embassy or a private address. With the gate locked and a tall fence, it remained private. I wondered if the driver had made a mistake, but he gestured for us to climb out and unload our bags, clearly sure he'd brought us to the right place.

"This is Aurora?" I stared at him.

"Yes!" He didn't look me in the eye because the rim of his cap got in the way. Yet he held out a palm for the fare, suddenly one hundred rupees more than we'd agreed. "Diversion take longer," he said by way of explanation, although there'd been no roadworks, nor any diversion.

Without so much as a squeak, the gate swung open and a man in a smart burgundy tunic strode out. He seemed to be expecting us, his lips pinned back into an enormous grin, and his nose upturned like he might be a royal prince greeting guests. Immediately I felt at ease, positive this would be a good place to stay. Fetching out my wallet, I paid the driver his surcharge.

Beyond the gate hid a little Garden of Eden. Palms and grasses, orchids and green-red-leaved shrubs, and in the middle of all this greenery a pleasant, two-storeyed building that, despite its size, felt like it was somebody's private palace. The man carried in our cases, then presented us with glasses of freshly squeezed pineapple juice. A pen and registration form too – something we had to fill in ourselves now Oshan wasn't here to do it on our behalf.

Our room was on the ground floor, its veranda adorned with flowers, and a novel, open-air bathroom at the rear. We could shower in privacy as we stared up at blue sky. Although it wasn't blue right at that moment but swaddled in low cloud that didn't look like it was shifting. We might be spending Christmas in the tropics yet that was no guarantee it wouldn't rain.

. . .

FRANK HAD ALREADY VISITED UNAWATUNA a few days earlier and kindly emailed me a photo of the beach. In his picture it was a mostly empty crescent of sand that curved towards a distant headland. Only seven beachgoers in all, most of them about to leave. If the beach remained that empty I'd be able to stroll, swim and lie down in peace.

And with a swim in mind, I sneaked out through the black gate to explore. The narrow lane twisted past mysterious other houses, all hemmed in by high stone walls and lush gardens. At the bottom of the lane, the busy highway exploded back into being. On my left a greengrocer, metal stands draped with fruit. On my right a wine kiosk. Except no wine on sale today, as I'd expected.

I overheard a backpacker asking why and receiving the reply, "All shops closed, all over Sri Lanka." My foresight had been rewarded, the bottle of wine I'd bought two days ago still unopened in my suitcase.

Crossing the highway was even more dangerous than in Galle. The road curved back like a bent banana, impossible to see more than a few metres in either direction. Buses whizzed from the left and trucks from the right. Never did the gaps coincide. It was no good following strangers across either, because most of them were other tourists following me. The monkeys had the best idea. They avoided the road by crossing overhead on telephone wires.

I couldn't climb the telephone pole though so, trusting my life to my feet, I eventually dashed over. Only to discover that the beach – the long crescent of empty yellow sand in Frank's photo – was anything but empty. A fleet of buses and tuk-tuks was parked at the end. In the water below, hundreds of people sang, danced, jumped and splashed. It was a hot day and a public holiday too. Where else would everyone go if not to the beach?

A little further on there was more space, the ethnicity changing from exuberant locals to more sedate Westerners. Yet here too were dive boats, placards for sea trips, sun umbrellas, and layers of overspill from all the beachfront hotels. I kept walking. But as the distant headland grew nearer than my starting point, it became clear the entire crescent – all one kilometre of it – was occupied. A corollary of one of the gas laws that says the number of available tourists will expand to fill every square metre of beach to approximately the same density.

I found a spot no more and no less crowded than anywhere else, where I waded into the sea. The water was warm and went down rapidly. I put my head under and swam. The further out I went, the fewer the people. Except there's a law for this too: don't swim alone.

AFTER DUSK we went out in search of a restaurant for a special Christmas dinner. Back in the UK, families everywhere would be tucking into their midday feasts of turkey and rich fruit puddings. In New Zealand, too, friends and in-laws would have gathered to sip sauvignon and eat freshly carved ham, crisp salads, delicious cheeses and berry pavlova. Even here in Sri Lanka, which is mostly Buddhist, Christmas Day is a public holiday. The seven percent of the population who are Christians attend midnight mass at their local church, and on the twenty-fifth enjoy a sumptuous family meal at home. Often they invite friends and relatives from other religions to join them. Catholics and Buddhists are reputed to get on especially well together.

Everyone else in the world might be celebrating, yet we felt a little disconnected, especially after so recently losing our new POM family – the crew of Oshan's eleven. Most of them had left the country, and now it was only Kate and me. Nevertheless we'd make the best of things: eat a nice meal somewhere and toast absent family and friends.

The weather had other plans. The sky darkened alarmingly with low, obsidian clouds. A storm was coming, a big one. Hurrying, we found a large beach hotel serving meals. Tall beakers of Tiger beer as well – despite my belief that all alcohol sales were banned. The à la carte menu, however, was disappointing. Only pizzas, one or two curries, and no seafood. Perhaps, it being a holiday, the fishermen didn't go out to fish.

As we waited for our food, both our phones pinged. A photo from Nelson, showing a golden turkey with stuffing, rolls of bacon around chipolatas, bread sauce, roasted potatoes, carrots and Brussels sprouts. I tried not to feel envious – after all we were still on holiday in a warm climate and he wasn't. But jealousy is an insidious thing. And as if to prick us deeper, there came a second ping. Another photo, this time from Beca – a panoramic view of mountains from her window, in front of which stood a table laden with food.

It would be around one-thirty in England, and everyone would be sitting down to their Christmas lunch. As a waiter brought over our meals – two large pizzas that could have easily been takeaways – we started to feel a little left out. Everyone else was with their families, eating traditional fare. Still, at least we had pizzas that, despite their bland looks, tasted rather good. Cheese, olives, ham and mushrooms – enough to fill our empty bellies. Anyway, it was our choice to be here, exploring a foreign country, rather than staying at home. No doubt our family and friends were thinking of us, envious of our chance to be somewhere different.

I wondered what Frank and Jerry were doing to celebrate their Christmas Days. Jerry had been due to fly out of Sri

Lanka yesterday on his way to some indeterminate resort – Cairo, Dubai or Tel Aviv – in the Middle East. Frank, as far as we knew, was still in Galle, dining at his hotel or maybe in one of those swish restaurants in the middle of town. We really should have contacted him and arranged to meet up.

I tried to forget about the others and concentrate instead on our own evening. And like a moody gate-crasher, the storm finally arrived, kicking and banging. Lightning flashed across the sea and rain plummeted so furiously it ricocheted off the concrete promenade and onto our table. The waiter rushed over to lower the blinds. On and on went the deluge, jets of water hosing from the sky. This wasn't a shower but a drenching. Too wet to walk home, though it was only two hundred metres. We picked at the olives and mushrooms on our pizzas, then ordered a tuk-tuk.

THIRTY-ONE

Driving Mrs Kate

In the morning, promptly at eight-thirty, we heard a car draw up outside the gate.

"It's Samid," said Kate straightaway, and sure enough, as a porter in a burgundy tunic pulled the gate open we caught our first glimpse of our guide and driver for the next seven days, standing in front of his burgundy car.

This was the juncture in our travels where we officially ended phase two – lounging like limpets on the seaboards of Galle and Unawatuna – and commenced phase three, a more circumspect, solitary journey back the way we'd come. Although that's a little inaccurate. We'd be deviating slightly from our original route with the tour. And we wouldn't be alone, because Samid would be explaining things as he drove us.

"Anything you want, you let me know." Samid smiled, shook our hands, then patted our shoulders. He sat us down at the breakfast table and went through the itinerary we'd planned with him by email. The elephants of Uda Walawe that afternoon. A train ride from Haputale the day after tomorrow. Even a four-thirty start one morning to see the sun rise at Lipton's Seat.

"You know we've already been up early for World's End." How could I forget that five o'clock start, traipsing through mist and drizzle?

He beamed. "This is much better."

Samid was a well-organised, friendly man, though he seemed a little tired. His family had hosted a big get-together at his house over Christmas, and he'd left Negombo at six that morning, driving for three hours along the expressway to Galle, then on to Unawatuna.

When we'd spoken with him by phone I'd envisaged a broad, slightly overweight, bearded man. Instead of a beard he had prominent eyebrows and a sharp moustache. He was thin rather than plump, his arms and legs as lean as strings on a fiddle. He was strong too. He had no problem lifting my suitcase, which just about filled his boot.

Plans made, we set off. East along the highway towards Koggala and Merissa, back over old ground. Kate sat in the front passenger seat, quizzing Samid, while I stretched out in the back, spotting things: the stilt-fishermen's stilts; the austere façade of the five-star Fortress Hotel. Over the next few days, we'd probably see many of the sights we'd seen on the bus but through a different set of windows and with dramatically improved weather. The clouds of Christmas had lifted, and now the sun shone.

At Merissa, Samid drew up outside a tourist hotel and ordered the big breakfast he hadn't had time to eat on the way down. As we sat with him I wondered whether he expected us to pay for it. We'd agreed on a fee for driving and guiding, but the details of his accommodation and meals had been vague. When the bill arrived – more for my coffee than his breakfast – he thumbed out the rupees he owed and smiled knowingly.

"I get special rates," he explained. "They know I am your driver and have brought you here."

Similarly, at many hotels he would be given a bed in the drivers' bunkroom, plus a free dinner and breakfast. This is how tourism works in Sri Lanka. The hotels fill their rooms, the drivers have work, and the visitors travel comfortably and easily.

Across the road, big white waves rolled up a sandy beach. For a moment I wished we could stay a little longer on the coast, rising late and chilling out, with no deadlines to govern our day. The bay here was more attractive than at Unawatuna, the sea turquoise, the beach golden and with hardly any people. Now that the public holidays were over the locals would be back at work. And the further east we went the fewer tourists there'd be anyway. But our itinerary was booked: hotels, trains and early morning starts. In four hours we were due at Uda Walawe National Park, where the elephants were waiting for us.

Uda Walawe is located in the middle of the southern plains. It is an area of grassland and bush famous for wild elephants. With luck we'd see a few of them after our zero sightings at Yala. The weather was good. The elephants had no excuse. No hiding away this time. They had to be out in force – all three hundred of them.

As he drove, Samid told us about his family. He had three sons, one living in Canada and two others still at his home in Negombo, near Colombo. On Christmas Day he and his wife had entertained over sixty people, relatives and friends. Samid had once been Buddhist but had converted to become a Roman Catholic when he married his wife. She had to be a very capable woman, I thought, with all the cooking she must have done over the holiday period. Yet she'd still thought of us – and had kindly wrapped up two pieces of Christmas cake as presents. I peeled off the layers of cellophane and baking paper from mine and, cupping my hand for crumbs, carefully ate the slice of cake as we travelled. It was packed full of fruit and nuts and tasted delicious.

At Matara, Sri Lanka's fifth biggest city, Samid turned inland and headed north towards Uda Walawe. We wouldn't be staying in a hotel that night but – the only occasion on this holiday – in a tent. Yes, we were camping! Although not camping-camping with a tent too low to stand up in, hardly any room for sleeping bags, and the ground as hard as a cake tin. No. We were glamping – or so I hoped – in a tent as grand as a palace, with a king-size bed, and a side-tent containing a bathroom and toilet.

As we drew up at the entrance of Kottowatta Village everything seemed very organised. A guard in uniform saluted us at the gate, and a girl tapped efficiently on a keyboard in reception. Two porters carried our bags in and showed us the way. Now that Oshan wasn't around we had to tip everyone, which meant having a wad of small bills ready in my pocket.

It was quite a walk to our tent, along a gravel drive between trees, then across a wooden-slatted bridge that spanned marshland and a lake. All habitat for local wildlife, I thought, hopefully not the sort that slithered into your bed in the middle of the night. No problem, though. The tent would stand above ground on a platform and have zips and mesh for Africa ... well, for Sri Lanka, ironically the country with the greatest number of fatal snakebites every year. Nothing would get in except us. There'd be no cockroaches, no spiders, no mosquitoes, and definitely no snakes.

Finally we reached our "tent", and it wasn't what I expected. Less a bespoke canvas house and more a Coronation-Street-style terrace. The right wall of our tent was the left wall of the next one, just as *their* right wall in turn was shared with their neighbour. No space for notions of being Redford and Streep in *Out of Africa* then, or even Don Estelle in *It Ain't Half Hot, Mum*.

Thankfully, however, all the tents here were pitched on a high platform. The snakes would get vertigo if they climbed up this far. In addition, a massive, sloping, metal roof shielded everyone above. Unless the rain fell horizontally we'd all stay dry. In fact, our tent was as comfortable as any hotel room. We had a large mattress veiled by a mosquito net plus a zip-up canvas door leading into our own en suite bathroom. Truly, Kottowatta Village was good value. The price of our accommodation included a generous buffet dinner, and a delicious breakfast in the morning. And not one but two large swimming pools to offset the heat. Really, we couldn't complain.

Bags dumped in our room, we quickstepped back out. Our entire rationale for coming to Uda Walawe was to spot elephants, and they weren't going to sneak into our tent. If we wanted to see one we had to go to the park.

Our safari jeep waited outside reception, Samid grinning down from the back. He'd changed out of the formal shirt he'd been wearing, and now clad in slacks, T-shirt and sunglasses he looked more relaxed. Plus he didn't have to drive. A park guide would take us around.

We climbed up a steep, four-rung ladder onto the jeep's deck to join Samid. Other than the aeroplane, this vehicle had to be one of the highest things we'd travelled in. As it set off, swaying and bouncing, we were able to gaze down on little villages with open fires and bordered by thick bush.

Then, reaching the stupendous Uda Walawe Dam, we drove several kilometres along a road raised on the top. To our left stretched a blue expanse of water with purple humps of hill country in the distance. To our right and beneath us, like a carpet of broccoli, were the tops of trees in the forest. With a breeze in our faces and sunlight on our heads, we felt a thrill of adventure. This was a place where mountains, water, forest and sky converged.

At the end of the dam several large trees grew out of the reservoir's smooth surface and towered, mirror-like, above their own reflections. A drop-jaw photo, except the jeep was moving too quickly. Already into bush again, we passed roadside stalls selling nuts and fruit, then turned left up a side road into the reserve. At the entrance hut the driver paid our admission, then drove through a gap in the electrified fence that surrounds the entire park. The fence is intended to keep elephants in and cattle out. It is only switched on at night, however, as a cost-saving measure and to avoid accidental harm to children.

Shortly after entering the park our driver stopped by a tree. He pointed out something that no one else, including Samid, could see. Yet the driver lingered, sure something was there. We used binoculars to scrutinise the tree – its branches, leaves, trunk and bark – wondering what he might have seen. A snake? A bird? An elephant in sunglasses? Eventually the driver turned around and told us. It was a chameleon, adept at changing the pattern of its skin and camouflaging itself. We studied the tree a bit longer, yet still couldn't see anything. For all we knew he might have been teasing us.

The driver backed up and drove for miles along a rough red track where, apart from one grey-and-blue Indian roller, we saw absolutely nothing. I wondered what sort of safari this was turning out to be. Chameleons that no one could see, and elephants that remained out of sight? There were echoes of Yala here, though the sun blazed on red, dry soil, and the sky shone cloudless.

Realising we were bored, the driver changed direction and took us to what at first appeared to be a pretty, tree lined lake. A couple of other jeeps were already parked on the shoreline, their occupants peering at something. As we drew nearer, a stench of death drifted over. And looking again through binoculars, perhaps the lake wasn't so picturesque. A floating pink object resolved into the ripped corpse of a deer. Two darker humps beyond were crocodiles with lots of teeth. They were guarding their pantry and would eat later. And as the smell worsened, I held my nose and wished crocodiles had fridges – or dentists.

We jolted away, the track as rutted as old ribs, and came across another herd of jeeps spying on – *hurray, at last!* – what appeared to be a corresponding herd of elephants. Four of the beasts. Two mothers, swinging their trunks and often glancing around, and behind them, weaving madly around each other like tiny animated toys, two babies. The mothers grazed close to the road, methodically tugging up tufts of grass and stuffing them into their wide-open mouths. The babies seemed more intent on playing. We had a clear view of all four and noticed how they stayed close together, none of them straying too far from the others.

The driver told us one baby was three months old and the other six. They fed mainly off their mothers' milk for their first two years, though some calves have been known to delay weaning for as long as ten years. Female calves stay with the herd for life, while males leave at fourteen to commence a solitary life.

The fumes from the other jeeps grew stinky, and we

drove on. Almost straightaway we came across another herd – seven animals this time. We watched these for a while, then motored on to discover another herd, and yet another. With each new sighting the numbers of animals increased. Altogether we must have seen thirty or forty elephants – perhaps ten percent of the park's population.

The day cooled and dusk fell. Other creatures came out to say hello: peacocks spreading their tails, black-faced monkeys jumping out of trees, an elusive fox and, best of all, a star turtle. Elated at everything we'd seen, we were driven back along the spectacular reservoir road. A fresh breeze caressed our faces, blowing bugs into our eyes along with the scent of charcoal fires. As the sun set, the water across from us darkened and the sky cracked open with fire.

This had been one magnificent safari.

THIRTY-TWO

Baby Elephants and Other Things

No snakes visited our tent in the night, though several dogs raced around the edge of the wooden platform, their tails shuffling excitedly against the canvas. When I switched off our light, an outside lantern painted strange, impressionist shapes on our door. With that combined with the French voices from the next tent, I fell asleep dreaming I was in a rakish arrondissement of Paris rather than camping in rural Sri Lanka. The next morning when I awoke, I found one of the dogs asleep in a chair outside on our balcony.

We left at eight forty-five sharp. Samid was a stickler for punctuality and we didn't want to disappoint him. Having our own guide was an entirely different experience from being on the bus. Now we didn't have travelling companions; it was strictly Samid and us. We could go where we liked, when we liked, and stay as long as we wanted. Yet we missed the others, their jokes and opinions. Oddly, we missed the predictability of a fixed itinerary as well. Some days it became quite hard deciding what to visit.

That morning, however, Kate had no doubts about our

first stop. We were going to the Ath Athuru Sevana, or the Elephant Transit Home, a short way from Uda Walawe. Around fifty orphaned young elephants live at the Home and are fed every three hours during the day with milk and palm leaves. The elephants originate from all over Sri Lanka and are usually orphaned as a result of an increasing conflict with people. As Sri Lanka's population grows, human activities – farming, cattle grazing, mining and timber – expand more and more into elephant territories. This leads to clashes between the two species, with adult elephants being killed and their young orphaned.

One such orphan was Sandamali from the region of the Handapanagala Tank, just to the north. After a new sugar cane factory was constructed in the 1990s the local authorities planned to relocate the elephants living there. But the elephants had different plans. They intended to stay. Predictable conflict followed, with deaths and casualties on both sides. Sandamali was one of the victims, losing her mother and becoming separated from her herd. Two villagers spotted her wandering aimlessly near the lake, and the local wildlife service rescued her – ironically from a herd of domestic buffalo – and brought her to the Elephant Transit Home.

Similarly, Bullet was a young male elephant orphaned in an area torn apart by the war in the north. Villagers spotted him limping and handed him to the police. He had a gunshot wound on his right leg – badly infected and needing months of treatment. This was how he earned his nickname, from the bullet that had entered his leg and passed all the way through.

We arrived just in time for that morning's feeding, luckily finding space at the end of the viewing platform. It was Saturday, school holidays too, and the benches were packed with local families, the children squealing in excitement. The baby elephants took no notice. They assembled on the other side of the fenced-off arena, patiently waiting for the keeper to open the gate.

He let two or three through at a time. The little elephants ran straight to the feeding bar where keepers draped plastic tubes into their mouths, then poured in milk from bottles. The milk is prepared using milk powder intended for human babies, though if an elephant has problems with cows' milk, then soya milk or rice broth may be fed to them instead.

One innocent-looking elephant decided to rebel. It ran in the opposite direction and chomped on some of the palm leaves laid out for dessert, before heading back for the liquid main course. Another more cantankerous elephant trumpeted dissatisfaction with its milk ration, but the keepers pushed it away so newcomers could step up for their share. Yet most of the elephants were well behaved, coming over in their little groups, gobbling down their two bottles-worth, then joining the others to munch happily on the loose palm leaves. By the time we left, there were forty or more animals in the arena, their trunks dipping and rising as they stuffed their mouths, their little eyes shining with delight. When these elephants reach the age of five they will be released back into the wild – usually to the neighbouring Uda Walawe National Park.

On the way out, people gathered around the skeleton of a full-sized elephant adjacent to the car park. These were the bones of Sandagiya, an elephant that had wandered the northern boundaries of Uda Walawe in search of food, all too often receiving bullets from farmers' guns. Sadly, despite medical treatment, one wound became infected and Sandagiya died. At least he isn't forgotten. In death he stands as a symbol of elephant defiance against man.

. . .

SAMID DROVE us to a little-known shrine at Buduruwagala, several kilometres along a rough track off the highway. The temple no longer existed, but seven magnificent statues had been carved on an elephant-shaped slab of rock. The largest central figure was an image of Buddha in the protective or *abhaya* pose. The others represented different deities, possibly Hindu, all one thousand years old.

Buduruwagala was a quiet, unspoilt place with few other tourists. The shrine had been covered by a lake for two or three centuries, only becoming visible again when the waters receded.

Back on the main road, Samid drove further north. The day took on a melodramatic feel, with ever more breathtaking vistas, one after another. Acres of verdant paddy fields followed by a terraced pit of mud – a new paddy field being sculpted from bare earth. Then the road rose rapidly as we ascended Ella Gap, the same scenic pass the bus had descended a week and a half ago with Nelson and Frank singing *My Way* in the back. We'd been lucky then to get down at all. Torrential rain had triggered a landslide the day afterwards, and now – as we ascended – two massive boulders, the size of family cars, stood like omens by the side of the road.

"You want to stop at Rawana Ella Falls?" asked Samid, and we nodded yes. There'd be hundreds of people hanging around this bend of the highway, yet we might as well see the falls again.

"You want to walk up to Little Adam's Peak?" Samid pointed at a hill on our right, at the top of which, apparently, awaited a wondrous view.

"How long does it take?" Kate was sceptical.

"Not too long. About an hour there."

She turned to me. "You go if you want."

I wasn't sure. I hadn't climbed the real Adam's Peak – Sri Lanka's most spiritual mountain – when we'd had opportunity on the tour. It would have meant missing an entire night's sleep. Also, after struggling up Lion Rock, I'd wondered if I was even fit enough; with five thousand two hundred steps, Adam's Peak rose much, much higher. Going up Little Adam's Peak could be my reprieve – a hill with a similar name, an almost similar view, yet without weeks of training and the likelihood of strained calf muscles and sore feet.

"What are you going to do?" I stared back at Kate. "If I do go up?"

"Wait here." She waved at the hillside. "Watch you."

I wondered again what to do. It was midday and the sun was hot. Slogging up there wouldn't be without sweat. And on the opposite side of the valley rose Ella Rock, a much more serious piece of work: better views, more of a workout, but four hours there and back.

Samid noticed me staring at the hard pinnacle of Ella Rock. "My last clients walked up there," he said in a quiet voice. "The route is tricky and they got lost." He paused as if something terrible had happened and they hadn't returned.

"Did they get there?" I asked.

He nodded. "But they had to use Google Maps. The man was so busy looking at his phone, he almost trod on a snake – a python, he said." Samid paused again.

"They're not poisonous, are they?"

"He showed me a photo." The ends of his moustache twitched. "And it wasn't a python. It was a cobra."

I abandoned going on either walk – Little Adam's Peak

or Ella Rock. We'd seen plenty of amazing views that morning anyway. This would only be one more.

Samid continued driving towards Ella as if my lack of courage – or energy – was normal. Instead he talked of Nine Arches Bridge, an architectural wonder that required zero exertion. Unlike other railway structures in the country, all British made, it had been designed and constructed by a Sri Lankan engineer. The British engineers, God bless their cotton socks, had surveyed the gap to be crossed, discovered a quagmire in the middle, and given up. The bridge was technically impossible, they said, especially when all supplies of steel were being diverted to World War I. Yet as things turned out, there was a way across. A traditional drummer and devil dancer, Mr P. K. Appuhami, took over the project and, using local labour, completed the bridge without the need for a single strand of steel. Boulders were tipped onto the swampy ground to make it firm, and the bridge's famous columns were assembled out of rocks, bricks and cement. When the first train travelled over the top, Mr P. K. Appuhami lay underneath one of the arches as a personal guarantee his creation wouldn't collapse. Samid told this story with a poker face, yet even I could tell that he was proud of what this local man had achieved.

We drove to the outskirts of Ella, then away again. Samid ignored the road signs for Demodara Railway Bridge – the bridge's formal name – and drove up a steep road with little traffic. After stopping at a roadside food stall run by a kindly old lady, he beckoned us to the edge of the decking to reveal a secret view of the iconic bridge. Far below us, the nine arches stretched like a Victorian sepia illusion above the green forest. Tiny figures walked between its rails, the tracks vanishing into nothing at both ends.

Suddenly I realised it was the same bridge from the front

page of my travel blog – a picture I'd downloaded from a photo stock library. This view was different, though. We were gazing at it from another angle – and there wasn't a train going over.

"When's the next train due?" I asked.

"In forty minutes." Samid blinked. "And it will probably be late."

Our stomachs were rumbling so we bought some biscuits from the lady and then went in search of lunch. First at the Eighty-Eight Acre Hotel, with its escarpment-edge restaurant and hair-raisingly expensive menu. The place was full, however. No tables with views, not even of the kitchen. We headed into the heart of Ella itself – a backpacker frenzy of cafes, hostels and happy-hour pubs that offered Lion beer on tap for two hundred rupees a glass. Samid recommended a place called Chill Café, where the food was allegedly hot and spicy. He and Kate chose chicken burgers; as a driver bringing customers to the restaurant, his was free. I went for rice and curry, which arrived as ten stainless-steel bowls of goodness all on one gigantic plate. Pork, chicken, jackfruit and eggplant curries; salted fish, pennywort salad, mango chutney and rotis. And, of course, rice. Ten out of ten for taste, and another gold star for endemic Sri Lankan cooking.

Exhausted after all that food, we skipped any further sightseeing and asked Samid to take us to our next accommodation at Haputale. He drove there via Bandarawela, of best breakfast fame, then along a road that seemed to perch on the edge of a precipice with million-dollar views of the lowlands far below. We were at a height of two thousand metres, and our ears popped. At Haputale, Samid kept going – along the town's pleasant one street and out the other side – then down another cliff-clinging road that descended in twists and sighs.

It turned out our hotel wasn't in Haputale as we'd thought but at the next town of Beragale. And it wasn't even there. We had to go further along another road that lanced out over nothing, apparently suspended in free space.

The Hotel at the Edge of Nowhere was a tall, stark, grey monolith of a building that clung to the steep hillside yet had a view that unrolled like a magical expanding carpet. From a silent grey balcony, we gazed down on the vast green and yellow plain below. A tiny blue oval glinted in the distance – probably that same enormous reservoir at Uda Walawe we'd visited only yesterday. How far, how high, we'd travelled in a day. Now we were perched on the top of those purple hills we'd seen from down there, looking back on ourselves.

THIRTY-THREE

Lipton's Seat

The next morning, as the car swung powerfully around dark bends, we could see almost nothing. Samid's headlights picked out snaking tarmac, while to our left a few lights twinkled. Nothing on our right apart from a deep, impenetrable void. I dared not think what lay in that direction. I feared it was a horrifying vertical drop.

It was four-forty-five. What on earth had possessed us to come on this bleary-eyed adventure when we could be lying comfortably in our beds?

"You sleep all right?" Samid glanced over from the driver's seat as if he could read my thoughts.

"Not too bad. You?"

"The other drivers got up a lot to use the bathroom." He sighed, then smiled. "But I got the lower bunk."

He'd already explained how he slept in accommodation provided by the hotels specifically for drivers. Often this was in a bunkroom with first comers bagging the more popular lower bunks. The washrooms and toilets were shared too, with the drivers forming an orderly queue in the morning.

Although this wouldn't have been a problem for Samid this morning – unless all the other drivers were rising at four-thirty too.

Outside the car, the road remained dark, twisting and ascending. Samid was driving us back up to Haputale, the little town perched on a precipice. Thankfully he seemed to know what he was doing. He drove the car confidently, neither too fast nor too slow. Reaching some momentary plateau, the road straightened out and flattened. Streetlamps and houses appeared on both sides. Haputale's main street, deserted of people. Swerving right, Samid ducked into a side-street. Past a foray of silent tuk-tuks, then into a narrowing lane of shutters and shadows. The sort of dead-end street where the car stops, the driver turns off the engine, and several masked men with machineguns step into the arc of the headlamps.

But this wasn't the movies. We weren't being driven in a battered black Mercedes-Benz by a hood. Samid had simply taken a wrong turning. After reversing up the lane until there was sufficient room to turn around, he drove back onto the main road and took the next right instead.

"They all look the same in the dark," he said in his pleasant up-and-down voice. "In the daylight I could drive this way with my eyes shut."

His car was warm and comfortable compared to the morning freeze outside. It was a well-kept burgundy Toyota Premio with cream leather seats and pleated beige curtains. A chill-box in the back was filled with bottles of drinking water. Had he been able to, he might have added a houseplant, a fish tank, even a recording of a Steinbach pianoforte to make his guests more relaxed.

"How much further?" asked Kate.

"A little way. Nearly there." He tapped the dash with his

fingers. No substitute for *Moonlight Sonata*, yet mildly soothing.

The new road ascended, zigzagging like an uncoiled bedspring. At this rate we'd be totally disorientated by the time we reached the top, unable to discern north from south or day from night. We'd be high too, perhaps at the same altitude as World's End, over two thousand metres up. Once again I wondered whether he was taking us to our destination or some hopelessly inaccessible place from which we'd never escape.

A mass of lights burst out ahead – a factory of some kind with a wire fence and a hum of machinery. Smiling again, Samid touched the brakes and brought the car to a stop.

"Where are we?"

"Dambatenne." He pointed at the factory. "Lipton's Tea Factory."

It didn't look like any branch of Lipton's I remembered from my childhood. In those days Lipton's had been a high-street supermarket that sold fresh cheese and sliced ham, plus sugar, biscuits and tea.

"Aren't we going to Lipton's Seat?" said Kate from the back seat.

"A little further."

Samid motioned for us to get out of the car. In the fresh night air, it was cold, almost a frost. Thankfully we were wearing fleeces, long trousers, socks and shoes. We'd have frozen to death in shorts and jandals. A few yards away a tuk-tuk waited, its engine chugging. Exhaling, all three of us squeezed into its back seat.

Immediately the tuk-tuk driver unleashed his fragile vehicle forward, roaring up another steep, winding road that led away from the lights and further into the night. We shook and swung against one another, the little two-stroke engine straining pitifully. Up, up and up, careening around hairpin bends so tight it felt that the four of us might tumble out and over the side. Left, right – right, left – the tuk-tuk's single front wheel performing impossible turns.

Then, just as it seemed we would never stop, red lights appeared ahead. A queue of similar tuk-tuks waiting at a checkpoint. We weren't alone. Other foolhardy tourists were going the same way. And as each tuk-tuk edged forward Samid whispered that the entrance fee was two hundred rupees, to be handed in notes to the man in the booth. In the dim light I pulled money from my wallet, unable to see if they were fifties or five hundreds, and handed the wad over.

Up we chugged some more, this track that was turning into a stairway. To the east the sky was lightening. Samid tensed, murmuring something about running out of time. He tapped the driver on the shoulder, and with a new burst of pain from its engine the tuk-tuk went into superdrive and charged past the three tuk-tuks in front. As the sky reddened the driver shouted and we stopped.

We jumped out, hoping this was it. We were at our destination. The hill where Sir Thomas Lipton, the famous Glaswegian tea magnate, used to come to sit and watch the incredible view across the plains below. Although in the nascent yellow light – like being inside an egg slowly cracking open – we couldn't see much. Just a layer of light bursting on top of a thick wedge of blackness. Like zombies we stumbled around in the last reaches of night, avoiding the dark figures of other sleep-deprived tourists who clutched blankets and cameras. Many of them leaned against a metal balustrade, craning forward to be inches closer to the emerging sun. In one corner gleamed Lipton himself – or at least his seated bronze statue, holding a bronze cup of tea.

Singlehandedly, Lipton had transformed the British tea

industry, first expanding his parents' grocery shop in Glasgow to a UK-wide chain of three hundred shops, then developing his own tea plantations and a factory here at Dambatenne in Sri Lanka. Ironically, his statue faced the wrong way. Rather than surveying his unseen plantations, this new Lipton had turned his back on them and now looked at us.

In another direction, people ascended a series of dark, winding staircases that led ever upwards. Following them, I discovered the true Lipton's Seat – a pinnacle with a three-hundred-and-sixty-degree view. To the east, the furnace-edge of dawn still burned, splashing a few bright nuggets in the black landscape. And behind us, a baby-pink sky had crept up unannounced, shining down on cloud swaddled in the valley below.

This was Lipton's Seat, no less, and we had arrived not a moment too soon. As the sunburst became sunrise, then bludgeoning daylight, we welcomed a new day, a new year, a new decade.

THIRTY-FOUR

Seven-Forty-Seven from Haputale

The big station clock read seven-forty-five and people paced up and down, glancing at their wristwatches and consulting their phones. Others knotted into family groups – mothers, aunts, children and baggage – as more people hurried through the ticket office onto the platform.

The minute hand on the big clock clicked onto seven-forty-six. The queue at the food kiosk dwindled and people began craning their heads, looking down the tracks to see if anything – a locomotive – was coming. Feeling excited, even a little apprehensive, we peered as well, breakfast packs clutched under our arms and tickets held tightly in our hands as we waited for the seven-forty-seven to arrive.

This was to be our inaugural Sri Lankan railway journey, travelling six stops from Haputale to Nanu Oya, the nearest station to Nuwara Eliya. The railway trip included on our tour had been cancelled due to bad weather – low-lying clouds and incessant rain. Often trains fell behind schedule for no other reason than it being customary to run late, sometimes hours and days beyond those on the timetable.

The carriages became overcrowded too, with no apparent limit on the number of men, women, children and chickens squeezed on board, with those who couldn't push their way inside clinging to the outer doors.

The railways in Sri Lanka had been built mainly by the British. That is to say the British supervised while local and imported labour forces constructed. This was Britain's typical way of saying thank you. Thank you for letting us stay here to grow tea and export it at vast profit to the Brits back home. Thank you too for all the spices like cinnamon and vanilla, and for letting our armies build roads and railways to conquer your interior. The railways, of course, were instrumental in transporting tea from the central highlands to ports such as Colombo for shipping overseas.

The British colonials left long ago; Sri Lanka gained independence in 1948. Yet the railways are still here, transporting goods and people all over the country. At Haputale modern diesel trains went in both directions – down the line through Kandy to Colombo, and up the line through Ella to Bandarawela.

Without anyone noticing, the clock clicked onto seven-forty-seven. No announcement came over the loudspeakers, nor did the rails hum. In no great panic, people drifted towards the edge of the platform. It was as if they knew something – although still there was no train. Perhaps like those elephants in Yala National Park they sensed vibrations.

With no great fanfare, a locomotive emerged from our left. It tugged blue carriages, one after another after another – too many, it seemed, to fit in the station. The last carriage slid to a stop directly in front of us and Samid motioned at the door, inviting us to board. He'd reserved two seats together halfway down – one by the window, the other by the aisle. A long-haired tourist already sat in the window seat. When he saw us coming, however, he rose and rejoined his girlfriend on the seat behind. They were both tourists like us and – as I realised when I gazed around the carriage – so too were most of the other passengers. Samid had booked us first-class, where we'd be guaranteed a seat, a little fold-down table and plenty of space. Indeed several seats were empty, and no one was standing. It certainly wasn't the sardine-can I'd half-expected but more like a typical train carriage back home – except without LED destination boards or those little pointed axes in glass cages for breaking the windows in an emergency.

We sat down, Kate next to the window and me by the aisle. Samid smiled at us through the opposite window, making odd gestures with his mouth and hands. Presumably this was sign language for *Hope you like your seats and enjoy the ride*. Samid wasn't coming with us on the train. Once we'd departed he'd return to his car and drive to Nanu Oya to meet us there.

With a jolt, our carriage moved forward. Samid gave a final wave and then paced to the station exit. Now that he didn't have our Western sensitivities to worry about he could put the radio on full blast and hot-foot every speed limit. Although I doubted he'd do that. He seemed too professional a driver to take a different approach. And we wanted him to arrive safely – he had all our luggage in his boot, and we needed his services for the rest of our trip.

The outskirts of Haputale petered out and we accelerated smoothly into forest. Kate had a first-class view of trees from her window while I, upon opening my breakfast pack, had an equally stunning first glimpse of my cheese and tomato sandwich. The bread was firm and slightly curled at the corners; the cheese sat soft and processed, and there was no tomato.

Across through the opposite window the hillside swept sharply downwards. Layers of trees and bush, and far below, a swathe of white mist. Beyond the high peaks of hills maybe there was that scary, sheer escarpment of World's End. Then, in a trice, our view vanished. We shot into cloud, only the gaunt limbs of trees striding past like stickmen. Until the train came to a sudden and unexpected halt.

"What's happened?" I stared through the window, seeing nothing.

"I think we're at a station." Kate stared out too.

There was no announcement of any kind, and as far as I could see there were no loudspeakers anyway. No one stood up or showed any interest in disembarking. Being in the very last carriage, we were too far along to spot any buildings or signposts – or even a platform. If this was a station rather than an unscheduled stop then according to the tiny writing on my large-format map it had to be one called Ohiya. Perhaps I'd glimpse something when we moved off. The lack of information didn't bode well for when, five or six stops later, we reached Nanu Oya. Hopefully other passengers would be leaving there too. Yet if we couldn't see the sign, how would we know we weren't at the station before or the one after? If we missed Samid and his car we'd be well and truly up the Swanee.

The train jolted again, moving forward. And, as I'd suspected, there *was* a sign for Ohiya.

A man came down the aisle selling tea and hot samosa snacks. They smelt delicious, but after the sandwich I was no longer hungry. The cloud outside dissipated, revealing the rounded green slopes of a tea plantation. Then another abrupt stop, again with no signage.

"This is going to be awkward when we get there," said

Kate, voicing what I'd been thinking. "Do you think we should go and sit forward?"

"The forward carriages looked full." They were all second-class and didn't have reserved seats. "Plus, we've got four stops to go. We won't be there for a while."

We were still gliding through tea country. The track curved sharply, and up ahead I could see the front of the train crossing over a metal viaduct. This was the stuff railway adventures were made of – the kind of journey one of the two Michaels, Palin or Portillo, would feature on their TV shows. We could forget we were Kate and Andy, and imagine we were a couple of hard-working, hard-drinking tea planters from the nineteenth century traversing the island's rugged interior. Later we'd have a pot of broken orange pekoe accompanied by thinly cut cucumber sandwiches and homemade chocolate cake.

The train stopped at three more stations, leading us to think the next one must be Nanu Oya. Yet when we *did* stop, an abrupt halt like all the others, there was no sign of anything to indicate where we might be. No one seemed to be moving either, everyone remaining in their seats. Yet, afraid we might have arrived, we grabbed our day bags and ran into the next carriage. Then the carriage after that, staring through the windows for any indication we might have reached our destination rather than a wayside hamlet.

The carriages further down were filled with local Sri Lankans, many with luggage, children, and containers of homemade food. Few of them were standing so we were able to sprint down the aisle unimpeded. None of these people were disembarking either. If this place really was Nanu Oya, a major stop, then we appeared to be the only passengers contemplating leaving the train.

We turned around and walked back up to our seats. As

we did so the train started moving again, swaying and rattling around us. Five minutes later, when it stopped once more, people did spring up, seize their bags and move to the end of the carriage. Now we had reached Nanu Oya. It was time to disembark.

Our epic railway journey had come to an end sooner than we'd expected. We'd been travelling for about an hour and a half, and with no delays – no tea leaves on the line – had arrived punctually. There was no brass band to greet us, no triumphant theme music, nor a string of TV credits, but a rush of everyone stamping off in the same direction. Ten paces to the door and three steps to the platform. Then everybody streaming to the station exit, colliding with new passengers who were rushing to catch an older brown-carriage train about to leave on another platform. We strode with the flow, looking out for Samid. Hopefully, he'd arrived too and was waiting for us somewhere.

Next time we'd travel further by train and turn it into a real journey. All the way from Colombo to Badulla maybe, hour after hour of scenery spanning an entire day, maybe two. Enough to make several episodes, a TV documentary – even a mini-series.

THIRTY-FIVE

Grandstanding the Grand

As the car slipped through the landscaped gardens, past a glittering fountain and trimmed green lawns, we knew we'd arrived somewhere special. And as we pulled up outside the grand entrance of an even grander building, a burly head porter already striding over in a distinguished red-and-black costume, I felt a new sense of importance – even of entitlement.

The head porter directed a squad of other porters in smart red uniforms to help us with our bags. We'd only been here thirty seconds – and the pomp, ceremony and excellent service of this place held our attention.

We were ushered through a long, panelled hallway, our shoes sinking into plush carpet. Then into a king's lounge filled with low antique tables and soft, cushioned sofas. A friendly lady in a grey uniform showed us where we could sit, then beckoned over a man in a white uniform who offered us hot towels. He was promptly followed by a teaboy in a white tunic who brought over cups of delicious vanilla tea and a generous dish of fudge.

Our room wasn't quite ready yet – hardly surprising considering it was only eleven in the morning. If we didn't mind listening to the automated piano playing Christmas tunes, then they'd make our room up as soon as possible.

Such a contrast to the piecemeal welcome we'd endured the night before at the Hotel at the Edge of Nowhere. Already I sensed the Grand Hotel at Nuwara Eliya was going to be a memorable place to stay. So much was here – four restaurants, several bars, a billiard room and a swimming pool – we probably wouldn't need to go out at all. We could put our feet up and relax.

The Grand is a famous hotel, one of Nuwara Eliya's must-see attractions. Outside, it has a mock-Tudor façade and immaculate gardens. Within, there is a wonderful collection of period public rooms. Originally we'd booked a room at a different hotel in Nuwara Eliya. Then, deciding to enjoy a last-minute splurge, the chance of a little decadence, we upgraded to the Grand. For one night only, along with all the other Western and Indian tourists staying here, we could continue our fantasies of the train journey and pretend we were celebrities like Lord Mountbatten, President Nixon, Roger Moore and Carrie Fisher, all of whom had stayed here.

The automated piano played a few more tunes, cycling through its Christmas repertoire, while we consumed the remaining fudge. Tourists in shorts and T-shirts shuffled into the lounge to take photos, ignoring us as we ignored them. Then, before we could ask for a second dish of fudge, the lady in grey whisked in and told us our room was ready. Another porter, this one in a brown uniform, loaded our cases onto a shiny trolley and pushed it out of the lounge and along the polished wooden floor of a long corridor. We followed, past a cabinet of silver tongs, a gold statue of the jungle fowl, Sri Lanka's national bird, and down a ramp. A workman was busily repainting the wooden banister, the smell of lacquer strong. Then around another corner, past an ornate metal goblet and towards a dark wooden door. Number one hundred and sixty-nine. Our room for the night – our boudoir of aspiring aristocracy.

The porter unlocked the door and wheeled our luggage in. He seemed very enthusiastic about the bathroom, demonstrating how the taps worked, hot and cold, the flush mechanism on the toilet, and the caps on the little shampoo bottles. Then he asked us if we'd enjoyed our breakfast – which I hadn't particularly, a cheese and tomato sandwich without the tomato. The porter didn't know this, however, and carried on showing us the safe, how the curtains could be opened or closed by pulling them, and the on/off button for the TV remote control. Amazing the things you learn on your travels – often things you have at home, yet experienced in a new and different way. We'd never had royal treatment like this on the tour. But then it had been Oshan dispensing gratuities from the kitty rather than us directly. So eventually I gave the porter his tip, if not for service then for sheer persistence, and ushered him out, explaining we could work out the rest of the room for ourselves.

The room was comfortable, though a little ordinary. Nicely furnished, yet with no easy chairs, no reclinable sofa, and definitely no view. Our window looked out onto an inner courtyard full of ladders belonging to workmen busy on the roof. To be fair, though, we'd booked one of the cheaper rooms, and we'd checked in early as well.

The hotel's grandness lay in its public areas – the many corridors, meeting rooms, lounges, high-tea galleries and restaurants that all came together like an episode of *Upstairs,*

Downstairs. Exploring, I discovered a wood-panelled wine restaurant, then through another doorway the sublime billiards room. Somewhere else was a saloon with a life-sized nativity scene and huge wall mirrors. Everything so old: dark, wooden floors and high, moulded ceilings; antique cabinets and chests of drawers; stately paintings and black-and-white photographs.

The most noticeable features were the staff. They graced every nook and cranny in white tunics and white sarongs, in brown and grey uniforms, their expressions officious and helpful. They strode purposely from one part of the hotel to another, or else stood to attention as if their sole duty was to greet guests.

Then there were the guests, tourists much like us, ill-dressed, badly shod, snap happy. All sorts of people: older couples, families with children, the odd backpacker. The place felt like a cross between a National Trust property and a busy hospital – something of a twenty-first century parody of what this grand place used to be. The guests here were no longer plantation managers, colonels or visiting dignitaries from the Foreign Office. The rules, too, though observed, had evolved into workarounds. Men still had to wear jackets and long trousers for dinner in the Barnes restaurant, yet their attire didn't have to be coordinated, and if they hadn't brought their own they could borrow clobber from the cloakroom. Likewise, in the billiards room, male players had to wear long trousers or a full-length sarong, with many would-be Ray Reardons winding temporary sarongs over their shorts.

Outside in the gardens, a quotation from Robert Louis Stevenson had been painted on a sign. "Don't judge each day by the harvest you reap but by the seeds you plant."

Strangely appropriate for this hotel and the people who came here.

As three o'clock neared we scouted the veranda, searching for the best table at which to enjoy another high tea. Thanks to my poor navigation we'd missed out on high tea here during our first visit to Nuwara Eliya so were particularly keen to try one now. My quest for the perfect cuppa was still in progress. We might have tasted the subtlety of Lover's Leap broken orange pekoe at Amangalla, yet who knew what stratospheric levels we might aspire to?

In 2005, to celebrate their diamond anniversary, PG Tips crafted a teabag worth fifteen thousand US dollars. On the outside the bag was encrusted with two hundred and eighty diamonds, while inside it contained Silver Tips Imperial Tea, the world's most expensive Darjeeling.

Then there is Panda Dung Tea, sold at two hundred US dollars a cup. Ironically, the tea isn't made of panda dung; it comes from a tea tree that is fertilised with the bamboo-rich poo.

Or consider Da-Hong Pao Tea which, at one million dollars a kilogram, is probably the world's most expensive tea. It is a dark oolong tea grown in the Wuyi mountains in northern China. It is more expensive than gold, and served only to the most honoured guests.

I doubted we wanted, or could afford, a cup of Da-Hong Pao. Anyway, they wouldn't serve it here. We weren't in China but Sri Lanka. The Grand, however, did list a Celebration High Tea on its menu, which at two thousand rupees had to be better value. So, sitting down at a table on the veranda overlooking the gardens, we put in our order with high hopes.

Around us waiters in beige uniforms rushed to and fro, carrying out trays containing pots of tea and tiers of sandwiches and pastries, somehow always destined for another table. We were in no hurry, though. The chairs were comfortable, and we had a fine view of the flowers and flags. Yet as the breeze increased, and the flags snapped rather than fluttered, we grew impatient. Then a waiter dashed over and carefully placed a flute of sparkling white wine in front of Kate and one in front of me too.

"But we ordered tea?" Surprised, I pushed my glass away. "Not wine."

"It comes with the tea." The waiter raised his eyebrows. "It is the celebration."

I realised we should have ordered one of the other high teas. In trying to be grand, we'd out-granded ourselves.

"It's too early for wine," I said. "There's no chance of swapping it for something else? More cakes? Extra scones?"

The waiter smiled and took the glasses away. Then, thankfully, he returned with our tier of savouries, sandwiches and cakes piled high. Even more welcome, he brought an extra plate of scones, with local berry jam and watery cream. Pots of tea too – a Ceylon cinnamon spice tea for Kate, and a Single Estate oolong leaf for me.

Hungrily we tucked in. As at the Amangalla, Kate delicately sliced each pastry, sandwich and cake into two so we could both sample everything. The portions were minuscule when halved, barely enough for a swallow, but the scones had more substance, especially when heaped with cream and jam. Plus, we had six of them – three scones each.

Even spinning things out, slicing, tasting and discussing, we devoured the fairytale feast in less than ten minutes. The tea took a little longer as we repeatedly poured from the white china teapots into white china cups, then when emptied, despatched the pots for refills.

"What's your tea like?" Kate gazed over the rim of her raised cup.

"Really good." I sipped and smiled. "What about yours?"

"Okay. But not what I thought it would be."

We swapped cups and tasted each other's. And realised that the waiter had announced the teapots wrongly. Kate had been drinking my oolong while I'd had her cinnamon.

A little underwhelmed – especially after the high tea we'd eaten a week earlier at the Amangalla – we made our way to the billiards room. If we couldn't be well-bred teetotallers we'd become hard-hitting snooker aficionados instead.

The billiards room was huge. Long, shaded lights hung from the ceiling, one over each table, while the walls gleamed dully, made of dark-brown, polished wood. The three snooker tables were full size, green baize over slate, the surface smooth and flawless. At the end of the room was a fireplace with a blazing fire. And underneath the windows were green-leather benches in case anyone wanted to sit down and watch.

We felt like we'd stepped into a prestige gentlemen's club. Sure enough, in time-honoured St James tradition, an attendant in an immaculate white tunic and sarong strode up to greet us. He told us his name was Harry and he led us to the furthest antique table. The balls had already been set up, the colours in position and the reds arranged in one perfect equilateral triangle. Harry smiled at us, handed us each a cue, then politely asked if I wanted to borrow a sarong. In my haste to get started I'd overlooked the rule about not wearing shorts.

It took only a couple of minutes to return to our room and for me to change into long trousers. I donned a long-sleeved shirt, socks and proper shoes too – just in case.

Harry hadn't seemed to have any problem with what Kate was wearing: a top, slacks and jandals.

We chalked our cues and walked around the table, taking our lie of the baize. It was ages since I'd last played, and I'd forgotten how big snooker tables are. I'd be lucky if I potted a few reds. No chance of putting many colours down or finishing a frame.

Kate took the first break, hitting the cue ball with force and dispersing the reds across the table. Then I surprised myself, putting a red down, followed by the black.

"Eight points?" Kate moved the brass marker on the scoreboard.

"Yeah." I knew it was a flash in the pan, a stroke of beginner's luck, and I was right.

After that I struggled to put anything down, red, brown or black. Kate, on the other hand, steadily knocked in reds, then colours, her score building. From the sidelines Harry watched us, saying little, other than the odd piece of advice for Kate and a congratulatory nod of his head when she potted.

It was a rout. Kate won ball after ball, while all I managed were misses, swerves and fouls. Once we'd finished – Kate the triumphant winner – Harry came up, shook Kate's hand and gave me a piece of paper. It wasn't a certificate but a tab for two hundred rupees, the small fee for table hire. Apparently snooker wasn't included in the room rate; we had to pay extra. Harry beamed as we quizzed him and he assured us he could add the amount to our room bill. He was a congenial man and, by all accounts, an excellent snooker player. He told us how the tables were very old, made of single slates, and similarly the balls were of ivory.

Suitably defeated, I followed my champion wife to the other areas of the hotel. The elegant indoor swimming pool, where a man and a woman in identical green bathing caps swam sedately up and down. Outside to the gardens – an ornamental fountain, tables and chairs around a teardrop lawn, and privet hedges sheared into the shapes of birds, deer and possibly a dinosaur or two. Then to a shop selling packets of leaf tea, postcards and other souvenirs. The lady shop assistant laughed when she heard about Kate's big win. Finally we wandered randomly along corridors that led nowhere, and through empty, chair-stacked halls that at other times would be used for conferences. Around us, fellow tourists, wide-eyed in shorts and sarongs, did the same. We were commoners imitating royals, ordinary people pretending to be famous.

The true stars here were the staff who, with their indefatigable smiles, fine uniforms and deferential service, kept the hotel functioning. Rather than the building or its trappings, they were the ones who truly made this place grand.

Exhausted, we retired to our room. There at least we wouldn't suffer delusions. We could be us once again.

THIRTY-SIX

Tea Factory Visit - Take Two

After the inertness of our last tea factory visit, we were both eager to see a real live working factory where people pulled levers on consoles, machines roared, and green fresh leaves were visibly processed into something resembling tea in a packet. There were dozens of tea factories around, many of them opening their doors to visitors. The Dambatenne Tea Factory near Haputale, for example, the lights of which we'd already glimpsed on the way to Lipton's Seat to watch the sunrise. Dambatenne had been established by Sir Thomas Lipton in 1890 as he created his own end-to-end supply chain, growing tea on his estate in Sri Lanka to process and ship to all his shops in Britain.

Unfortunately we'd had to skip Dambatenne because we had a train to catch. Anyway Samid had suggested a different tea factory: the Damro, otherwise known as Labookellie Tea Factory, on the road to Kandy. We were driving that way, plus it was situated in the middle of beautiful tea country.

So far, so good. Then I read our guidebooks. Neither

gushed good things about Labookellie. One described the tours as being too brief, while the other used words such as quick, rushed and hurried. I began to doubt Samid's judgment – even wonder if he had an ulterior motive. Another tea factory lay a few kilometres further on, the Blue Field Tea Factory nearer to Kandy. In fact there were tea factories everywhere. If we had the time and the will we could turn this into a tea factory crawl. A pot of broken orange pekoe here, a pot of oolong there. Such a pity Jerry, Nelson and Frank weren't still with us. I imagined the three of them sampling the various brews to loud harrumphs and smackings of their lips, a heated discussion about aromas and tastes, then entering marks on a quiz sheet.

"Red tea wins hands down," said Jerry, after slurping from the saucer.

"Fannings! They've the best flavour." Frank as honest as a day.

Then Nelson smirking and saying nothing. He spoke with his shirt, no longer an elephant but a motif: "Tea is at its strongest when it's in hot water."

The three funny men weren't with us, though. One was back in Blighty and the other two somewhere in-between. And rather than mess up Samid's recommendation, we ignored the guidebooks and went to Labookellie. To my surprise the factory was welcoming, informative and leisurely.

It was a big place. In conspicuous white letters, "Damro Tea" was signed on the green hillside. Opposite this a serious-looking, four-storey building stood by the road. As we walked into its foyer a slim lady greeted us, her smile hinting at inner mischievousness. She held no green pinafores for us to wear. Nor did she recite any warnings about taking photos. In a clear, easily understandable voice she said hello and told us her name was Shiroma. We tried repeating it and she laughed. No doubt we were pronouncing one, two, possibly three syllables wrong.

Taking command, she waved us outside. At a small tea bush she plucked a top bud and its two adjacent leaves – known as a flush – and held the foliage up like a charm.

"These are the leaves we use to make tea," she said in a well-practised manner. "The outer two for white tea, the inner bud for golden tea, and all three for green tea, all *unfermented*!"

Then as if we hadn't understood, our faces blank, she said exactly the same thing again in a louder voice. "The outer two for white tea, the inner bud for golden tea, and all three for green tea, all *unfermented*!"

We repeated "unfermented" several times as if it was an incantation.

Eyes twinkling, lips rising at the ends, she explained how black tea – most of the tea we drink – is made from all three leaves after a process of withering, rolling, fermentation and firing. Today the factory was manufacturing black tea, so she would show us how first-hand.

We followed her up some steps and straight into the withering room. As at the Pedro factory, several long metal troughs stretched out. The ones here, however, weren't empty but were brimming with green-brown leaves as they dried out or withered. Shiroma dipped in her hand to demonstrate. The layer of brittle leaves was several centimetres deep. "They have to be turned every few hours," she said, waggling her fingers. "It can take days to wither them completely."

Next she led us to a viewing gallery. From behind a large Perspex screen we saw the next stages of the process: the leaves being rolled to wring out their juices, then left to oxidise – or *ferment* – during which the tea's enzymes combined with oxygen. Finally the leaves were fired – or heated – to stop the oxidation, then cut and sorted.

Below us, plenty was happening on the factory floor. One lady in green overalls adjusted a machine that shook or rolled the leaves like a tumble drier. This process bruised and tore the leaves to aid natural fermentation. On the opposite side, a couple of men worked other machines: one that heated the leaves to stop oxidation; another that cut the leaves; and at the end, one that sorted the tea into grades and removed any loose stems.

This was so different from the previous tea factory. Here all the machines were in use. There was an air of purpose, of something being made.

Shiroma explained how they only produced one type of tea at a time, for instance a specific run of black tea one day, green another, then white or oolong the day after. The sequence of processes for each type of tea varied. White tea was simply plucked and withered; there was no fermentation. This makes white the most delicate tea. Green was plucked, withered and rolled, then fired without oxidation. This gave green tea its distinctive grassy colour and taste. Oolong was the most time-consuming tea to make, with rolling and oxidising repeated several times under heat, producing a tea that was partially fermented. Oolong is midway between black tea and green tea, and has the most complex flavour of all.

Shiroma led us into a large warehouse where the final products were packed into paper sacks like cement bags. These would then be shipped to Colombo for auctioneers to sell on to brokers. Labookellie Factory was highly mechanised, a large-scale operation. It was surrounded by acres of plantations and produced high tonnages of tea.

We followed a line of white cups out of the factory. Each cup contained a particular variety of black tea: for instance, broken orange pekoe which consists of larger pieces of leaf and produces a light orange tea; or flowery broken orange pekoe, a coarser broken tea with more tips; or broken orange pekoe fannings, the smallest pieces of leaf left after the higher grades have been broken down; and finally dust – the remaining black tea powder that is used in so many blended tea brands.

Now thirsty, we raced into the tearoom. Samid was waiting for us at a table, looking very relaxed. We'd already agreed with him that once he'd dropped us off at our hotel in Kandy – the Twee Sri again – he could take the night off and go visit his family in Negombo. There was an important church service that evening he wanted to attend with them. It was no trouble for us; we'd only be strolling around the centre of Kandy.

As we joined Samid, a waiter came over to take our orders. What type of tea did we want to drink? And more importantly – for Kate anyway – what type of cake? There was a choice of two: chocolate or teacake.

We chose a plain pekoe to drink. Samid, clearly a connoisseur of these things, insisted we also eat teacake. The waiter returned with a large teapot, three cups, and three plates of cake. The tea was orange and delicious – maybe not the finest in our travels, yet certainly not the worst. The cake, however, tasted of nothing much and was dry. Perhaps that was the point. It was a counterbalance to the tea rather than a distraction. Samid seemed to enjoy it though, picking off big pieces with his fingers and gobbling them down. Kate too, her plate suddenly empty.

"You like the cake?" His own cake finished, Samid watched me.

"It's not bad."

"The tea here is the best, better than other factories." He smiled and brushed crumbs off his chin. Had he suspected my earlier doubts about Labookellie? That I'd thought of suggesting the Blue Field Tea Factory instead? I could never tell with Samid. He was a master of courtesy, of influencing things without ever contradicting us.

We found Shiroma to say goodbye and thank her. We were both impressed by the tour – I for the insight gained and Kate for its overall clarity. Shiroma couldn't have escorted the writers of our guidebooks, otherwise their comments would have been kinder. For us everything had been perfect. We'd fulfilled one of our objectives for coming to Sri Lanka – we'd seen a working tea factory in action and now had a good understanding of how tea is made.

And I had a new appreciation for all the work needed to prepare the tea that my father had loved. So many *many* steps before he even began *his* process of warming the pot with hot water, refilling it, stirring in two spoonfuls of loose leaves, then letting it brew. Tea, like cricket, is a game of patience. It has lots of rules, takes several stages/days to complete, and does not always attain a definitive conclusion. Who is to judge when one pot is finished and a fresh to be brewed? How many cups – runs/overs – are enough?

Our time in Sri Lanka was almost at an end as well. We had two days left and we'd hardly skimmed the surface of this complex, rich country with the tiniest teaspoon. Like cricket and tea, we needed a replay – we needed a refill.

THIRTY-SEVEN

Back to Kandy

Kandy was our favourite city, an amalgamation of Kate and Andy. It's a hot city – a busy city. Yet like Wellington where we live, it's a city where sky, water and forest juxtapose, a frenzied tapestry of people and loose ends. Once again, as we sat in the warm, dusk heat of our hotel balcony, flocks of white/black birds swooped down onto the lake while crows cawed in trees and unseen traffic hummed.

Overall, five of our twenty-eight days would be spent in Kandy, more than anywhere else. I liked the city's anonymity, how it wrapped its limbs around green hills, embracing inhabitants and visitors alike. I liked its nonlinear messiness too – how its roads converged, condensed, then wound away.

After dark the city twinkled, the stars of the sky reflected in its lake. The red/green disco lights of a big hotel pulsed opposite and, further down the valley like a second moon, shone a huge white Buddha statue. Later, as I lay in our eyrie room, I dreamt of an earlier Kandy, the capital of Sri Lanka's unconquerable third kingdom. Not the city we saw now – the steep valleys, the tiny muddy lake, the white boxy houses sleeping in forest – but a more rural city where time circled, beginning to end, king after king, in a kind of perpetuity unto itself. In one version the sun smiles and life is kind, prosperous and happy. In another, it is pitch-black night, filled with the smoke of war. Perhaps it is a vision or merely the feng shui of our room, perched so precariously on the edge of everything, looking down on trees, birds, the fish in the lake, and all the tiny buildings, so near and yet so far.

WE HAD CHECKED back into the Twee Sri after a swift, slightly tense drive from the Damro Tea Factory. For Samid to be able to return to Negombo, we had to arrive in time for his bus. He didn't want to take the car; he'd park it at our hotel. Presumably it was cheaper that way, or less stressful, maybe faster. He'd come back tomorrow on the bus again, ready for our last day's sightseeing before we too hastened to Negombo for our flight home.

At the hotel reception I asked for our old room, remembering its transcendental qualities. Sadly, it wasn't available. Someone else had taken it. The receptionist offered us a better room – at least she said it was better. It was even higher up, a soaring nest on the fifth floor.

"It has a bath in the bathroom!" She seemed to think this was something all Westerners craved.

"What about the view?" I was worried we'd see only clouds.

"The view is better too."

In the end I accepted her word. Not that we had much choice. When we reached the room, the layout was identical to the old one – the bed in the same position, the same style of sofa and coffee table. Plus there was the ballroom-sized bathroom with a rickety-looking bath. Neither of us intended to use it. We'd stick to the shower.

Unlike our last time in Kandy, we weren't part of a tour group. No alarm call in the morning, no big communal table at breakfast, no packed itinerary. We could get up when we felt like it and go anywhere we liked. Although being back in the same hotel did feel a little odd without the others. No Nelson to spring out of a lift with a wry grin, no Jerry with his astute remarks, and no Frank to nod and laugh.

We had no Samid either. We were truly on our own, able to go as fast or as slow as we wanted. And after a respectable amount of time doing nothing in the room we strolled into town – not for its temples, gems or even elephants, but for some good, old-fashioned pastry shopping.

"We'll go to Devon, shall we?" Kate named our favourite bakery.

"Sure." I wasn't going to object.

Devon was packed with local women eyeing up the goodies inside the long glass cabinet. So many delicious-looking cakes and pastries that our eyes enlarged. Kate took charge of buying the sweet stuff while I selected savoury: four vegetable samosas, two egg rotis, and one sausage roll. We emerged with several stuffed paper bags, plus one gigantic cardboard box. Enough to feed an army in our room that night – though not of macaques if we were to believe the red warning sign on the balcony door, "Do not feed the monkeys."

I headed for the bottle shop next, hidden like a speakeasy at the back of the supermarket. The counters were made of concrete and the windows were iron bars. It was the sort of place where you pulled your hoodie up, thrust your hands in your pockets, and came out po-faced with a clinking brown paper bag.

Then we tried our luck in the modern shopping mall, three floors of Western retail bliss. Except the shops swiftly became mundane – the same kinds of clothes shops we'd find back home. On the top floor was a Burger King, the first we'd seen anywhere in Sri Lanka. And after three and a half weeks of beef abstinence I gobbled down a Texas Burger, though the patty was less like the kind of patty I was used to and more like jerky.

The main street remained busy as we waded single file through a turmoil of people. At the lake the pavement widened and we were able to walk side by side, admiring the birds and the tiny flowered islet in the middle.

"You know we've got the keys to Samid's car in the room safe?" Kate grinned in a way I'd learned to fear. "If we get bored tonight we could always go for a ride."

I shook my head. "I thought it was a tuk-tuk you wanted to drive, not a Toyota Premio?"

"Anything will do." Her grin broadened. "Anyway, who said I was driving?"

Back in our room, I deliberately kept the safe closed. No doubt Kate knew the code though – I'd used it in front of her often enough. Trying to keep her occupied, I suggested we eat the cakes out on the balcony as we watched the sun go down. Hopefully she was joking about the car but if not, surely she wouldn't want to drive it in the dark?

THE NEXT DAY SAMID – always a consistent and reliable time-keeper – returned promptly at noon. He'd had to set off from Negombo at seven and take two buses, connecting at the interchange town of Kurunegala. This was the town where we'd had our very first break on day one of the tour, and also the home of several rocky outcrops shaped like animals – including an elephant after which Kurunegala was named. Samid seemed happier than yesterday, his expression less tense and his eyes brighter. Seeing his family again, even for only a few hours, had been good for him – and hopefully for us too.

We had to do something new today. We couldn't lounge around the hotel when this would be our last full day. Kate wanted to visit the Bahiravakanda Buddha that gazed over the city from its hilltop setting – the same illuminated Buddha we could see at night. I wanted to go to the Commonwealth War Cemetery where many Allied soldiers were buried.

Samid drove us to the giant Buddha statue first. It was located off a steep street to the west of Kandy, full of parked buses and cars. The man at the ticket office smiled as we paid for our entrance and asked where we came from.

"New Zealand," I said. "You know, the home of the All Blacks, the Blackcaps and Kane Williamson."

"Ahh, yes. Kane Williamson." His nod implied he knew the captain of the Blackcaps personally. Then, as if to catch me out, he recited the names of other New Zealand cricket players: Martin Guptill, Tom Latham and Trent Boult.

Now it was my turn to nod sagely. I wasn't a cricket buff. I truly had no idea.

Fortunately Kate came to my rescue. "And don't forget Karunaratne, Malinga and Gunathilaka," she said, naming players on the Sri Lankan team.

"Aah, yes. Dimuth Karunaratne!" His smile grew broader as he counted out *sīya, desīya, tusīya, harasīya* rupees in change

There was an important lesson here. It pays to learn

28 DAYS IN SRI LANKA

elementary numbers in the local language. And even more vital, the names of a few well-known sports people.

A flight of steps led upwards to the statue, but before climbing a single one of them I stopped to look at the moonstone at the bottom, its semi-circular bands of elephant, lion, horse and bull carved in the Anuradhapura way. A fifth creature lay half-on, half-off the moonstone. A recumbent, living dog. As I gazed at the creature, wondering if it realised what sacred company it was keeping, I felt the sun on my head. It was a hot, fine day. Quickly I put on my hat. Only for Kate to nudge me a second later and tell me to take it off, and my jandals too. The Buddha statue was next to the Sri Maha Bodhi temple, and that old rule Oshan had kept reminding us of – no hats, no shoes – came into play.

We climbed the steps, their surfaces hot against our soles. A bright courtyard dazzled at the top, in the lap of the giant Buddha. Sunglasses weren't forbidden, so pulling them on, I admired the view. The city of Kandy spread out hazily, a vast, pixelating map: tiny buses and trucks circling the puddle of the lake; a squadron of mosquito-sized tuk-tuks stalled alongside the matchbox clock-tower; cubular hotels and office blocks stacked along the valley sides; and the red arms of the old Bogambara high-security prison encompassing the grey-and-brown roofs of the central market.

I let my eyes feast. So much history. So much evolving structure. The frieze-frame of a city in an eyeball of time. I spied the green expanse of Udawatta Kele Sanctuary, and then the barrel end of the lake. Somewhere in-between the two of them lay our hotel, from where I'd gazed up at this statue. Now I stared back down, unable to pinpoint our balcony.

Turning, I looked up at the Buddha statue above me – so

bright, white and vertiginous against the blue of the sky. A switchback staircase was attached like a fire-escape to one side. I beckoned Kate over and, still barefooted, we climbed around and around. At each level we stopped to enter the statue and explore small rooms inside. In one we found a tableau of Buddha, seated and serene, as he overcame the invasion of Mara's squirming, bug-eyed army. In another was a glowing ceiling of pink, purple and yellow lotus flowers.

We didn't climb to the very top, yet we went far enough. Sufficiently high to appreciate its height – twenty-seven metres – and realise what an important icon it is for the city. The statue was only commissioned after years of fundraising and petitioning by certain monks in the temple next door. It was completed quite recently, only in 1993, and depicts Buddha in the classic meditation or *dhyana mudra* pose.

The man at the ticket office stretched arm over shoulder as we left, a mock fast-spinner that followed us out to the road. There was no sign of Samid or his car, and for a moment I wondered if he'd left us and gone back to Negombo. Then, as we stood in the intense sunshine, he drove down the road, smiling and waving.

"I was parked further up," he said, the ends of his moustache going up and down. "Too hot down here."

We jumped in, and he handed us each a small bottle of water. He seemed to have an inexhaustible supply of them – far more than the icebox on the back seat could ever accommodate.

"Cemetery next?" His eyebrows rose.

"Yes, please." Gratefully, I drank from the bottle.

The Commonwealth War Cemetery reposed like a distinguished war veteran reflecting on the comrades-in-arms he'd lost. The verdant lawn was as smooth as a well-brushed tunic, with red shrubs as shiny as medals. White headstones formed orderly lines, each one identical save for its name.

The head gardener came over to say hello. He told us he'd looked after the cemetery for twenty years and pointed out how the different nationalities and religions were buried in sections: Muslims in one, Sri Lankans in another, and the British in a third. There were two hundred and three graves all together, all but three of them casualties from World War II. Many had been killed in the Japanese attacks on the ports of Colombo and Trincomalee in 1942. Others had died during training in the jungle as troops prepared for active service in Burma. The average age had been exceptionally low. One soldier had died at only eighteen.

Kate was happy to chat with the gardener while I roamed in aimless circles, reading individuals' surnames, watching where I put my feet and soaking up the cemetery's sunlit stillness. This was a place where it seemed natural to reflect, to ponder on these men I'd never met, and how each one of them had ended up here. The quiet was deadening and deceptive. This was a peace born out of battle, a field covering bloodshed. Yet a place that would stay with me, for the slain men who lay here and the living man who tended them.

AT THE CENTRAL Market we met Mr Pressure Salesman, closely followed by Mr Hyper Inflation. Ever since our first foray here while on the tour I'd wanted to buy a handmade, embroidered batik of an elephant. They came in lurid colours – scarlet, mauve, turquoise and pink – with silver sequins sewn on as eyes and gold lamé fabric as ears. Some were as psychedelic as the amazing murals painted on the subway walls.

At the first textile stall a plump, balding man hauled us in like a pair of hoodwinked schoolchildren.

"You want a shirt?" He dangled a cheap, printed shirt from a hanger. "I'll give you a discount. How much do you want to pay?"

Straightaway I didn't like him. Or the way he glared like we were dollars on legs, his beady eyes scouring the creased shirt I was wearing and probably the bulge of the wallet in my pocket too. I wondered if Samid would say something – a word of advice – but he stayed behind us, his lips closed.

"Please can we look around?" I stared back at the man and he picked up more shirts, waving them in my face. Had there not been several elephant batiks hanging in a corner I would have shaken my head and walked out.

I went in the direction of the batiks, trying to seem uninterested. Salesmen like him were the same the world over. Once he realised I wanted something he'd raise the price and never budge.

Yet Mr Pressure Salesman was sharp. He could read the mind of a tourist from the merest tic on their face. Clicking his fingers, he beckoned over an assistant who unfolded several batiks. One in fire-engine red that stood out prominently. Another in green that was more subtle. I avoided looking at them and picked up a pale-blue scarf instead. It was similar to one Kate had bought in the market last time, though from a different stall.

"That would look nice on Madam." He snatched the scarf from me and held it like bait in front of Kate. "If you buy two I can give you a discount."

"I've already got two." Kate laughed. "I don't need any more."

He didn't know what to say to that, his eyes darting up, then down. I jumped in quickly and asked his assistant the price of the green batik.

"Nineteen thousand rupees!" shouted Mr Pressure Salesman, pushing his assistant aside.

"Nineteen thousand?" I nearly had a heart attack. This was way, way more than the initial seven and a half thousand a man in another shop had asked for a similar batik last time we'd visited the market.

"Make me an offer." He grinned smugly as if he recognised a fool with money when he saw one.

I shook my head and began to walk out. I wasn't going to be drawn, not when he'd started at a price twice the height of Everest. No matter how well I bartered, or badly, his final price would still be steep – and well above seven and a half thousand.

He followed me, grabbing several more shirts on the way. "These then? Ten thousand for three?" That was thirty dollars a shirt, more than I'd pay for a better shirt at home. He was determined to sell me something. I sped up, accelerating onto the walkway outside.

Still he pursued, gesticulating loudly. "Some tablemats, then? An elephant shopping bag? Come back and make me an offer."

In desperation I ran along one side of the quadrangle that formed the upper market and, panting, dodged into another textile stall. Surely he wouldn't enter here – into the lair of one of his competitors?

He didn't. But Kate followed me in, then Samid. And as we all looked at one another, then at the batiks surrounding us, I realised it was a shop we'd visited on our first time in the market – the same one where Kate had bought her two scarves. On the wall was an elephant batik I'd admired then, still for sale. I shouldn't have bothered with that other place but come straight here.

A different man from the one who'd served us last time stood behind the counter. His glasses and lips formed rigid straight lines as he explained to another couple in front of us how excursions on Kandy Lake were a waste of money.

"The boatmen are greedy." His eyes were squares too. "Conmen who charge more than they should."

As the couple left, he spotted me and raised his eyebrows.

"How much are the batiks, please?" I waved my hand around, trying not to single a particular one out, yet expecting a similar price to last time – around seven and a half thousand rupees.

"Which one?" He didn't smile.

"That one?" I pointed at the elephant batik behind him.

"Twelve and a half thousand," he said without compunction.

"Twelve and a half? Are you sure?"

"Twelve and a half."

"You know, we came in here two weeks ago and it was only seven and a half then."

"Ha! Anyone could say that. And prices go up."

"By sixty percent? In two weeks?" I was gobsmacked.

Then Kate spotted the man who *had* served us last time. Finding a scarf similar to one she'd bought, she held it up adamantly. "You remember me, don't you?" she said to him in a loud voice. "How I told you about Kane Williamson from New Zealand and Trevor Chappell from Australia? How you sold me two of these scarves and told my husband the batik was seven and a half thousand?"

The man – shop assistant, relative of the owner, whoever he was – nodded sheepishly.

"Well, Kiwis don't like people who bowl underarm!" In full swing, Kate turned to the first man, Mr Hyper Inflation. "Now you tell us it's gone up to twelve and a half? TWELVE AND A HALF! It's not those boatmen who are conmen. It's YOU!"

The man looked angry, his face reddening. He reached up and shook his don't-give-a-damn glasses as though they were to blame. "How much will you pay?" he said, his voice hardly contrite.

"Seven thousand." My offer was a token five hundred less than the asking price two weeks ago. It wasn't that I wanted to beat him down to an absolute minimum, for I recognised the hard work that had gone into making the batik, plus he had overheads as well. Yet I didn't want to be ripped off blatantly, and by asking one price one week, almost doubling it the next, then boasting he was honest, he seemed like he was taking us all for fools.

Quickly I counted out seven thousand notes and set them on the counter while his assistant folded the batik and slid it into a bag. I felt quite awkward about how the bargaining had gone, and by the scowl on his face Mr Hyper Inflation didn't look pleased either. Had he been fairer, less contemptuous of his customers, I might have bought two batiks, possibly three.

Eager to leave, I grabbed the bag, muttered goodbye, and left. Kate followed, then Samid too, as quiet as he'd ever been.

THIRTY-EIGHT

John Key and the Cobra

It was our last morning in Kandy – our last day in Sri Lanka. Every holiday comes to an end, and so too had our time here. Samid would drive us to the international airport at Negombo, then very early the next morning – at a bleary-eyed quarter to one – our plane home would accelerate down the runway with us sitting in seats forty-two A and B.

We ate a quiet breakfast, then packed, repacked, and finally dragged our cases down in the lift. In the lobby we met Samid. Before driving to Negombo he'd take us to Kandy Hospital, and then Peradeniya Royal Botanical Gardens. A fortunate order of proceedings, for had it been the other way around then I might have been in Kandy longer than I'd expected...

Kate wanted to visit the hospital on behalf of her grandfather. He'd recovered there after his injuries during World War II. As we drew up to the main gate of the General Hospital, however, all the buildings appeared to be relatively modern. None of them looked seventy-six years old.

A security guard in a light-blue shirt and bright-red tie came over. He smiled and asked what we wanted.

"My grandfather was a patient here in 1943." Kate held up her phone, displaying an article about soldiers in Kandy during the war. "We wondered if we could see his ward?"

The guard pointed at a grassy slope leading up to the multi-storey car park. "The old hospital used to be there. But I don't think any soldiers are up there now."

The hospital had been redeveloped. Hardly a surprise, really.

Our next hiccup was that photos weren't allowed, though the kindly guard permitted one token snap. Swiftly, Kate aimed her phone at the General Hospital sign over the entrance and clicked. Something to show her family that we'd paid our respects. Then, on the way out, Samid took a sly photo of the grassy slope that once had been a temporary home to all those New Zealand veterans.

Hospital ticked off, we continued south to Peradeniya. The highway was a crush of traffic – four lanes of vehicles hemmed in by ever-careering tuk-tuks. Rather than waste an hour trying to reach the botanical gardens entrance, Samid let us out on the opposite side. Like rabbits, we dashed over between slow-moving cars.

Last time at the gardens we hadn't had to buy tickets because admission had been included in the price of the tour. We found out now that there were two prices – a pricy one for overseas tourists and a cheaper option for Sri Lankan nationals.

We were becoming garden specialists in our own green ways. Kate wanted to see the orchids again. And I was looking forward to wandering in the wide green spaces under bright blue skies.

I'd dithered earlier about returning – a second visit might

disappoint after the gloss of the first. Yet as we strolled past the spice garden, dived into glasshouses full of orchids and cacti, dipped beneath a trellis of dark-green, trailing plants, the gardens didn't disappoint. They spread out with tranquillity. They transcended space and time.

Then – solitude pierced – we encountered a knot of Asian ladies, all busily chattering and photographing one another at the end of Palm Avenue.

"My foot hurts." Kate stopped to adjust her jandals.

"What's up with it?" I was impatient. I wanted to explore. We'd told Samid we'd be only an hour.

"I don't know. It's sore."

The Asian ladies flowed around us, cutting off all routes of escape. We waited until they'd passed, then agreed Kate would walk slowly back to the entrance while I – one fast foot in front of the other – whizzed around the longer way.

Scooting across the diameter of the Great Lawn, keeping a lookout for any sticks that might not be sticks and avoiding patches of longer grass, I made my way further into the gardens. I wanted to revisit the Great Circle where seventy-eight dignitaries had planted seventy-eight trees. I wanted to see the lake again too, perhaps now full of water.

In this methodical way I reached the Great Circle where a sign listed all the trees – plus who'd planted them and when. The first had been by Edward VII in 1875 and the seventy-fourth – *surprise, surprise* – by the Right Honourable John Key, Prime Minister of New Zealand, in 2016. As luck would have it, John Key's tree was nearby. Scrambling back through the grass, up a slope, left a bit, then right, I found his sapling – a *Mangifera zeylanica* that seemed to be growing quite well.

I felt like a proud Kiwi, spotting something that the real

Kiwi, Kate, had missed last time. Although she wasn't much of a tree person, just as John Key's tree, compared to all the older, mightier behemoths, wasn't really much of a tree.

As I framed the tree on the screen of my phone I noticed the time. In all the excitement I'd overlooked that only ten minutes remained before we were due to meet Samid. Hotfooting back onto the path, then along Cook's Pine Avenue, I hurried past the bamboo grove towards the main entrance. It wouldn't do to be late. Kate would be displeased. And Samid was a stickler for punctuality. We had a four-hour drive to Negombo; I'd never hear the last of it.

Rounding the bamboo grove and accelerating down the final tarmac path, I saw Kate ahead. She was smiling and waving, her blue shirt prominent against green trees. She seemed to be happy, her foot recovered. Perhaps I wasn't late either, a minute or two left. Speeding up some more, I stamped the last few yards.

Then slowed, curious, as a rustling sound came from below me. Looking down, I glimpsed a six-foot-long black stick zigzagging its way past. It was only there for a moment, a helix of motion hardly touching the ground. Too quick to evade, to react, to panic or scream. Yet it was close – *too bloody close* – barely inches from my sandaled feet. Then as I looked again it had gone, vanished into bush. Waves of emotion swept over me: excitement at finally seeing a snake, then relief, gratitude even, at having avoided standing on it – or worse, being bitten. I had no idea what species it was – a rough-sided snake, a rat snake, a cobra – but thankfully it had had the good sense to go one way while I went the other.

Afterwards Kate told me it had provoked warnings and screams around the entrance as it shot from one bed of plants to another. When I described it to Samid he nodded matter-of-factly as if snakes were routine and said it might have been a cobra.

THIRTY-NINE

The Man in the Wedding Photo

On a shelf in Samid's kitchen, alongside jars of spices and long, spiky cooking utensils, sat evidence of the time when he wore his hair long. A framed portrait from his wedding day, it showed him with Jimi Hendrix hair and his wife glorious in a pretty white dress. As we scrutinised the picture, the shorter-haired, more rugged Samid of today lifted the photograph up and laughed as if to express how things had changed. He couldn't pretend he wasn't older – in fact he looked nothing like the man in the wedding photo at all. He was thinner, both his body and his hair. Little creases had crept underneath his eyes and he wasn't so serious but smiled more.

"How long ago was this taken?" I asked, noting the photo was in black and white.

"Too long ago. We were very young."

Of course I tried to work out how old he'd been – indeed how old he was now. Perhaps younger than the photo implied, for his three sons were all still in their twenties.

Earlier he'd introduced us to his wife and two younger

sons. Then to his youngest son's wife who'd shown us *her* wedding video – a singing, dancing pre-nuptial extravaganza as different from Samid's photo as turmeric is from salt. To the music of a popular crooner, she and Samid's son had smiled at each other, line-danced, then boogied South American in front of a classy, landmark hotel in central Colombo. It was like the video we'd seen being filmed in Galle. Apparently this style was now the vogue for all premier Sri Lankan weddings, something the young couple could replay over and over again.

After the long drive from Kandy we'd arrived in Negombo around four. Samid had kindly invited us to his home for dinner – a last chance to relax before heading to the airport in five hours' time.

His house was in the Catholic part of Negombo, close to his church. It was an affluent-looking suburb, the roads neatly laid out and the houses modern and well-spaced. He pointed at his church as we drove past and told us how it had seated thousands of worshippers at mass on Christmas Eve. His religion was important to him – and to his family as well.

A few minutes later we reached his house. It was far larger than I'd imagined, though since this was the first Sri Lankan home we'd visited I hadn't been quite sure what to expect. He stopped the car to open two metal gates, then drove into a pleasant, paved courtyard. We climbed out, now a little less certain of our roles. We were no longer paying clients but house guests, with all the intricacies of etiquette that entailed. We needn't have worried though. He was the perfect host. He led us into a large, airy lounge full of heavy wooden furniture and sat us down on a sofa in the corner.

"The bathroom is upstairs, if you want a shower?" He

pointed up an open staircase that led to a mezzanine with three doors.

"Thank you, but I think we're okay." A shower would cool us down, especially as it was hotter here than it had been in Kandy. But despite his hospitality, as well as a very clean modern bathroom, both of us felt a little awkward taking advantage of his family facilities.

Samid was noticeably more relaxed now he was at home. "First we will have drinks," he said, smiling. "Then dinner."

He offered us glasses of red wine from the bottle I'd given him – the same bottle I'd bought a week ago in Galle and never opened. Later, Samid told us with a grin, once he'd dropped us at the airport and returned home, he'd drink some of the rum from the other bottle I'd given him. Despite what I might have thought, he enjoyed a wee tot.

I knocked back my wine, and he promptly refilled my glass. I didn't want to drink too much – besides, it was his wine now, and after driving us for a week he deserved the bottle to himself.

His wife brought out cake, then a plate of savouries. His middle and youngest sons shook our hands and his daughter-in-law played her wedding video. Then it was time for dinner, and Samid led us into the kitchen where his wife had prepared a feast. A big bowl of rice and smaller bowls of fish balls, prawns, chicken, pork, potatoes, dhal and poppadums – way *way* more than we could eat. We'd stopped for a lunch of samosas and *kiribath* rice cakes at a café on the Kandy-Negombo road, and our stomachs were still full. Nevertheless we tried a spoonful of everything, wanting to be polite. The food was delicious, and had we not had the deadline of leaving for the airport I would have eaten more.

Samid and his wife didn't join us but stood on one side of the table watching.

"When will you eat?" asked Kate.

"Oh, later." Samid grinned again, no doubt looking forward to his wife's good cooking.

We finished dinner, and it was time to say goodbye. First to Samid's friendly family: his wife, his two sons who lived in the house and his daughter-in-law. Then half an hour later to Samid, shaking hands, hugging and patting shoulders after he'd dropped us outside departures. We'd known him for just over a week, yet it felt longer, almost as if he'd been on our original tour – another comrade alongside Nelson, Jerry and Frank.

Samid had certainly looked after us, always punctual, reliable, trustworthy and – in a land of runaway buses and kamikaze tuk-tuks – a safe driver. Along the way he'd shown us many interesting things, from simple sights such as nascent paddy fields to beautiful viewpoints few other people knew about. He'd told us stories of his country, from elephants that were bred for temple duties to monkeys that rode on trains and cobras that disguised themselves as sticks. He'd arranged train tickets, an elephant safari, endless bottles of water, and those two appetising pieces of Christmas cake. A couple of times he'd manhandled my suitcase too, no mean feat.

Hopefully one day we'll see him again, when we – *as we must* – return to Sri Lanka.

FORTY

The Last Buffet

Dinner at Samid's would be our last meal in Sri Lanka, carefully and lovingly prepared by his wife. We'd enjoyed the medley of tasty dishes, yet I was looking forward to some plainer Kiwi fare when we reached home. Robert Harris instant coffee in place of the strange brew that dripped from hotel cafetières. Marmite on toast for breakfast instead of rice and dhal, and bacon and eggs that tasted like bacon and eggs rather than the spicy white omelettes we'd sometimes been served at the hotels.

If there was one aspect of Sri Lankan cuisine of which we'd had a stomachful, then it was buffets. One for breakfast and another for dinner. In the beginning they'd seemed wonderful and offered clear advantages over à la carte. We could choose what we wanted, when we wanted and how much. If we were hungry afterwards, we could go up and fetch more. What was there to dislike about that?

Nothing.

Yet as each buffet merged into the next, then the one

after that, we started to become a little bloated. We still kept eating – try taking away our knives and forks – yet secretly longed for something simpler: egg on toast, a cheese sandwich, even a bag of greasy chips. The buffets were always varied and plentiful, yet sometimes the components didn't fit together. In what other circumstances would you serve spaghetti bolognese with battered fish fillets, or stir-fried eggplant with hard-boiled eggs?

We couldn't complain though. We hadn't starved. We'd eaten very well. Nor had we gone down with the lurgy. Far from it – after four weeks my tummy was bulging and I needed to diet. So it would be good to return to our own kitchen – all those green salads and trim milk in the fridge.

At the airport security was tight. Even before the terminal building Samid had to stop the car at a checkpoint where the guard wanted to see our passports and itinerary, and before we could enter the departures lounge we once again had to show our documents. Inside, a huge X-ray machine hummed. We fed our bags wholesale into its maw and submitted ourselves through scanners. Then, after a short arcade of shops and money exchanges, we came to another row of x-ray machines and guards.

I realised we were going to be checked several times before coming anywhere near our plane. Without a doubt, these enhanced and highly visible security measures were a response to the tragic Easter Sunday bombings.

We passed through the second level of checks and into the departure lounge proper. Here, people queued at airline check-in desks while others, newly bereft of their hold luggage, marched to Emigration. We couldn't do the same. Our flight didn't leave for another three and three-quarter hours so our check-in desk wasn't open. Instead, luggage in tow, we made several orbits of the only bank of chairs, a mere twelve places to sit, all occupied. One seat became free and Kate sat down, while I perched on my case. For once, its size helped. It was probably more comfortable than any of the hard-plastic seats.

For forty-five minutes we sat in limbo. Every minute dragged, apparently unable to move onto the next, no matter how many times I glanced at my phone – that curious phenomenon of time dilation spent waiting in a foreign airport.

My ears pricked when I heard my phone ting and Kate's too. Then a sense of apprehension as I wondered what it was – *who it was.* A message from the airline to apologise for our flight being late? Or worse, one from Samid to inform us we'd left something important – our passports or the elephant batik – at his house?

It wasn't from Samid. Or the airline. Instead it was a photo from Jerry – the entire Blighty crowd gathered together in a pub, holding glasses and smiling as they blinked at the camera. Jerry wore a red Santa hat while Frank sported an All Blacks shirt and Nelson cocked a bicorn. Beca and Amy had fastened aviator goggles on their foreheads, and Lucy and Bruce stood with orange robes draped over their shoulders. Linda and Tom were there too, standing proudly with their lenses, also a huge photo album – *their wildlife pictures* – in their arms.

"They must have all met up," said Kate, gazing at the same photo on her screen. "Every one of them's back now."

"Yes." It would be Friday evening in England, just after five. "They look like they're having a good time."

"Not as good as we're having." Kate smirked at me.

Eventually our desk opened, and after gratefully surrendering our hold bags we made our way to the next security checkpoint – *more x-ray machines and scanners, hurray!* – and into level three of the airport. Here, at least, were plentiful chairs and a café where we could eat and drink.

One last rice and curry – *if we wanted it* – one last buffet. Then home.

FORTY-ONE

Rubber Band

We learned a great many things during our twenty-eight days in Sri Lanka. How tea is grown and manufactured, where to eat the perfect fish curry, and why Duran Duran's pop video of "Save a Prayer" must have been so difficult to shoot. Plus, all our many different meetings with elephants, spending several days in a working heritage site like Galle Fort and climbing the island's number one drawcard, Lion Rock. Yet our trip would be memorable for many reasons besides the ones we'd first gone to Sri Lanka for – all the incidental things such as storms, tuk-tuk rides, cheese and tomato sandwiches, even snake encounters too close for comfort.

There was all the history to start with – far, far more than I'd ever expected. The ancient kingdom of Anuradhapura predated Stonehenge and lasted a millennium. The succeeding kingdom of Polonnaruwa lasted several hundred years and was followed by invasions and colonisations, one after another. Far too much information to absorb in a few short weeks. Out of all the historical sites, temples, caves, churches and museums on the island, we barely brushed our knuckles on the door.

Then there was the culture. With so many ancient invaders – and modern ones too – Sri Lanka is a tapestry of contrasting ideas, ethnicities, religions and languages. Many peoples have flooded the island, each eroding, silting, and changing the cultural landscape. From the north, ancient Indian princes bringing Buddha's teachings, then Hinduism. From the west, Arab traders with Islam, followed by Portuguese with slaves. Later came the Dutch, then – more holistically – the British with soldiers, railways and cricket.

We were like children straying into a sweet shop – one in which all the glass jars have been broken and their contents, every candy known to infant-kind, scattered like gems across the floor. So many different shapes and flavours all mixed up – turquoise with cyan, orange with gold, yellow with silver – that it was impossible to tell what had once been a fruit pastille and what a wine gum. It was similar here in Sri Lanka: Buddhist man marrying Catholic woman, Hindu temple standing next to Protestant church, Sinhala shop-writing next to a road sign in English, and the Dutch Hospital serving coffee arabica with Key Largo lime pie. Everything, everyone, was made of bits from somewhere else.

In Galle Fort alone we visited Buddhist and Hindu temples, a mosque, Catholic and Protestant churches, plus a bank all in the space of one day. Too much for our senses to absorb. Too little capacity in our heads to understand. The best we could do was pick out the highlights and promise ourselves we'd return for another twenty-eight days in the future.

Most worthwhile of all had been the people we'd met. The courteous staff at the hotels, restaurants and cafes, and

28 DAYS IN SRI LANKA

the helpful, friendly strangers in the streets – even our bogus fish chef, Ranuga. The guys who'd led our tour – Oshan, Chanuka and Sakan – and of course our personal driver/guide Samid. Then there were the other members of the tour, the nine POMs from diverse occupations and stages of life who'd so easily and seamlessly bound together. They were like pencils inside a loose rubber band. They didn't always point the same way, nor were they all as sharp as each other, yet they each made their mark, some broad, some fine, and producing one picture – this wonderful country made into an image we would all remember.

Everyone had the same motive: an appreciation of new places and the desire to explore. And admirably, despite an election taking place in Britain on 12th December, only four days into the tour, no one discussed the "B" phenomenon that had divided their country. When people did speak of Blighty it was only in passing – the town they lived in, the best route to work, their favourite meals, and once, the Dutch band Focus from the 1970s. We never did find out what Nelson did, if Amy was an author, but it didn't matter. This was a band of Brits at their best, demonstrating how good humour, regional accents and unselfish cooperation made for enjoyable and rewarding travel. For me as an expat POM it was like old times, sharing observations and laughs with fellow country men and women, once treasured, never lost.

Believe in the old African proverb. "If you want to go fast, go alone. If you want to go far, go together."

About the Author

Andy grew up in Stratford-upon-Avon, England, spent too many years in the fog of London, then followed the long white cloud – and his wife – to Wellington, New Zealand. Always wanting to write, he completed a Graduate Diploma in Creative Writing. He writes contemporary fiction, science-fiction and travel blogs. After living in Samoa for three months in 2017, he published the travelogue, *One Hundred Days in Samoa*. He's also published a novel, *Making Meredith*.

You can visit Andy's website at www.andy-southall.com

If you enjoyed this book please let others know by leaving a review on GoodReads and Amazon. Reviews are vital for new authors to become better known. Imagine you've just been somewhere new and want to let others know. Please pass the sunshine on.

Printed in Great Britain
by Amazon